I
am
jennie

I am jennie

JENNIE KETCHAM

GALLERY BOOKS

NEW YORK   LONDON   TORONTO   SYDNEY   NEW DELHI

Gallery Books
A Division of Simon & Schuster, Inc.
1230 Avenue of the Americas
New York, NY 10020

First Gallery Books hardcover edition July 2012

GALLERY BOOKS and colophon are registered trademarks of Simon & Schuster, Inc.

For information about special discounts for bulk purchases, please contact Simon & Schuster
Special Sales at 1-866-506-1949 or business@simonandschuster.com.

The Simon & Schuster Speakers Bureau can bring authors to your live event. For more
information or to book an event contact the Simon & Schuster Speakers Bureau at
1-866-248-3049 or visit our website at www.simonspeakers.com.

Designed by Jaime Putorti

Manufactured in the United States of America

10 9 8 7 6 5 4 3 2 1

Library of Congress Cataloging-in-Publication Data is available.

ISBN 978-1-4516-4476-0
ISBN 978-1-4516-4478-4 (ebook)

To the people I've hurt,

and the people who helped me

figure out why.

INTRODUCTION

Jennie Ketcham is a special person—and I knew it from the first moment I saw her.

Of course, the irony is that the first person I saw when I showed up for work at the Pasadena Recovery Center on April 6, 2009, was Penny Flame—a vivacious, outrageous, camera-ready professional in the adult entertainment industry. Penny showed up for her stint in rehab with a suitcase full of sex toys and a plan to use her reality TV exposure to fuel her destructive quest for a dysfunctional definition of success.

Don't get me wrong. I liked Penny; I was charmed by Penny, often amused by Penny, and—to my chagrin—initially deftly played by Penny, who used her wit and humor to keep any real connection at arm's length. But it wasn't long before I came to love and respect *Jennie,* the brave, real, and substantial woman hidden behind the facade.

Penny may have decided to come to rehab, but it was Jennie who decided to commit to recovery. Her story is the story of the road to health. This unsparing retelling of how she came to be sitting across from me in rehab and her journey into the real world as an authentic participant sends a loud and clear message to anyone who is struggling with pain, confusion, and choices that have led down a dangerous road. Choices have consequences, and in this book those choices play out in real time. Jennie's story makes explicit that there is a point of no return. It also makes explicit that you don't need to be rescued, or cast out of society, or emotionally numb. You don't need to die of addiction. There is a way out.

Jennie's story shows how people recover. Simply put: we all affect one another profoundly. I made the effort, and spent the time, to not be distracted by Penny Flame and to tune into Jennie. I paid attention to who she actually is, rather than who she was projecting out into the world. Jennie was brave enough to risk the scrutiny. She could have turned and run from it. But for whatever reason, she was surprisingly willing to allow me to be present with the real Jennie.

As a doctor, I can't expect that my patients will give me what I hope for them. I have seen those who are too destroyed—they look at the carnage of their behavior and shrink away in shame. In treatment, all the stuff, all the manipulations Jennie had used to survive could have gotten in the way, if she hadn't been willing to risk abject honesty.

Jennie never allowed her false bravado to take over. Instead she channeled it to face her shame, to withstand the discomfort of allowing me to see her real self, and then found the strength to reach out and meet me from that very real self.

This is the nature of a healthy, intimate interpersonal exchange. Our soul, our spirit, our core self is able to grow because another person is there to touch it and we allow them to see deeply into us. We become better people, and the self literally emerges through our exchanges with others. I know this is true, because knowing Jennie taught me something important about myself. Her commitment to truth held up a mirror to a weakness that still makes me cringe when I recall it.

When I first began working on reality television, the producers told me they had to do things to the environment to make the show interesting—to get outside of the same four walls. It was an argument I had become familiar with, and one I pushed back against every day that I went to work. I appreciated their point that hours of talk therapy and one-on-one counseling was not highly dramatic; in fact it can be about as exciting as watching hair grow. But as an addiction specialist, I know what I need to do for my patients in order to help them heal.

In this book, Jennie vividly details a moment in which I learned a wrenching lesson in what could happen when I blinked and did not follow my instincts. Her description of a moment in treatment when she almost lost faith is so graphic and heartbreaking that I could barely read it. Her uncompromising commitment to tell the truth about her journey required that I relive one of the lowest points of my work on television. Jennie's treatment—which she was taking so seriously—was compromised for a moment, and she reacted with the full fury of someone who had experienced a violation of the honesty of her program.

Everything that Jennie writes about here that involves me happened precisely as she details, and so I trust that everything else in this book happened exactly as she says it did. Jennie is the rare real deal: someone who dares to report things about themselves exactly as they happened. Usually when people write stories like this from within their condition, there are distortions and manipulations. By the same token, when they write about it from a position of recovery, they can be judgmental and disdainful of how they were—and of others who are like them. Not Jennie. Reading this book is a real journey, in the moment, with no posturing or spin. You don't get a commentary on an experience; the story isn't filtered or flattered by carefully crafted recollections or the hope of sidestepping personal responsibility. This book is more than a memoir of recovery, however. Jennie's story throws into relief the kinds of options society provides for people who are in pain. She holds a mirror up to the things our current culture tells us have value—fame-seeking, sex, and money—and she shows us the damage they do to people when distilled down to their numbing core.

Jennie is on a rare journey. In my experience, people who have been in this kind of situation either are rescued and hobble along in dependent dysfunctional relationships, or burn out. They take on other psychiatric ailments later in life as they continue with unresolved issues. But Jennie has gone to the mat to do what she needs to do to start over and heal. I've rarely had a patient who has committed so fully to life and to recovery. With each letting go of the trappings of her condition, she became a richer human being and more joyful to be with.

It's exciting to be around Jennie. I look forward to interacting with her. Part of the excitement is in witnessing such a dynamic work in progress, but there is much more I gain from our relationship. There is a kind of excitement from seeing someone's spirit come to life that you can't get anywhere else. Jennie's gift—not just to me and to others close to her, but to anyone who wrestles with painful demons—is the knowledge that such resilience exists. It fuels me to go back to the difficult patients. And it gives hope to a thousand other patients who are not ready to start the journey to recovery.

As I write this, I've known Jennie for nearly three years, and I would have said that I knew a lot about her and her life. Reading this book filled out her full experience. To be honest, there are stories here that make me uncomfortable; there were times when I wanted to avert my gaze from her raw honesty. In the end, however, the whole of the picture is astonishing and well worth momentary discomfort.

This book is an extraordinary gift, yet it is only a small part of Jennie's story. It is clear that she now understands that every choice is a chance to find out more about herself. I can't wait to see where she goes from here. There are so many things she might contribute that will have massive impact. This is a woman who can and who will make a difference—and it is a pure pleasure to be a part of her story.

Dr. Drew Pinsky

1

"I HOPE THE MONEY FILLS THE HOLES 'CAUSE,

SEE, THE ROOF IS CAVING IN."

—THE HORRIBLE CROWES, "BLACK BETTY & THE MOON"

I flew into Phoenix on a Thursday to work an Internet porn convention. I was trying to promote my webcam studio, a new webcam company that I couldn't seem to get off the ground, even though I'd been running it for nearly four months. My boss, Del, wanted me to hang out, drink with affiliate managers, accompany him to dinners and parties, and be the arm candy he thought would help generate traffic to the site.

By Sunday, I had been awake for two, possibly three days. After the first twenty-four hours without sleep, days bled into weeks, which condensed into minutes that could have been years. Time did not matter, because I had a singular purpose in life, and it was to find more cocaine. I had called various random numbers from the Craigslist hooker sections—the sections listed under "Adult Services" or "Casual Encounters"—until, on the other end of one particular number, I recognized my girlfriend Camilla Bangs's voice saying, "Leave a message and I'll call you right back."

So I did. I knew that, if I could get her on the phone, she could probably get some blow. I wasn't concerned that it was 4:00 a.m. or that she might recognize my number and decide to press the IGNORE button. She knew I abhorred her hooking, let alone selling herself on Craigslist. I didn't feel like I had a choice.

Del had started pacing. He walked fifteen feet to one wall and then fifteen feet to the opposite wall, shooting nervous glances from me to Kagney, a superhot blond chick I was in the process of seducing. I either had to find more blow, or leave the hotel room so he could find something else.

Del was hunting for something other than cocaine. Just like the last time I worked for him in Vegas, he wanted to watch girls fuck themselves until he fell asleep, usually with a tired and hopeless look in his eye. It was the same tired and hopeless look that visited a drug addict at 7:00 in the morning when he realized that the day would proceed and he had yet to sleep a wink.

In his hotel room in Phoenix, as Del continued scanning the personal ads, I tried to read his face. I also tried to read Kagney's, to figure out how much time I had to appease his bossly desires before she got sick of the hunt and went to bed. I had been trying to get into her bikini bottom since I saw her at the pool earlier that morning. She was fairly new to the business and didn't have the stamina of us old pros, so I wanted to take her to bed before she was too blasted to be of any good.

I might have offered up her services to Del, but I didn't think Kagney was hooking. While many porn stars end up "escorting," which is just fancy talk for prostitution, she was still new enough in front of the camera that she was being booked for plenty of scenes, and so she didn't need the extra money.

It amazed me how quickly a girl would be "shot up" simply because she'd been booked solid for three months and ended up flooding the market with images or videos of herself. Then nobody in the biz could shoot her because she'd been "shot out." Some girls were cleverer than others and only took two or three bookings a week, understanding full well that $3,000 a week was a ton of money, and if they put too much product out at once, their porno shelf life would be nil.

Kagney seemed fairly clever. She was savvy enough to sense the discomfort in Del's hotel room that morning and to understand it was time to go. She gave me a searching look as Del called yet another Craigslist phone number.

"Bedtime?" I asked her quietly.

I didn't do the escort thing for a wide variety of reasons. For one, I understood the laws of supply and demand. With the insane amount of porn stars, Playmates, and career girls who supplied pussy to the market of lonely, vagina-hungry men, I would never be able to charge an amount of money that I thought would make prostitution a rewarding experience. Additionally, I enjoyed the formality of going to work, filling out a W-2, signing waivers, getting tested, and having sex with tested people. I felt like I was a step higher than a regular old hooker. I managed to rationalize my way out of any suggestion that pornography equaled prostitution. Being an escort simply felt shadier than being a porn star, perhaps because there weren't any Internet conventions for prostitutes.

Kagney reached her hand out and touched my thigh, meeting my eyes with her big blues, a nonverbal yes.

Del held his hand over the mouthpiece of the phone as if he were trying to hide something from the empty ring on the other end.

"Wait one moment, girls," he said, his posh accent making him sound much more refined than the pornographer he was. "Will you try your friend again?"

"She probably recognizes my number, but I'll give it another shot," I said.

Kagney let out a little "Harrumph" and settled down into the chair as I called Camilla again on my cell.

Voice mail.

"Hey, dude, it's me again," I said. "Listen, sorry to keep bugging you but I've got a little business proposition, one or the other if you know what I mean. Just, uh, give the hotel a call for room, uh, 307. Okay? Love you."

I hung up the phone, feeling a bit traitorous hooking her up with a hooking gig.

"She'll come over, yes?" Del asked, hope dying in his eyes with each passing second.

"I mean, she might, but it's, like, 4:15 in the morning, man," I said. "She's probably on a call or too messed up to drive."

I saw his desperation and tried to reassure him.

"I gave her your room number, so she might call back," I said.

He sat forward and lit his fiftieth Marlboro Red.

"Did you tell her I only want the masturbation?" he asked, sounding way more proper requesting masturbation than any American ever would.

"No, but she'll do whatever you want," I said. "If it's only masturbation, she'll be pumped."

I took one of his cigarettes.

Camilla had been in and out of the business for quite some time, struggling with a cocaine problem and then a weight problem, and felt uncomfortable in front of the camera and contrived in the bedroom. She hated hooking but did it anyway, because she needed the money. *Rolling Stone* magazine had even named her one of America's worst hookers, although it was phrased a bit more eloquently. And while I was always interested in making more money, I was uninterested in becoming an unhappy hooker like Camilla, and so her example was enough to keep me out of the game.

"I think you're more likely to get her to bring blow," I said.

There was nothing more telling than the lost, forlorn look in Del's eyes. I grasped Kagney's hand, the soft, perfectly manicured hand that had been resting on my knee. We both stood to make it apparent that we were going to leave. I prepped the final few lines of coke on the table.

"So I'll see you tomorrow at the show, right?" I asked. "Around one?"

"I doubt I'll be sleeping until then," he chuckled. And then the manic desperation returned. "Do you think she'll be able to get in?"

He dropped his cigarette into a very full ashtray. He knew damn well that the entire hotel had been reserved and closed down for this convention and that unless his special guest had a pass, she would be left out front with her tiny purse and plastic heels.

"I kind of don't think so," I said. "I mean, you can try, but security is no joke. I guess be ready to get another room at a different hotel?"

I patted Kagney's ass. She took her rail as I held her long blond hair off the cigarette-ash-and-coke-dusted table.

"Leave your pass, mate," he said.

He was simultaneously asking me and telling me, knowing that the next day was my final day of the show and that I wouldn't be needing it to get back into the hotel. I bent over, snorted the final rail, then lit my cigarette.

"Be careful, man," I said, handing over the small plastic badge that allowed conventioneers onto the grounds. "Arizona isn't down with drugs."

I HAD A secret gram of blow stashed in my bra. Where the drugs in my bra had originally come from, and whether or not they'd been bought, borrowed, or taken were mysteries to me, and questions I didn't bother asking two hours before dawn. The weekend had become a disjointed mess—a blurry, choppy jumble of memories.

I led Kagney out of Del's room and down the hall to my own, which I unlocked with my small key card. Once inside, we tossed our purses, clothes, bras, and underwear to the ground. Then we were naked, with our heads at the foot of the bed and a magazine for cutting the secret cocaine into rails. With each line I tried to account for my whereabouts over the weekend, and with each line the weekend memories continued to slip and blend.

The previous morning I had hosted a beer pong tournament, where teams of grown men battled one another over flimsy poolside Ping-Pong tables. Before the game I had done blow with Porno Dan, a producer, director, performer, and my favorite drinking companion, and when I felt too gacked out to be a proper beer pong host, Porno Dan had personally escorted me to the bar for successive shots of Jack Daniel's and Jäger. I finally went back to the tournament and evened out: the high was not so high and the drunk was not so drunk.

"Don't you all do anything besides throw tiny balls into gaping, dirty, wet orifices?" I cried over the loudspeaker.

And then I led the girls at the pool in an arousing version of the Little Chicken Dance.

When my hosting duties were done, I happened upon Aaron Carpello, an ex-fling with easy, seductive eyes and the smug grin of a twenty-something-year-old guy who had already amassed a cool mil for his bank account. I had momentary imaginary heart palpitations when I remembered that we'd met at that same pool the year before. I still cared about him. But in lieu of saying hello, I pretended he was invisible and returned to the bar to meet Porno Dan, the drinking love of my life, who was totally visible. Carpello and I hadn't seen each other in months, and the last time we'd hung out, we'd been out of our minds on E, and I was in no shape to do the "catching up" thing with cocaine and Jack running through my blood.

BACK IN THE hotel room with Kagney, another fat line brought me out of my memories, and I wondered how long I'd been spacing out.

"Okay, sexy Penny?" she asked.

She ran her fingers down my naked back, opened her body to me, and slid the cocaine-covered magazine to the side of the bed.

"Yeah, just trying to remember where I left my shoes," I said.

This wasn't a total lie because I *had* lost my shoes at some point during the day, and during my poolside Carpello memories it had crossed my mind to wonder where they were.

"Here, baby, let me fix you," she cooed.

She kissed my ear ever so gently, flicking her tongue to the soft skin along my hairline, her fingers still tracing my tattooed back down to the curve of my ass.

But I still couldn't shake thoughts of Carpello. I had been warned about him before we met through a feminist, sex-positive sex education director friend of mine named Tristan Taormino, who had offered me a gig directing my own line of sex-ed videos for Vivid. Tristan had run up against Aaron in the past, and thought he was an arrogant pig. I took that as a challenge and decided to fuck him.

Kagney swept my hair back to the left side of my body while she pressed her naked skin against my right side. "Do you want me to lick your pussy?" she whispered delicately. "I'll make you come all over my pretty face."

I doubted she could make me come after a three-day cocaine binge, but I wasn't against her trying. I wasn't against the idea at all.

"You sexy little whore," I said.

With my left hand, I moved the magazine to the floor. With my right, I grabbed her crotch.

"I've wanted to taste your wet little cunt since I saw you this morning," I said.

She squealed with delight.

"No, no, no, me first," she said.

I rolled over to my back while she dove between my legs. As I looked down at the mess of blond curls, I thought of the thousands of other blondes who had been down there and wondered if she would surprise me and do something extraordinary with her mouth.

Lexi Belle, Love, Tyler, and Marie had all been between my legs with their beautiful, bouncing blond curls. I'd had an Elexis, an Alexis, a few Torys, Eves, and two Tiffanys, one redhead and one brunette. There had been so many of them that they all blended into one moving mass of pleasurable curls, small ringlets, big waving tendrils, highlights, lowlights. While Kagney worked her sweet tongue over my clit, I thought of the first night I'd fucked Carpello in one of these hotel rooms. It was even on the same floor we were on now.

We had been lying next to each other in bed, smoking a joint, when we started kissing. Because kissing is the gateway drug to fucking, I knew I had to bring up a very important matter before things got messy.

"I'm bleeding right now, but I'll still suck your dick."

I was breathless and ready, my hands already searching his pants.

"I'm good with that," he said with a smile.

I performed for him with one hand attached to my mouth, the best that I could do while using the other hand to tuck the tampon string away so I could show him my pussy. When I was sure everything looked perfect, I maneuvered my body so that he could watch me masturbate while I continued to suck his cock. I played my clit like turntables and he threw his head back, pleased he'd ended the evening in my mouth. When he came, it was warm and thick. I swallowed it without tasting his essence and casually excused myself to the restroom to clean the spit from my face.

After washing my cheeks in the sink, I sat on the toilet and started to pee with the door to his room wide open. "How long do you normally fuck a bitch before she pisses in front of you?" I called out to him through the darkness, smiling, because I was sure very few women in his life called other women "bitches" or talked about their own pissing.

"What?" he said.

The silhouette of his naked body came into focus in the doorway, lit only by the dim table lamp by the bed.

"I asked: How many times do you have to fuck a bitch before she pisses in front of you?"

Without a word, he walked to where I sat on the toilet and shoved his cock again into my mouth and down my throat.

While I thought about Carpello, Kagney was still between my legs.

"Do you like this, Penny?" she asked.

I shifted my hips into her face, grabbing the back of her head and holding it firmly but gently.

"Yes, I most certainly do, my little beauty," I said. "You like the way my pussy tastes?"

I was only with her for a moment, though, before I quickly faded out again to the night with Carpello the year before. As much as I tried to remain present, I'd done too much blow to keep my sexual escapades straight.

"Are you really bleeding?" he asked.

He lifted me at the armpits and thrust my body and ass onto the cold bathroom counter.

"Yeah, but I don't care," I said. "I'll make a fuckin' mess with you." He walked from the bathroom to his luggage, rummaged around until he found a condom, came back, and pressed it against my tit while pinching my nipple and pushing his mouth to my neck and ear.

"You're gonna make a mess with me?" he said. "Be my messy girl?"

I had already taken the tampon out in super-stealth mode, wrapped it in toilet paper, and tossed it while he was condom hunting, so I was ready for him.

"I'll be your filthy fucking mess," I said. "Be your messy little girl."

He fucked me in the dark, standing there with his balls driving into the counter and my ass cheeks. And then he carried me to the bed, and we fucked until he worked himself into a heated frenzy. I watched him attentively and listened to his breathing crescendo, matching my own breath to his. We came together, on and with one another, and fell asleep, exhausted, on top of surprisingly clean but damp, sweaty sheets.

Kagney brought me back to our moment.

"I don't think you're really coming," she said.

I sat up, grabbed her by the throat, and brought her perfectly structured face an inch away from my own.

"You think I'm lying to you?" I said.

She laughed and licked my lips.

"Hit me," she hissed. "Fucking hit me, you slut."

I smiled down into her face, eased her hair from her forehead, and slapped her. The force of my open palm shifted her gaze away from my eyes to across the room.

"You like that, don't you, you little fucking whore?" I growled.

She giggled and looked back into my eyes. Still holding her throat, I slapped her again. That time I grabbed her face and kissed her mouth, biting her fat, pink lips, which threatened to turn blue from my choke hold.

"I love it," she said.

"Put your lips on my cunt and show me *how much* you love it," I said.

I pressed her back down between my hot, wet thighs, her perfect curls now tangled and drenched in dewy pussy juice.

"Whatever you say, sexy Penny."

She bit my clit and then flicked her tongue until I came in her mouth.

I can't remember if my orgasm was because of her mouth or because there was nothing left to be felt.

Panting and exhausted, she slithered her glistening body up against mine. The sixty-plus hours we'd spent awake, drinking, laughing, and now fucking, finally hit her. With her back against me, I held her hips, my fingers following the curve of her abdomen while I inhaled the smell of her damp honey hair, which fell across my pillow.

As I listened to her slow breathing, my mind continued to piece together events from the weekend, searching for a linear explanation of my time in Phoenix, the work I'd accomplished by being there, and where in the hotel I might have left my shoes. When I started praying for sleep, for the cocaine to finally disperse into my system, for the depressant alcohol to finally win the battle for my blood, I realized that because the shoes were brand-new, I couldn't remember what they looked like. Kagney was sound asleep. If I could fall asleep as well, I might be ready to enter rehab in thirty-six hours, like I was supposed to do.

"IN MY BEGINNING IS MY END."

—T. S. ELIOT, "EAST COKER"

Most people believe porn stars were molested as children, and while some probably were, neither my dad nor my mom was abusive. Even though they were both addicts at one point in my childhood, they maintained a certain level of normalcy that isn't possible in the majority of homes struck by addiction.

My Cabbage Patch Kids and I had homemade matching frilly dresses and patent leather shoes. On my birthdays, Mom would bake fantastically detailed cakes, creating Big Bird and Cookie Monster from little star-shaped dabs of frosting. Dad traveled a lot for business, and on the rare nights Mom would scold me, I'd lie in my king-size water bed with its white mesh canopy and downy comforter, pretending to be a princess awaiting her father, the King, who would return to save her from the punishing solitude of "Go to your room, Jennifer."

I was nine years old when we moved from Evanston, Wyoming, to a little house on Spring Valley Way in Concord, California, a move that came only five years after our move from Denver to Evanston. The big companies for which Dad worked often restructured their workforces, and whenever Dad was restructured out of a company, he would apply for a job in a different city, and the family would up and move.

I never fully understood what he did at work. I knew he was a safety inspector of a plant or facility, but I had no idea what that meant. All I knew was that when he wasn't traveling, he left for and returned from work at the same time each day, and once he was home and settled into his comfy jeans, we'd share a big glass of milk and eat peanut-buttered saltines in front of the television until dinnertime. I had no reason to believe he was anything other than perfect.

In fact, up until my parents' divorce, my entire life was perfect. Like, super-perfect. Or at least it seemed perfect, until the problems that lurked below the surface made themselves known.

A few months after we moved to Concord, my mom went to Boston for a weekend to attend a training course in forensic science, which she was thinking about as a career choice, leaving my dad to watch my brother, my sister, and me. He came home from work early that Friday afternoon. After our usual peanut butter and saltines, followed by a special kung pao chicken dinner, he disappeared into his bedroom. This was fine with my siblings and me, because we had the run of the house. James, Lyss, and I ran from room to room, first jumping on the couches in the living room, then to each others' bedrooms for bed jumping, and then back to the couches. The jump circuit continued for about an hour, until we had digested dinner and had room for dessert.

"Ice cream?" I asked my sister.

She nodded excitedly and continued bouncing on a couch.

I ran through the house, back to where Dad was, slowing to a snail's pace only as I walked into his bedroom.

"Dad?" I said.

I expected to see him sitting in bed, illuminated by the glow of the TV. But the bed was empty. I started to wonder where he'd gone and why he hadn't told us.

"Dad?" I said again.

"What's up, Jen?" he said.

His muffled voice came from the bathroom, and my heart quit its million-mile-a-minute beat when I realized he was just going potty. I stood right at the door.

"Can we have some ice cream?" I said.

"Sure, Jen, go right ahead," he said.

I took off at full speed for the kitchen with visions of mint chocolate chip dancing through my head.

We piled onto the freshly jumped couch and ate ice cream straight from the container, something Dad did but Mom hated, while watching *Are You Afraid of the Dark?*

I was awakened sometime later that night by the noise of the television. When I realized that the three of us had fallen asleep on the couch, I woke up James and Lyss and herded them off to bed. After I kissed Lyss on the forehead, I went into Dad's room to say good night, but the bed was still empty. A little sliver of light beamed from underneath the still-closed bathroom door. I thought it was strange that Dad had pooed twice in one night but was too tired to bother saying anything about it.

"Night, Dad," I said.

"Good night, Jen," he said, his voice audible over the whirl of the fan.

I zombied off to bed.

Early the next day, we rose to watch Saturday morning cartoons. When Dad hadn't gotten up by the time we finished our bowls of cereal, I padded back to his bedroom to see if he was awake. The bedroom door was closed, so I quietly cracked it open and poked my head in.

"Dad?" I whispered, not wanting to wake him if he was still sleeping, because I remembered that he'd been having a poo super-late the night before.

"I'm in the bathroom, Jen," he said.

I slowly approached the bathroom door.

"Do you want some cereal?" I asked.

"No, I'm fine," he said. "I'll be out in a bit."

I went back to watch cartoons with Lyss and James. It was near lunchtime when Lyss finally pulled her attention away from the TV.

"Where's Dad?" she asked.

"I don't think he feels good," I said.

I went back to check on him again.

"You sure you're okay, Dad?" I asked.

This time I pressed my nose to the door to see if there was the smell of barf coming from the bathroom.

"Yeah, I'm okay," he said. "I'll be out in a bit. Make your brother and sister peanut butter and jelly sandwiches."

Revived with my new lunch mission, and feeling a bit like the queen of the house, I took Lyss and James to the kitchen. Once I had made the sammies and fed the kids, I sent them to their rooms to play. The afternoon turned into early evening, and not having seen Dad for nearly twenty-four hours, I started to get really worried about his stomach. I went to his room to check on him.

"Everything is fine, Jen," he said once again.

But this time I heard a slightly more frantic tone in his voice, and I decided to call Mom. She had left the phone number of her hotel right next to the phone.

I sat at the kitchen counter, dialing her across the country. After the third or fourth ring she picked up.

"Hi, baby," she said, sounding glad to hear my voice.

"Mom, I think Dad is really sick. He hasn't come out of the bathroom since yesterday."

"Will you go tell him that I'm on the phone and I'd like to speak with him?" she said very calmly, in her standard Mom fashion.

I ran to their room and shouted at Dad through the bathroom door.

"Mom wants you," I said.

I heard the odd shuffling of papers and other objects inside.

"Tell her I will call her back."

I returned to the kitchen and picked up the phone receiver once again.

"He said he'll call you back later," I said. "Can I use the stove to make dinner, Mom? I want to cook some soup."

I twiddled the spiral phone cord around my fingers, unraveling it as I waited.

"No," she said. "Tell Dad you're hungry and then wait for him to come out of the bathroom. Then tell him to call me."

I hung up with Mom and checked on James, who was happily playing on his race car bed. Then I checked on Lyss, who sat on her bed listening to my Walkman. And then I ran back into Dad's room to sit on his bed and wait for him to emerge.

When the bathroom door finally opened, he was as shocked to see me as I was to see him. His eyes were wide and wild, as if I had caught him doing something naughty. He had a ton of newspapers in his hand, crumpled and rolled up, and his fingers were covered in the rubbed-off ink. I hesitantly made eye contact.

"We're hungry, Dad."

"Where are your brother and sister?" he asked, his voice rushed.

"Their bedrooms," I said. "Dad?" His tone worried me.

"Jennifer, I need you to come with me."

I thought perhaps he wanted my help making dinner. But then he slowly opened his bedroom door and began to creep down the hallway like some superspy.

"What are we doing?" I asked.

"We need to check the house," he said.

I wondered what we had to check the house for as we crept out into the living and dining rooms. I stood beside him as he pressed his body against the wall.

"Dad, are you—"

"Shhh," he said. "I need you to crawl over to that window and make sure the police aren't out front."

Now officially terrified, I did as he asked and crawled across the living room to the window. I lifted the soft, translucent curtains and raised my small freckled face to peer through the window-pane.

"Dad, there's no police," I whispered.

He cautiously opened the front door in slow motion and edged his way out onto the porch.

"We need to check the front," he said.

I stayed inside the house, careful not to reveal myself to anyone who might be outside. I was afraid because police were the *good guys,* but now my dad's behavior said they were bad.

"Dad, why would police be here?"

"Just stay close," he said.

He crouched down and darted across the yard to the hedges that lined our driveway. I bent over and followed.

"Dad, what are we—"

"Shhhhh."

We checked the entire front yard for police. We looked up trees and in bushes. When we ran back inside after checking the back-yard as well, he finally settled into the kitchen and started rummaging through the cabinets. He found a bottle of codeine cough syrup and threw back a couple of swigs. I sat on the counter, clutching my knees to my chest.

"I think I'm having a heart attack," he said.

I had seen enough TV shows to know that when someone was having a heart attack, it was important to call 911.

"He's been in the bathroom since yesterday and he just drank all our cough syrup and said he's having a heart attack," I cried to the police operator. She asked that I stay calm until an ambulance arrived.

I must have called my mom at some point as well, because it was arranged that my younger siblings and I would spend the night at a neighbor's house. My mom came home on the first flight out of Boston the following day. She never became a forensic scientist, and Dad never locked himself in the bathroom again.

That Sunday night, when my parents both thought I'd gone to bed, I crept down the hallway to the entrance of the living room and listened to them fight. I don't recall much of the details, but I do remember my mom shouting.

"*How dare you* do cocaine instead of watching your kids?" she yelled at him.

Monday morning in Miss Hasegawa's class, I wondered if any other fourth graders' fathers did cocaine instead of watching their kids. Did other kids have to call 911 so their dads wouldn't have heart attacks? What had happened to the dad I knew and loved? This new Dad was scary and unpredictable. To me, at nine years old, he couldn't be trusted. And it would be decades before I would trust him again.

IN 1995, PARAMOUNT Pictures released *Clueless,* a movie that changed my life. When Alicia Silverstone, Stacey Dash, and Brittany Murphy hit the big screen, I fell in love with Jeep Wranglers, the word "whatever," and schoolgirl uniforms better suited for a stripper pole than academic life. After the movie came out, I threw away every pair of ultrawide JNCO jeans I owned. I tossed my lame skater shoes and awkward baggy T-shirts and said hello to knee-highs, penny loafers, and unbelievably short plaid miniskirts.

I related all things, people, and events in my life to those in the movie, and though the similarities generally fell short of being even remotely comparable, I decided that if I could get myself a brand-new wardrobe, I'd be that much closer to living the eye-opening characters' life. So I made a list of things that set me apart from the mythical girls of Beverly Hills, and even though I primarily identified with Murphy as Tai, the not-super-totally-hip transfer student, I felt like I had the potential to be the "It" girl if I could just change a few minor things.

Things Going Against Me at Twelve:

1. Braces. Stupid, hideous braces.
2. Freckles. Stupid, hideous freckles.
3. Mousy-brown, not-curly, not-straight hair.
4. Good grades.
5. A four-bedroom house without a fountain or drive-through driveway.
6. Mom drives a caravan. Totally not a Jeep Wrangler.
7. Nobody wants to be me. Not even me.
8. No boys want to be near me.

As a rule, I gauged my coolness levels by watching Isabella, Pine Hollow Middle School's very own "It" girl. She used Victoria Secret's Pear Glacé before any other girl wore scented lotion. Her body looked great in anything, even baggy overalls. She had almond-shaped eyes, straight jet-black hair, and perfect white teeth. I, on the other hand, smelled like the cigarettes that I borrowed (read stole) from my mom, looked like a slightly ghetto and retarded farmer in overalls, and had to carry one of those fuzzy teeth pickers to clean my braces post-lunch. Isabella was a trendsetter, but when *Clueless* came out and she failed to pick up on the superhot schoolgirl look, I thought, *Hot damn, this is my chance to beat you to it. Fuck your smelly lotion, your straight hair and teeth, your perfect overalled body. I'm gonna look like the girls in Beverly Hills.*

I made a list to counter the "Things Going Against Me at Twelve" list and began to plot my middle school takeover.

Operation Beverly Hills:

1. Amass all necessary clothes, jewelry, and shoes through Mom or thievery.
2. If necessary, wait for Christmas and request needed items from Santa.

3. Check out Mom's/Santa's secret presents hiding spot.
4. Act surprised Christmas morning.
5. Take over Pine Hollow Middle School and be eternally remembered as the most popular girl ever.

The biggest thing I'd ever stolen was a pack of cigarettes, so accumulating all the necessary clothes, jewelry, and shoes as a result of thievery was out. However, when Christmastime came and my wish list contained skirts as opposed to giant baggy jeans, Mom was thrilled that her wannabe gangster daughter was transforming into a plaid- and button-up-clad lady.

The first day after break, Dad drove me to school. After I bounced from his car, I rolled my new blue, green, and black plaid skirt up three times, unbuttoned the top three buttons of my blouse, shoved two shiny pennies in my loafers, and proudly walked my confident new look onto school grounds. As I crossed the first threshold, past the gate that kept truant kids in and sketchy people out, I nearly vomited into a sea of red-, yellow-, green-, blue-, and black-skirted girls who'd all apparently asked for the same Christmas gifts. In the middle of the quad stood Isabella, in a skirt not unlike my own. However, it rested gently on her hips, the hem grazing just above her knees, as if she were making a statement directly to me about how hard I had to try to look cute and how naturally it came to her. Heartbroken, I unrolled my skirt two times, fixed my knee-highs, and went about the morning totally unnoticed.

A few weeks later, the *Clueless* schoolgirl craze died down. I was never sure whether parents got sick of their daughters dressing like exotic dancers or if the fashion police sent out the memo from which I'd once again been excluded, but Isabella returned to her overalls, and other girls followed suit. But because I'd thrown out all my other clothes in a dramatic moment of complete *Clueless* devotion, I was stuck with the skirts, the loafers, and the white button-up blouses, which now had small stains in the armpits.

Normally when Dad dropped me off at school, he turned down his Republican talk radio station and patted me on the knee or head. "Have a great day, pumpkin," he'd say as I climbed out of the car.

That was it in the way of father-daughter bonding.

However, one fateful morning, in the frosty, Republican-rhetoric-filled, coffee-scented car, he turned down the radio about ten minutes away from school.

"How long are you going to keep wearing these clothes?" he said.

I was pissed that I had no other suitable clothes to wear and unfazed by his concern.

"Until I can put my pajamas on and go to bed," I said.

He slowed the car slightly and looked over at me.

"That's not what I mean," he said. "You know, the way we dress says a lot about who we are."

"So I'm a plaid skirt?" I said.

I shook my head at him while keeping my gaze on the road. There was nothing worse than being indirectly scorned for my fashion choices.

"No, you're not a plaid skirt," he said. "This is a risqué outfit. It says stuff you might not want to say."

"Dad, please."

I knew where the conversation was going. The birds-and-the-bees talk should have happened years before I'd been allowed to see *Clueless*, before I figured out "the birds and the bees" was just an awkward euphemism for an even more awkward conversation. By then I'd already kissed, like, four different guys and was working on kissing more. The time for parental intervention had long passed.

"Jen, guys are gonna want one thing from you: sex," he said. "I just want you to be careful."

He pulled into the middle school parking lot, and I gratefully leapt from his car.

"Got it," I said. "But plenty of guys want to be my friend, Dad. So thanks anyway."

I slammed the door and walked into school, trying to wash the conversation from my mind. In the process of doing so, I shifted the context and meaning of his words entirely. His comments morphed from being the sound, fatherly advice of "No man will take you seriously or want to be your friend" to meaning "Men are easy and only want sex" to meaning "If you use your sexuality in certain ways, you can elicit certain responses in men, and then, you can control them."

This final interpretation fell directly in line with Operation Beverly Hills. I started thinking that perhaps I'd missed another powerful message in *Clueless,* so I returned to the film for a review.

There were plenty of hidden messages in the movie, messages that ranged from "Flirt shamelessly!" to "Command attention, at any expense!"

Then came the moment when Alicia Silverstone's lead character, Cher, said: "Sometimes you have to show a little skin. This reminds boys of being naked, and then they think of sex."

I finally got it. It didn't mean a thing if you simply dressed like a girl who would get naked with a guy. To elicit certain responses from boys, I needed to start sleeping with them. Not that any sleeping would occur. So I tweaked the plan to include item #6:

Send out some "Fuck me" vibes.

And then, I got busy fine-tuning my mega-awesome skills of flirtation.

I practiced flirting everywhere I could. I practiced in the morning before class, sending out sultry, sexy looks to the bathroom mirror as I washed my hands post-pee. I "accidentally" brushed my hips against a seated male student as I took my own chair. I bent over to pick up a book, keeping my legs straight or better yet, bending my knees, letting my hair fall in my face, and looking up gently at whoever was sitting nearby with the come-hither look I assumed they'd use in *adult* situations.

I practiced, practiced, practiced.

And finally, the summer after seventh grade, I had a chance to make good on all these "Come fuck me" vibes I'd been emitting. My bestie, Melanie, and I started going over to the divinely hot Alex's house for hot-tub sessions. Mel and I both wanted Alex, and he was as much of a player as any thirteen-year-old could be. We sat in the hot tub together, and he put one hand between my legs and one hand between Melanie's legs. And though Mel and I never spoke of how he put his fingers inside each of us at the same time, we let it happen like it didn't matter.

We also gave Alex and his buddy, Matt, massages back at my house, using my room instead of Mel's because my mom had a new job and was never home, and Mel's mom was a fundamentalist Christian who didn't even believe in spandex pants.

Then one day Alex came to my house alone. Soon I was sitting on top of him, rubbing his back. His shirt was already off. He rolled over and looked up at me.

"Should we have sex?" he asked.

I didn't want to seem ungracious or suddenly and inexplicably prudish.

"Sure," I said.

He pulled a condom from his pocket and wiggled out from beneath me, leaving me sitting on the bed, looking to him for guidance.

"Take off your shorts," he said.

He dropped his pants. I did the same, leaned back on my elbows, and curiously watched his hands. He moved closer to me, placed one hand on my knees, and fumbled as he self-consciously slid inside me. I shut my eyes for a moment, and when he started moving his hips, I reopened them to see what the hell was going on.

For the briefest moment our eyes met. I then looked away to the ceiling to count the glow-in-the-dark stars I had put above my bed. It didn't hurt. It wasn't orgasmic. And when it was over, I wondered what all the fuss was about. He shoved the used condom in his pants pocket, we got dressed, and we rode our bikes back through the neighborhood toward his house. He seemed to look at me and the road all at once.

"I guess we aren't virgins anymore," he said.

"Guess not," I said.

I was pumped to have lost my virginity to him, because he was the school's hottest boy, besides his best friend, Matt. I did not, however, want word of our little thirty-second fling to get around. But when Matt showed up for a massage the following week, totally solo, I knew that Alex had talked, and that word of my sexual escapades would be all over the middle school as well.

That didn't stop me from taking Matt's virginity, though. He was much more educated in the world of sex than Alex. We did it doggy style on the carpet, and there was some blood that wasn't present the first time.

I never talked to Melanie about having sex with Alex or Matt. She may or may not have known. She may or may not have had sex with both of them as well.

By the time fall came, I'd totally captured the minds of a few different young "men," and knew that each boy I slept with would be thinking about me, and only me, come back-to-school-shopping time—knowledge that gave me the upper hand when it came to the generalized insecurities that go along with being in eighth grade. While I'd settled into my well-worn and scuffed-up penny loafers, I'd forgotten that the rest of my classmates hadn't had sex yet. But they didn't let me forget that I was different for long. As I walked into the quad on the first day of school, wearing my favorite black, red, and white plaid skirt, Coolio singing "1, 2, 3, 4, get your woman on the floor" came blaring through the lunchtime speakers. A large group of kids I thought of as my friends sang along with the song, only they replaced the words with their own:

"*1, 2, 3, 4, Jennie Ketcham is a whore.*" I walked straight through the crowd into the cafeteria with my head held high. I bought a

Cup of Noodles without saying one word to anyone. I met Mel in the same place we ate lunch every day, where I sat down and stifled pained whimpers.

"Fuck them," she said. "Don't let them see you cry."

That night I went home and begged Mom to take me shopping for new jeans, plus some big, even moderately baggy clothes—anything that didn't make me look like a whore. She did as I asked without ever asking me why. Dad never brought up the clothing issue again, and I never told either parent about how I'd become the shame of the middle school. Instead, I kept my head down, ignored the fact that, inside, I was screaming for a hug, and pretended like everything was just fine.

———

THE ART OF hiding one's feelings is fairly complex, and something I probably learned from my mom. She and Dad had married at eighteen, and by the time I was in my *Clueless* phase, they had become two separate adults, living two separate lives, even though those lives happened to intersect under one familial roof.

When Mom got preggo with me, she quit her job to be a full-time mother. She kept that position until James was in elementary school and then decided that it was time for her to return to the workforce. She found a place and employer she liked and began spending all her time at work. Dad kept the same regular hours he always had and tried to encourage her newfound enthusiasm for her job, but the vibe in our home had started to shift. She and Dad were barely in the same room, except to sleep, and so they never seemed to fight. I don't even remember them talking about adult-type things or having conversations that didn't involve us. But I knew shit was going down.

It was a collection of little oddities that added up to a big, obvious explanation. I noticed how short Mom had become in answering Dad's questions and how late she stayed at work. I noted that she checked her cell phone like crazy on her days off, and that her eyes lit up when she talked about her boss.

On Christmas Day, the year I was in eighth grade, Dad confirmed my suspicions of her affair. He was so full of Christmas spirit that he shared a video with me that he'd hired a private detective to take as proof. It had been filmed in a park across the street from an office building. Through the window I could make out a man and a woman, pressed up against a desk, kissing passionately. I didn't have to see my mom's face to recognize her. I knew the office, the desk, the spot from which the video had been captured. I also recognized the man as my mom's boss. I don't know if Dad showed me the video because he doubted what he was seeing, or if he wanted to drive a wedge between my mom and me, or if he just needed someone else to be as heartbroken as he was. But I do know Christmas was never the same again, and neither was my family.

I felt betrayed by both parents, but even more so by Dad, because when I looked at him I saw a dad. When I looked at my mom, I saw a friend. I couldn't understand why he wouldn't let Mom tell me herself. Why he had to share something so damning. I felt like my mother was a beaten woman, like she'd settled with a man she didn't love because it was her civic duty to raise children, when all she really wanted was to feel and be loved, which were wants I totally understood. While the marriage had started to crumble in less evident ways many years before that Christmas Day, after Christmas it avalanched out of control and ended in a flurry of vileness and anger.

Mom had bought a new Taurus at the end of February and, being the cool mom she was, let my friend Matt—yes, the same summertime-doggy-style Matt—drive it. He had recently gotten his learner's permit, so she let him take us around the block a few times. Other friends of mine, all boys who happened to be much older than myself, had taken to standing outside my house during that school year and "kickin' it." That particular day, Jack, Craig, and a slew of troublemakers stood on my corner smoking cigarettes and drinking forties while we were out for our joyride. As Matt turned the corner to head down the hill to my house, my dad walked out the front door and down to the sidewalk, cocked his arm back, and clocked Craig square in the jaw.

"Stop!" Mom screamed as she watched the scene ahead unfold.

Matt obediently punched his foot to the brake, but Mom grabbed his shoulder.

"No! Go!"

He smashed his foot into the gas, whizzing past our house and farther down the street until out of my dad's sight. I was sitting in the backseat, frozen and unsure of what was going to happen next. Matt pulled over and stopped the car.

"Get out and go home!" Mom said to Matt before scrambling into the driver's seat. I hopped up front. The two of us drove back to the house, where all the homies had scattered. Mom tried to play it cool and mellow, but when she pulled into the driveway, Dad came flying out the front door again and started banging his fists on her new car.

"Whore!" he screamed. "You fucking whore! You let a kid drive that car?"

I knew the anger wasn't about Matt driving the car, although I figured that was probably bad news too. I knew because when *I'd* been called a whore, it was about sex. And so I knew my dad must have meant it in a sexual context as well.

"What the fuck is wrong with you?" he demanded.

As Mom opened the car door, she looked at me. "Stay here," she said. "We're leaving."

Time seemed to stand still as their mutual verbal assault unfolded in the driveway for the whole neighborhood to hear. I have no memories of what they screamed at one another. I don't recall going inside to get my things. I'm not sure at what point James and Lyss ended up in the back of the car. But I do remember, as we drove away, my dad was in the driveway with tears streaming down his red, wailing face.

"Go with him, you whore!" he yelled. "Just go!"

As we pulled up the hill that took us away from our little house on Spring Valley Way, I looked back at my dad one last time. His body was folded over, crumpled into the driveway and the darkness of the night. His head was in his hands. As he faded from view, I thought of his comment about men only wanting sex from me, about the video that he shared with me of Mom and her boss, and about him screaming "Whore!" at my mother, just like those assholes had sung at me. I thought, *I don't need them, and I don't need you.*

"AMERICA I'VE GIVEN YOU ALL AND NOW I'M NOTHING."
—ALLEN GINSBERG, "AMERICA"

The evening before I checked into the Pasadena Recovery Center, Jacob and I went to dinner at Firefly, a sultry, tea-light-lit restaurant with an attached library that also functioned as a bar. Jacob and I had remained friends ever since I dated his friend Logan in high school and gave him a secret midnight peep show while I was taking Logan's virginity. Jacob had been living in San Diego since a year after I started school at State, and though he was a year younger than me, we were the best of friends. Jacob was a big facilitator of my adult get-rich-quick schemes, and I sought his approval on my new webcam management gig, my personal website, and the *Sex Rehab* idea, by which I thought I could use the show to change my life in a positively pro-porn way.

My pal KB, a sex tape broker and a guy Hollywood loves to hate, got a call from a guy named David Weintraub who was looking for people to cast for a new VH1 show. Dr. Drew was expanding the addiction focus from his *Celebrity Rehab* drug-oriented shows to one about sex addiction. Being that I fucked for a living, I figured it was the perfect opportunity to get national attention for my floundering webcam studio.

"You a sex addict, Flame?" KB asked, with Weintraub still on the line.

"Sure, dude, I love the cock," I said. "I masturbate obsessively. I cheat like it's my job. I think of myself as a workaholic."

KB giggled. Weintraub asked that I check out the Sex Addict website and take the test.

After failing the sex addict test miserably, I knew I was in.

Sex Addict Test:

Q. Do you often find yourself preoccupied with sexual thoughts?
A. Yes. Penis. Penises. Penis-tration.

Q. Do you sometimes believe your sexual behavior is not normal?
A. I know tons of porn stars and whores, and this all seems fairly normal. However, not many of them have trained in the art of nonsexual orgasm like I have, which results in the oversexualization of all things. So, yes.

Q. Do you ever feel bad about your sexual behavior?
A. I feel bad that I don't feel bad. Which makes me feel really bad. Yes.

Q. Has your sexual behavior ever created problems for you and your family?
A. Ha. Next question. Family questions blow.

Q. Has anyone ever been hurt emotionally by your sexual behavior?
A. Double ha. Every boyfriend I've ever had. Ever. They've all been hurt. All of them.

Q. Are any of your sexual activities against the law?
A. Oh, like sex in public? Yeah, that's totally illegal.

Q. Have you made any effort to quit this sexual behavior and then failed?
A. I did move to San Diego again to go back to school. But I'm expensive and ended up stripping. Then back in porn because stripping is hard work.

Q. Do you hide your sexual behaviors from others?
A. Hide the Internet? I wish.

Q. Have you traded sex for money and gifts?
A. It's not trading if you fill out a W-2, right? Then it's, like, a job, right? Fuck this test.

Later, I reviewed the sex addict test again, unsure of whether I was pleased to qualify as this kind of addict. Not because the test was right or wrong but because I had a difficult time feeling uncomfortable.

I went to my garage and pulled out all the giant pieces of poster board I could find, plopped down on the cement driveway, and lit a cigarette. Whenever things felt down or ugly, I'd paint, or throw paint, or make lists with fantastical plans that provided some sort of sunshine in an otherwise dreary life.

Operation Sex Rehab:

1. Get cast for reality show.
2. Sabotage reality show with sexiness.
3. Wait for show to air.
4. Show airs and webcam studio is huge success.
5. Money falls from sky and I'm fucking rich.
6. Move to Tahiti, drink rum, run bitches. Ad infinitum.

"I can't believe you're going to Dr. Drew rehab tomorrow," Jacob said, his words bringing me back to the present. "Seriously, Bleeze? You're gonna make dumb money!" Jacob had started calling me Bleeze in college because I smoked a ton of blunts. I retaliated by calling him "my blunt."

Jacob knew I wouldn't be making dumb money as a result of filming the show, but from the national attention my webcam company would receive as a result of my doing the show. I had been offered 10 percent of the studio's profits. As long as people who masturbated also watched *Sex Rehab with Dr. Drew,* when I went back to porn and running the studio, money would flow like honey, and I'd be queen bee of my pornographic hive.

"That's the plan, little Blunt," I said. "Make dumb money, and no more fucking on camera, or fucking performers with screen names, or mandatory AIM [Adult Industry Medical Associates P.C.] testing. None of that. Maybe we should move to Tahiti and open a studio there. Get new beautiful babes to work for us while we just paint and drink and live like Gauguin. Shit will be ill."

Here was yet another plan whereby I thought that life would, thereon in, be super-awesome.

"You know they're gonna call you Jennie, right?" Jacob said, smoothing his long turning-salt-and-pepper hair.

"Not a chance, homie," I said. I had signed every contract as my porn alter ego Penny Flame. "The producers are all calling me Penny. There isn't a chance for Jennie."

I'd fucked guys on camera for approximately five years, fucked women on camera for nearly seven, and fucked myself for eight. Most of the people I had sex with used fake names, and on the rare occasion that I did know his or her real name, industry custom prohibited me from using it. We referred to one another only by our porn identities. Even when we called the testing center to verify another performer's clean STD test, we chose to pull up that performer by pseudonym. The real name only confused things.

Jacob grinned and swilled his wine, pleased that he'd caught me so off guard.

"Okay, Bleeze, but I think you're gonna be surprised once you get there," he said.

I lit a Parliament and shrugged my shoulders, dismissively shaking my head.

"Nope, Jennie doesn't even exist," I said.

I'd been using the pseudonym Penny for eight years, and very few people called me Jennie. Mom, Lyss, James, and Dad, who I'd just reconnected with after not talking to him for years, called me Jennie, but that was about it. Just the fam. Jacob called me Bleeze. My best girlfriend, Angel, called me Pie. To the rest of the world, I was Penny. Penny Flame.

Over dinner, we discussed the real possibility of moving to Bora Bora or Moorea. While we talked, I reviewed all of the problems that would arise if people on the show were to call me Jennie and not Penny. Jennie had no financial future—no current existence, even; thus, it would not be financially beneficial to be Jennie instead of Penny.

Jennie could be stalked, captured, and hurt, all very easily, whereas Penny was not a real person and could disappear, run away, or smile and fuck it off. On the other hand, Penny did have a buttload of commitments when it came to the show, to people, to real life. The webcam company expected me to be Penny. My fans expected me to be Penny. I expected myself to play Penny, which itself meant that Penny was an act and that Jennie was only playing the part of Penny. But that all seemed fairly complicated by my fifth or sixth glass of wine.

When Jacob and I left the restaurant, we gave the valet ten bucks for my car and hopped in my E350 Benz. Jacob plugged his iPod into the speakers and we slapped Mac Dre while doing eighty down the 101 northbound. As I drove, he handed me the blunt, a grape-flavored Swisher Sweet that I'd ripped open and stuffed with OG Kush dank, a crazy expensive strain of pot.

We went home to hide dildos in my bags—knowing they'd be found—alongside my Jack Kerouac and Henry Miller books and *The Tibetan Book of Living and Dying*.

As he sat down, Jacob asked about the high-powered Magic Wand that rested next to him on my couch, eternally plugged in for anytime fun.

"You wanna bring that, Bleeze?" he asked.

"Naw, I couldn't even turn the thing on without getting caught," I said. "Sounds like a fucking lawn mower. Besides, I have enough dick for twenty-one days."

As we talked, I placed a hand-blown glass cock into my running shoes before packing them in my overnight bag.

"Such a minimalist, Bleeze," he teased.

We hit the bong until we both fell asleep on the couch.

EACH PERSON ENTERING rehab on the show was assigned his or her own field producer, the make-it-happen captains of all reality television shows. My field producer's name was Louie, and he e-mailed me to request that I send him my health insurance info, clothing sizes, bra size, weight, and height ("in case the art department needs to purchase clothing for an episode for you"). He wanted pictures of me as a child, preferably at age seven years or younger. He told me I'd be fed three meals a day but could bring money for snacks. And he asked how I would be arriving at the Pasadena Recovery Center.

I laughed as I wrote: "Porn stars don't have health insurance!" I gave him my sizes and closed with: "I gotta ride, don't worry, but I don't have any pictures. At least childhood pictures. Naked pictures, yes. Childhood, no. See you soon!"

Jacob, Angel, and my boobalicious, totally vivacious, and totally unruly porn girlfriend Tory Lane had agreed to drop me off at the PRC. Tory, while over the top and as pornorific as a porn star can be, had a heart of gold and was taking care of her sister, extended family, and self with the money she made in adult. She was one of the few responsible girls in the biz, and when the camera shut off, her sensibility and compassion turned on. She was scheduled to arrive around 10:00 a.m. By nine, I was pacing anxiously around my three-bedroom Sherman Oaks house, venting to Angel and Jacob, who both sat watching my neurosis unfold.

I had a sudden moment of clarity that living in rehab did not sound like the best idea.

"Do you think they'll let us drink?" I asked.

Jacob choked on his bongload, laughing.

"Bleeze, you're going to reeeehaaaaab," he said. "There's no drinking in rehab. You silly Bleeze."

Angel stood and smoothed her long dress, one of the millions of long dresses she owned.

"Pie, you'll be fine," she said, reminding me that my dog and cat were the only things that really needed to be cared for while I was away. "Saucerton Dogsworth is going with Jacob, I'll be here with Kitty, and since that's all you need to worry about, you don't need to worry about anything. You'll be fine."

I remembered the multiple bottles of alcohol in the freezer.

"Should I take a shot?" I asked.

"No, Pie," she said. "No shot. Just be mellow."

Tory pulled into the driveway and honked the horn. I felt all of the blood drain from my face and upper body.

"Oh, shit, what am I doing?" I said.

Angel laughed, grabbed a bag, and ushered me out the door.

"You're going to rehab, Pie," she said. "It'll be fun."

"Let's go, bitches!" Tory yelled from her teenage wasteland Toyota Sequoia.

As we climbed in, we found that the interior of the car was littered with stripper heels, McDonald's bags, and a few three-ring binders.

"Sorry, we went to Disneyland yesterday," Tory boasted. "It's a little messy back there!"

Her giant tits nearly flew out of her tube dress as she spun the wheel and pulled out of the driveway.

"To rehab!" she yelled.

I lit a cigarette, yielding to the next three weeks, the unknown, and that which I could no longer control.

It was abnormally hot for April, and when I stepped from Tory's Disneyland kidmobile and onto the black, sunshine-smothered asphalt outside the Vagabond Inn Executive Pasadena, I remembered how much farther east we were, and how the ocean breeze failed to blow past Interstate 5. Louie greeted me as Jacob and Tory hopped out. A bear of a man, on the shorter side of tall, he had a grin that went ear to ear and an embrace that was equally as disarming as his smile. Disagreeing with the hot temperature, Angel continued to sit in the car.

"Let's get a mic on you, girl!" Louie said.

He herded me toward one of the small hotel rooms, with Tory and Jacob following close behind. When Louie opened the hotel door and revealed a slew of production guys, I laughed.

"Ah, I see you brought me some entertainment," I said.

The room shifted, uneasy with the overt sexualization. Jake, the microphone guy, stepped forward to prepare me for battle. He strapped a battery pack to my bra and delicately and unobtrusively ran a fingernail-size microphone down the front of my blouse, connecting it with sticky white tape to the inside of my shirt and plugging the end of the cord into the battery pack.

"You can move this around if it's uncomfortable," he said.

"Really?" I said sweetly, running my hand over the outline of his shoulder. "I do squats on cock for forty-five minutes each day I go to work. Sometimes get fucked upside down while doing handstands. I think I can handle a little battery pack. Thanks, though, buddy."

He stepped back, surprised. Smiling an awkward smile, he turned on his heel and went to mic Tory.

Tory, who wore a tube dress sans bra, laughed at him as he approached.

"I don't know where you're gonna put that thing, but I can think of a few places!" she said.

Then she whipped out her giant fake tits and gave him a solid bend-over-to-display-the-vagina stance.

"We can . . . uh . . . just put it . . . here . . . ," he said, hooking it to her underwear, a string that was barely even there.

"We good to go?" Louie asked Jake.

Tory and I played with the microphones.

"Testes, testes, one, two . . . three?" we said.

The room shifted again. Muffled laughs led to Jake's response.

"Yeah, they're good," Jake said.

Tory and I bowed, both pleased with our intentional, hyperbolic performance. The show was just getting started.

We got ourselves arranged in Tory's car with Jacob driving, Angel riding shotgun, and Tory and me squished into one seat in the back. Louie hid in the trunk so the cameraman could film Tory and me, then Jacob, then spin to get Angel. Tory and I kissed, rubbed each other's legs and tits, and then paused so that I could look out the window, pensive, unsure of what was to come. It was such a production. The movement felt contrived, the dialogue rehearsed.

"Dude, whatever you do, don't come out of rehab and be all anti-porn and shit, okay?" Tory said.

Both Angel and Jacob glanced back in the rearview mirror as I lit a cigarette and delivered the lines I'd already written in my head.

"I won't be different, baby," I said. "I'll be the same freaky, horny girl that you love. Besides, ain't nothing out there for me but porn."

Another porn star, Mary Carey, had done a Dr. Drew show, and when she came out and quit, it was the joke of the industry. We made bets on how long it would be until she was back. She tried to stay away. But she needed the money, so she ended up stripping again, and then, slippery-slope style, she was right back to porn. But there was a big difference between her and me: She had hoped to become mainstream famous by doing the Dr. Drew show. I wanted to become porn famous. As far as I was concerned, it was impossible to go mainstream after you'd made a career out of fucking for money. Not to mention socially unforgivable. So I wasn't even going to try.

"I'm just gonna take a little me time," I said, pulling a long drag off my smoke. Jacob threw his glance to me through the rearview, his already crow's-footed eyes smiling and his jaw slack, poker-faced except for the eyes, and repeated his question from the night before. It was the question that I'd dismissed and tried to forget.

"How do you feel about them calling you Jennie?" he said.

"They aren't calling me Jennie, dude, so stop it," I shot back at him, slicing through the mirror and into his driver's seat with a look of my own that said, *Shut your fucking mouth.*

"Yeah, they *will* be using Jennifer," Louie whispered from the trunk.

My heart dropped.

"What?" I said.

I turned my head back to Louie, even though I'd been instructed to ignore his existence entirely.

"What do you mean, they'll call me Jennifer?" I prodded.

We pulled up to the Pasadena Recovery Center, and I unsteadily hobbled out of the car in my shiny black stilettos. Tory hopped out of the car and we embraced and shared a dreamlike, hazy kiss. I hugged Angel and Jacob and walked up to the front door of the facility. When the cameraman cut, a production assistant took my bag and led me around the center to a back entrance.

The arrival shot was complete and it was time to check into sex rehab.

NO CAMERAMEN WERE allowed to film in the loading room, so they took off my mic and then I was left to my own devices. It was a kind of ~~prison~~ holding cell for rehab patients who hadn't been processed yet and needed to be given a rundown of what was about to happen. The small, dank room was pastel-Easter-egg yellow, as if the soft color of muted sunshine would ease my worries. There was an old scratched wooden table in the center of the room, and stiff-backed chairs lined the walls. The chairs had ripped green seats with itchy yellow Styrofoam poking out, and none of them were the least bit comfy. I climbed on top of the table and sat obsessively sending texts until that, too, became uncomfortable. There was a small cooler loaded with bottled water and granola bars. I started thinking that if they were going to leave me in there for more than twenty minutes, I could chug a bottle of water and fashion an ashtray from its plastic remains for some smoking entertainment. I called this plan Operation Make an Ashtray and Smoke and was halfway through draining a bottle when the program director came into the room.

"I'm Mike Bloom and I run this bitch," he said.

That's probably not what he said, but I couldn't hear him over the roar of nicotine withdrawal inside my mind.

"Hey, man," I said. "Nice to meet you."

Seemingly unsettled by my pacing, he offered a seat and produced a contract.

"We are having all the residents sign contracts upon entering the facility," he said. "There will be no drinking or drug use. No physical touching, no sex, no masturbation, no sexual inferences, implications, or conversations."

He reviewed the remainder of the contract with a super-serious face, the kind of face that said: *If you break the contract, I will kick your horny, cock-loving ass outta here so quick your ovaries will burst.*

The only problem was I didn't know how to interact with people in a nonsexual way.

"Do we get warnings?" I said. "Like a yellow card or something?"

He raised his thick eyebrows and tilted his head ever so slightly to the right.

"You'll get a warning," he said. "One or two. It will be up to the rehab technicians."

I signed without reading, because I didn't have time to get a lawyer in there and review the agreement. And I needed a fucking cigarette.

"I'll get a copy?" I asked.

Clutching my purse and the cigarettes inside, I stood and smiled warmly at him.

"Yes, you'll get a copy," he said. "Would you like to go smoke?"

Unsure of how he had accessed my innermost thoughts, I hid my surprise and followed him to the parking lot, where a watchful production assistant shadowed my every move, suspicious of the girl in heels and full spandex, chain-smoking cigarettes and checking her phone obsessively. In the time I'd been in the Easter egg room, I'd texted nearly sixty people saying:

"When I get outta this bitch, I'm gonna fuck you silly."

The responses came in like a flurry, and as I smoked cigarette after cigarette, I arranged my future fuckfest for when I got out of rehab.

"They're ready for you now," the PA said.

I flicked my cigarette butt into the graveyard of butts at my feet. I followed him back to the front door. Once inside, I waited in the hallway until Jake reappeared and re-microphoned me. Then I was introduced to Tommy, "cat herder" extraordinaire. He was called a cat herder because people in the industry (both porn and mainstream) like to think of organizing celebrities like herding cats: virtually impossible with a high probability of being scratched. Tommy and all the other staff wore FBI-style earpieces and he gave me a countdown as I walked through the double doors and onto the floor.

"Five . . . four . . . three . . . ," he said.

I'd had no clue that there would be so much hoop jumping.

I guess that's why I loved porn. All I had to do was get a guy hard and then fuck him. The cameras were always ready.

BY THE TIME I was led into my room by a tech named Selma, it was late afternoon or early evening. Selma was a headstrong, pastoral type of woman with a voice like wind chimes who made me think of collard greens and corn bread. She was very welcoming, and took both of my hands as she walked me down the hallway to my room.

"Would you like to be called Jennifer?" she asked.

I knew I was on camera and that my answer had to be affirmative, but for the briefest moment—even with all the time I'd spent in front of a lens, tits out, with my legs wide open—for that fraction of a second I felt more naked than I ever had before. Jennifer had never been on camera, and even just the thought of it made me feel revealed and vulnerable.

"Yeah, that will be better," I said.

Selma scrunched her face and smiled at me, and it was done. I was Jennifer. Not Penny. There was nothing to be done about it now. So I sucked in my stomach, pushed out my tits, and grasped my hands delicately at my waist as I sat down on the small single bed.

"So this is it?" I said.

If I couldn't be Penny Flame in here, I would have to create a Jennifer that was prim and proper yet sexually impossible to resist. Only, she would have to exist within the confines of this particular space and without violating whatever contract I'd just signed. She would have to be a watered-down version of the porn star, the sexy piece of ass behind Penny Flame.

In the room, *Playboy* model Nicole Narain slept in semidarkness. The lights were controlled by the production crew, who had placed cameras in each corner of the room, mounted indiscreetly on the ceilings. I was used to rooms filled with cameras, and I had worked plenty of live webcam shows, so the cameras didn't bother me at all. Quite the opposite: I loved the idea of a stranger sitting in a room no more than one hundred feet away, watching my every move. I made a mental note to perform a live striptease for this godly, omniscient person.

Selma kneeled down on the cheap wood flooring next to my bed.

"I'm going to check your bags for paraphernalia, okay, Miss Jennifer?" she said.

I had been waiting for this moment. When I packed my bags full of cocks, I knew it would be a great moment for the show's editors and line producers when they found the mold of Ron Jeremy, the six hand-blown dildos, the kneepads, and the plastic cock with a suction cup at the end. I had planned to hold them up for the camera to see, as I said: "Oh, tee hee hee, you caught me." I hadn't expected to be disappointed that she would find everything, even the one stuffed into my running shoes, and I wasn't. But I had expected to have the most confiscated cocks of all the patients. I couldn't believe what I was hearing.

"You weren't the worst," she said. "Don't worry, Jennifer."

She kept saying my name, the real one. Each time she addressed me, she made a point of starting or ending each statement with Jennifer:

"Jennifer, what are you doing with all these?"

With every Jennifer, I thought, *PENNY PENNY PENNY. I AM* PENNY.

If I could have put my fingers in my ears and sung to drown out her name-calling and cock-finding, I would have, but I feared looking childish. My goal was to look sexy.

"I'm not the worst cock bringer?" I said.

As I did so, I unwrapped a Blow Pop and smiled on the inside that she hadn't noticed and confiscated my oral flirtation devices.

"We aren't saying that here, Jennifer, because it's inappropriate language," she said. "What I meant was, someone else brought more paraphernalia than you. You shouldn't be ashamed."

"Cool, no shame," I said. "Got it. I'm gonna go smoke, is that okay?"

I left her in my room, repacking my bags, and walked to the outdoor patio to meet some of my fellow patients.

THE PATIO HAD a smoking table, two lounge-style bed things, a long picnic table, and some greenery. Some of the bushes were real and some were big fake flowers to spruce up the set. I was acutely aware of such details the first day, and yet I became oblivious to them in the days that followed.

The patio was also home to two boys, which I was super-excited to find. One looked like a surfer, the other a rock star. As usual, my surfer-slash-rock-star radar was on point.

James Lovett marched back and forth along the patio, his long, scraggly dirty-blond hair flopping as he tossed his skateboard to the ground, did a trick, and then jumped off with a yelp. Phil Varone, all hard spiky hair and tattooed arms, sat calmly taking in his surroundings, seemingly expending as little energy as possible.

"I'm Penny. Fuck. Jennie. I'm Jennie," I said.

"Hey, Penny Jennie," he said. "I'm Phil."

James continued back and forth across the patio. His spastic movements made me edgy, even a bit frightened.

"Is he okay?" I asked Phil.

"Yeah, just horny, I think," Phil said.

I immediately felt like this James person was like me and had ulterior motives. He seemed like he didn't give a fuck about treatment and was probably there to get some green.

"You?" I asked Phil, wanting to know if James and I were the only con artists.

"Yeah, but I'm fine for right now," he said. "I'm not gonna go crazy or anything."

"I wanna be the first guy to do, like, an action sports porn," James said. "Like, some little baby is skateboarding, and then she, like, falls, and I'm, like, 'Whoops!'"

As he talked, James looked to us and made a motion as if he had fallen and his penis had fallen into a woman's vagina.

"Girls on skateboards sounds like girls getting hurt," I said. "You don't want to make porn that hurts girls, do you? Then the girls can't perform."

James stood with his back to the wall, like a caged animal unsure of its surroundings.

"Some girls like to get hurt," he said, smiling coyly.

"Some girls like to *hurt*," I said.

An hour or two later, the last patient arrived. He was an older British man who dressed as if he awoke each morning with the specific purpose of looking fabulous. When he walked onto the patio, wide-eyed and curious as a child, he said, "Hey," to six people all at once and introduced himself as Duncan Roy. His gayness was already quite apparent. *There is no way this beautiful, impeccably dressed man would be jerking off all the time if he liked vagina,* I thought. Gay men often struck me as being impossibly choosy when it came to their food, clothes, friends, and orifices.

Duncan sat down on one of the outdoor daybeds as Dr. Drew, along with an unidentified woman whom I later came to know as a therapist named Jill, and some other rehab techs stood on the patio and addressed the patients. Here was the rehab welcome wagon.

"I just want to say welcome and thank you for really showing some immense courage to step up and drop the veil of secrecy and shame that surrounds this condition," Dr. Drew said. "Now, you've all signed a celibacy contract, which means no pornographic materials, no seductive behavior, no inappropriate dress, no masturbation, and no touching in this program, right?"

I looked to Duncan, who nodded his head at Drew as if Drew were mentioning a grocery list that was unnecessary because Duncan had already memorized it.

"Nobody touches," Drew repeated. "At most a handshake if the other person gives you permission. The first order of business is to create a boundary around yourself and your body. Also, there are some things that are highly slippery for people with this condition, like computers. We can't have that. Cell phones, too, are off-limits."

Selma had already confiscated my cell phone, and as I looked down at my dangerously low-cut shirt, I knew I'd be asked to change when the welcome wagon concluded.

"Cell phones are often loaded with numbers and other things that you may have visited that could easily be triggers," Drew continued. "Sexual addiction is an interesting thing to treat; it's a little different from straight substance addiction."

I was sitting next to Kendra Jade Rossi, a stunning and petite mega-breasted woman whose eight-by-ten naked photos I'd seen plastered across American strip club makeup rooms. As the feature dancer, it's tradition to leave a signed, eight-by-ten photograph of yourself for the picture wall, and when I traveled the country, dancing in the nation's finest titty bars, I'd seen her photo on many walls and imagined she'd be lovely in person, which she was.

Amber Smith, a dewy-eyed and soft-faced forty-something model who had appeared on *Celebrity Rehab with Dr. Drew,* was also sitting on one of the daybeds. She had signed up to deal with a love addiction that Drew believed was the root of her drug addiction. There was also Kari Ann Peniche, who kept talking about going home to her pets and was very obviously high on meth or speed or some sort of serious upper.

I looked at Amber. *That chick is way too hot to fall in love with guys who don't love her back.*

Jill, the therapist specializing in sex and love addiction, broke my momentary reverie.

"This is way harder than any other addiction," she said. "I would say this is the last frontier after people have addressed food, drugs, and alcohol."

Drew concluded the welcome party with these closing words:

"We are here to make this an important experience."

"What the fuck am I doing here?" I muttered, lighting another

cigarette and looking from the doctors—who had walked away
from their sexually addicted patients and gone back into the rehab
facility—to Kendra, and then to Duncan, and then to the sky.

⸻

THE ROOM DESIGNATED for therapy wasn't part of the Pasadena
Recovery Center. It was a large double-wide trailer the production
crew brought into the parking lot of the facility. It was equipped
with exterior lighting to keep the interior perfectly lit. The room
felt colder inside than outside, perhaps due to the specific seat loca-
tions: the two chairs were not clustered together but instead face-
to-face, and Dr. Drew wasn't within reaching distance, which was
generally how I gauged appropriate standing, sitting, or sexing dis-
tances. For group sessions, we were invited to a semicircle of white
chairs, which created a bit more warmth, a semicircular sense of
community. But, for the one-on-one sessions with Dr. Drew, or
Drew and Jill, I sat in a solo chair, separated from their chairs by a
square table that held flowers and Kleenex. When I sat down for
my first one-on-one, I crossed my legs primly.

"Welcome," Dr. Drew said. "So we're gonna call you Jennifer;
you getting used to that?"

I recrossed my legs and placed my hands delicately in my lap.

"I'm trying," I said.

He looked to his papers.

"Good, you're trying," he said. "Now, we're a program to treat
sexual addiction and compulsion. How do you see that manifesting
in your life?"

I was thrown by the quickness with which he immediately
jumped into therapy, without any "How ya doin'?" or questions
about my family.

"Uh, well, I'm an adult performer, so I have sex on camera,
and, uh, I'm incapable of caring about any of the people I have sex
with," I said.

Suddenly, I wasn't so sure about this. A quality I had thought made me invaluable and hot now sounded cold and appalling. In my head, I was used to thinking, *I don't give a fuck about these people.* I had always thought that was different from *I can't care about people.* In a flash, I knew they were the same thing, and for the first time that knowledge hurt. I don't know why I never realized that "not giving a fuck" could be equivalent to "unable to give a fuck" or why it hurt, but in that flash, sitting face-to-face with Dr. Drew, I thought, *I bet this guy can care about people. And I bet he's not ashamed of caring for people, either. I can't even care for myself.*

Dr. Drew nodded emphatically, which made my feelings even more difficult to brush away, which was exactly what I wanted to do. It was the same nod I had seen and doubted on television, but in person he was able to make his charisma and understanding tangible with only three simple nods of his head.

"Well, you know, sex addiction is, for the most part, an intimacy disorder," he said.

I was the one to nod at him now, not because I knew what he said was true, but because I knew I couldn't be intimate. There was no place in my realm of understanding in which the idea of intimacy fit. It certainly didn't fit into porn star land, and I didn't exist anywhere else.

"I create it, and I run from it," I said.

This was true for every person I'd dated, cared for, loved.

"You run," he said, and paused, looking up from his pad. "What do you think that's about?"

I had never allowed myself to wonder why I ran from people, from connection, from what Dr. Drew was labeling as "intimacy." I had never questioned why I habitually hurt the men I dated, or the people in my family. I had never thought: *Jennie, why are you doing this?*

In the past, I had simply acted and then moved forward. If I felt like crying, I shut the emotions down or explained to myself what was happening physiologically, so that the emotional side of the tears somehow seemed less important than the biological. This quality made me a good porn star. But it suddenly didn't seem like a great way to live.

"It's a wall," I whispered. I felt a surge of emotion and used every ounce of strength I had to admit my separation from all things human while keeping the salty water from covering my perfectly made-up cheeks.

"What do you think is behind that wall?" Drew said.

He looked directly in my eyes, though it was not a stare I could maintain without breaking. The thought of something existing behind this impenetrable wall was horrifying, exhausting. I grabbed a Kleenex and began folding it into small triangles, thinking if I could make the perfect triangle, I could dab my inner eyes without disrupting the glue that held my fake eyelashes in place.

"Hopefully, a caring, sensitive person that can have meaningful relationships," I said.

I continued tissue folding and inner-eye dabbing.

"I think we can help with that," he said, smiling diplomatically, carefully, as if I were a fragile, breakable creature. As if I hadn't had the weight of hundreds of men and women on top of my small body. As if whatever hid behind that wall still mattered.

The rest of the evening felt like swimming. Like walking on the bottom of a pool with weighted shoes and no goggles. The rehab floor felt like sand, the sky ripped open, my vision blurred and my breath caught. I couldn't stop thinking about the person behind the wall, a person that—like sunlight in the depths of the Pacific— barely survived beneath the tons of watery weight up above.

AS I QUICKLY learned during my time on the show, interesting things begin to happen when you place multiple quasi-famous people in a living facility together. The ego-driven desires of "real life" became mundane nonissues. Things like rent and car payments faded away under the influence of family-centered therapy sessions in which Duncan and Kendra both revealed they'd been molested and abused as children, and Kari Ann and Nicole denied, denied, denied there had ever been any problems whatsoever.

Nicole, my roommate, very quickly began to dislike me because of the thin, wavering gray area separating our professions. She considered herself higher on the food chain than me, more of a model than a sex worker. For my part, I always wondered where all of her money came from. I doubted her modeling paid so well.

Soon Kari Ann became increasingly difficult to handle. She made demands for juice early in the mornings and refused to get out of bed. She was definitely coming down from a crystal meth binge and was seemingly ~~unwilling~~ unable to participate. Phil's feelings started to bubble up, pushed to the surface by his inability to masturbate. He revealed a deep-seated need for love and suffered unresolved hurt from his mother's death, which would only be alleviated through a conversation with his father. Amber also had an unquenchable need for love, thanks to abandonment issues left over from her father and an inability to sort it all out with her mother. James continued on his quest for attention. While that was the original, inauthentic reason I'd come to rehab as well, my intentions had shifted dramatically with the reintroduction of Jennie and the notion that Penny Flame was indeed "the wall" behind which my real personality was hidden.

Kendra's husband, Lukas, came to visit one evening, and we sat around listening to him sing. He had won a reality show called *Rock Star: Supernova* about the search for a lead singer for Tommy Lee's band. As he crooned sweetly to his darling wife, Duncan and I sat back in awe, astonished that two people could love so deeply, so honestly, so entirely.

"The concept of being loved so fully by someone—anyone—so completely overwhelms me," Duncan said. "I laugh in people's faces when they ask me if I want a relationship, as if the thought of loving someone and being loved by someone is laughable."

I identified with him on a devastatingly intrinsic level.

"It is possible to love someone, Duncan," Kendra said. "It is possible for someone to love you."

"Let's hope so," Duncan said.

To me, those words were a brush-off and also incredibly complex. I could relate.

Because we had signed contracts that we would make no physical contact, Kendra and Lukas were unable to embrace one another, and so he was left to show his love for her in song. Powerless to formulate a cohesive reason for my loveless life, I left the group and returned to the solitude of my room. Once there, even with an occasional shift in the angle of the cameras in the ceiling, I completely forgot that I was being filmed. I was too absorbed in writing in the thin journals provided on our nightstands, along with varying Anonymous groups' books on addictions ranging from alcoholism to sex.

I took to the empty pages and wrote: "Sad, cold little girl, always running away."

I decided that if I could speak as strongly as Duncan, love as selflessly as Kendra, be as open and honest about my wants as Phil, and have as much awareness of my fears as Amber, the possibility of loving anyone, including myself, could rise from zero to one in a gazillion. And even that would be quite the improvement.

In an afternoon therapy group led by Dr. Drew and Jill, we were asked to write a list of six valuable things about ourselves. I wanted to write Duncan's list instead of my own. Finally, I admitted to Drew what I knew was wrong with me.

"My heart is as damaged as goods can be," I said.

"Your heart is only wounded, not damaged," Drew said. "'Damaged' implies it cannot be repaired. You just need some work."

When Jill talked about the precious inner child in each of us, I laughed. But she insisted that the adult Jennie and the child Jennie must live in harmony, that it was the adult's responsibility to take care of and provide for the child.

Later that night, Duncan and I lay under the Pasadena stars on the cheap patio furniture, chain-smoking and laughing until we cried. We talked about falling babies and inner children until it kind of made sense. Maybe we could see how Duncan re-traumatized his inner child each time he acted out, and how I had quit caring about the innocent child within my own soul long before I began selling my body for money.

ON ONE PARTICULARLY warm evening, everyone from the show waited outside of a meeting related to our treatment, which Dr. Drew and Jill had thought would be good for us to attend because they hoped it would help us prepare to be sober in the outside world. I stood talking with James. We were joking and flirting totally inappropriately, and I was floating somewhere in between Penny the porn star and Jennie, the young girl who needed help learning how to feel.

"I would rape the shit outta you if we weren't in here," he jokingly said.

"Ditto," I said.

I didn't know how else to deal with the comment.

We went to the meeting, said our thank-yous and good-byes, and went home. Afterwards, I sat outside, smoking cigarettes until midnight, unable to stop thinking about what he'd said or close my eyes and go to bed.

I knew he wouldn't actually rape me, but the inappropriateness of the comment and my inability to maintain a boundary I'd been trying so hard to create bothered me. His word choice was also particularly troublesome because I'd been raped on a train to San Diego when I was twenty-one. I had been on a five-day cocaine binge at the time, and I had never mentioned it to a soul. I simply exited the train afterwards and vowed never again to ride anywhere when I was that fucked-up, a vow I broke the second I had some more coke and needed to get to Los Angeles.

When we came back home from the meeting, sitting outside on the smoking patio, at the small table next to the fake bushes, I confided in Duncan and Kendra, my two rehab soul mates, about James's comment.

"He didn't mean it like that, you know," I said. "Besides, I've used 'rape' as a way of telling someone I'd fuck 'em, too, so it's not like I can be mad at him for something I've done. I'm more concerned about my inability to tell him, 'What you're saying isn't appropriate here.' Why couldn't I stand up for myself?"

"Just because you couldn't stand up for yourself doesn't make it your fault," Duncan said.

He was fuming that the word "rape" had been used in a facility where the majority of the patients had been raped.

"That little fucking prick," Duncan said. "I can't believe him. Such a phony."

Kendra was also fuming.

"You have to say something to him in group tomorrow," she said.

It hadn't ever occurred to me that what had happened to me on the train to San Diego was not my fault. When I woke up, blurry and drunk, to a conductor between my legs, I immediately blacked out again. When I woke the second time to him fixing my panties, I brushed his hand away.

"Leave me alone," I mumbled.

When it was time for me to get off the train, I walked by the vile conductor and shook my finger in his face.

"I know what you did," I said.

However, I also knew what *I* had done: I had gotten so fucked-up that I couldn't stay awake, and I had let myself be raped by going to sleep on the train in an empty car. And so I blamed myself for what had happened more than I blamed the man who raped me.

The next morning, sick to my stomach with nerves, I brought up the comment in group, where I felt it was safer to confront James than one-on-one.

"It wasn't appropriate," I said to James. "I'm not mad at you, because you didn't realize it was inappropriate. I'm grateful I get to exercise a boundary and say that this isn't okay. So thank you, and please don't say things like that anymore."

It turned into a bigger fight than it should have, because he had swimmer's ear and a difficult time hearing what I was saying.

"You think I'm going to *rape* you?" he yelled at me, cupping his hand over his mouth, astonished.

"No, dude, I'd cut your balls off if you tried," I retorted, somewhat frustrated that he had the hearing of an old man. "I'm just saying it's not the right place to use that word loosely."

"You're going to cut my balls off?" he screamed, moving his chair as far from me as possible while still being a part of the semicircle.

"No. Jesus," I said. "Fine, yes. Fuck. Never mind."

I gave up the fight, but the overall resolution was positive, the group supportive, the lesson incredible. Some words should never be used lightly, and just because I'd had a difficult time saying "No" once didn't mean I couldn't ever say "No" again.

OVER THE COURSE of the nineteen days we ended up spending in the Pasadena Recovery Center, a close bond was formed between these people who had originally started off as horny strangers. Friendships were forged that would not be undone when the show ended. Five days before we were to be released into the world, I sat outside with Duncan, drawing sketches of him in my notebook using charcoal pencils.

"You know, you don't have to be a porn star," Duncan said with a hint of seriousness in his voice that I hadn't known existed. "I think you can do anything else you want in the world. Be a writer, director, candlestick maker. You're very good, Jen."

"Stop moving," I said. "I'm trying to get your nose."

I may have been in therapy for nineteen days, but compliments still made me uncomfortable.

Later that day, in a one-on-one session, I sat across from Dr. Drew, feeling at once confident and disoriented.

"I don't think I can go back to porn," I said. "Not like this. I have too many feelings."

I sat still as I talked, having managed to keep the Kleenex triangle folding under control, as it was one of the little things that Drew and Jill had both picked up on and said I used as a distraction from the task at hand, like talking about feelings.

"I think that is a good idea, Jennie," Drew said. "We can help you figure out where to go from here."

He gave me his nod of approval, the same nod he gave me on the very first day when he explained the "wall." After the session, I went back to the rehab floor and told Duncan what I had decided while finishing the portrait of him I had started.

"I'm not going back," I said. "I'm going to quit porn."

Dr. Drew, Jill, Duncan, Kendra, and the rest of the patients weren't the only ones excited to see me quit porn. The production crew—which had managed to blend like wallpaper into the background of heartbreaking therapy sessions and genius "Aha!" moments—was super-excited to film my departure from adult business. They loaded me into a production van and we headed off to Chatsworth, the porn capital of the world, so I could properly resign from the webcam manager position. The first time they'd ever filmed me there, earlier in the show, I was adamant about including shots of the exterior of the building and a giant sign that displayed the company's name, so it would appear on the show and I could ultimately profit from the shot. This time I didn't care. I was on a mission, and I had to do it while the courage flowed. I walked into the studio and sat down with Del.

"I can't come back here," I said. "I can't do any of it anymore. I quit."

"What's this about?" he asked, his accent heavier when he was stressed.

"It's fucking me up, Del," I said. "My insides, my soul, they're fucked. I mean, I have a huge alcohol and drug problem, and the sex-for-money thing makes me want to use. I have to quit it all. Everything. I'm sorry."

I cried, pushing his Marlboro Reds toward him so he could smoke, even though I knew he wanted to take the box and throw it against the wall.

"I know you have a problem," he said. "I've always known."

I laughed, surprised by how aware he'd been of my internal devastation.

"Awesome," I said. "Thanks. Okay, so I have to go now."

I walked out of the studio and ran to the van, where Louie stood, tears shining in his eyes. As Louie hugged me, the pain of the moment and the fear of my insecure future all came tumbling out, and I sobbed in his arms until I couldn't sob anymore. I felt somebody tap me on the shoulder.

"Uh, Miss Penny?" a man's voice said. "I mean, Jennie?"

Tom, the studio's maintenance guy, stood behind me, looking to the ground and holding his hands shyly in front of him, unsure of whether to put them in his front pockets, his back pockets, or to extend them to me for a hug.

"I just want to say what a pleasure it's been working with you," he said. "You're gonna do it all. I know you can."

Then he swept me up in a solemn embrace.

"Don't you come back, you hear?" he said. "Don't you forget me, either."

The next morning, the same production crew drove Jill and me out to my house in Sherman Oaks. We threw away three bottles of vodka and two of Jack Daniel's. Dumping them down the drain was much easier than I'd expected. When we went into what I deemed my "porn room," I climbed into the mess of DVDs, stripper shoes, feather boas, and shoot clothes—the plastic and pleather skirts, fishnet panties, and bra sets I wore to shoot porn scenes—the silly, cheap things that had made me *me*. One shoe at a time,

I filled Tupperware tubs until the room was clean and my house and life had been de-porned. It felt good while Jill was standing there watching me, and yet, my mind had already drifted to the hows. How to live here alone, how to afford the $2,400-a-month rent, how to continue in life without the exaggerated hyper-numb persona I'd created and called my career.

It hadn't been easy, but I had found a way to be Jennie in rehab. But now that I was about to get out of rehab, how could I *not be* Penny Flame?

4

When Ira Levin wrote *The Stepford Wives,* I'm fairly positive he had Moraga, California, in mind as the setting. It's a small town of less than fifteen thousand people. There is barely any crime, so parents and kids don't lock their houses, cars, or bikes. Grazing cows cover green, rolling hills. As we passed Campolindo High School and the fat spotted heifers, my mom rolled down the Taurus windows and smiled as if we'd arrived someplace special.

"The air smells terrible here," I said, defiantly placing my feet on the dashboard and crossing my arms. It was a few days after my dad's driveway tirade.

"That's what clean air smells like, Jennifer."

I laughed, a sarcastic, snarky, thirteen-year-old laugh, incapable of equating the abstract idea of clean air to a clean start.

"Clean air smells like cow shit," I said.

For our first month and a half in town, before Mom rented an apartment on Ascot Drive—one of the two streets in Moraga with apartments—we lived in a residence-style hotel, the Hillside Inn & Suites, in the neighboring town of Lafayette. During the course of our hotel living, I became increasingly irate about the late nights my mom was working. Each evening I perched in the hotel window and waited for her to come home, leaving my post only long enough to put my brother and sister to bed. When she finally rolled into the parking lot, followed by her boss, Samuel, in his Jeep, I watched them get out of their cars. They embraced, kissed, and then parted. She double-checked her car lock before walking toward our room. Most nights I went back to the bedroom before she got into the two-bedroom suite.

One evening I worked up the courage to confront her lack of parental attentiveness. It was midnight when she got home and found me in the kitchenette.

"Jennifer, I have to take two and a half hours out of my work-day *each day* to take you and your brother and sister to school," she said. "I have to work late."

"Whatever," I said.

I glared my best eye-daggers glare, arms crossed defiantly, and stormed into the bedroom, where my siblings slept quietly, and tried to sleep off the hurt.

Another night she came home and caught me sitting in the window, my nose pressed against the glass, backlit by the hotel's cheap lamps.

"Why are you sitting there?" she asked, sounding incredulous that I would wait up for her each night.

"Why does Samuel follow you here?" I asked.

Returning a question with a question was the best defense I had.

"Because your father is furious that I took you guys away and is looking for you," she said. "If he knows we are here, he'll take you away from me. He's dangerous. I'd never see you again."

"So we're hiding from Dad?" I said.

I was a bit worried that we were hiding from the man who raised me, who created me, who was half of me.

"Jennifer, go to bed," she said.

I did as she asked, but I couldn't sleep. While my sister snored softly next to me, I imagined Dad showing up at the hotel just as furious as he'd been the night we left. I replayed my memory of him hitting the Taurus and screaming: "Whore, you fucking whore!" I imagined us kids kicking and screaming, begging to be left with Mom. After he had taken us away with him, I imagined Mom crying hysterically when she returned from kissing Samuel, realizing she'd chosen to work and fuck him instead of protecting her children, who had sat in a cheap Lafayette hotel room, as terrified of being found as they were of being left alone.

I'd been sleepless since the "dangerous dad" conversation. When we finally moved into the apartment on Ascot Drive, Mom tried to reassure me.

"It's safe here," she said. "You little babies will be safe."

Moraga *was* a safe town. The worst thing happening there was the occasional burglary, and because there were only three streets in and out of the area, burglars were often caught before they could hit the freeway. Samuel's family lived in Moraga, in a beautiful sprawling home on one of the beautiful rolling hills, and they didn't worry about theft, either. It took his wife years to recognize that my mom had stolen her husband away from her in broad daylight.

I SPENT THE entire summer taking the bus and BART out to visit Melanie in Concord, where we prepped ourselves for high school and messed around with the Concord guys, Alex, Matt, and Jeremy.

As the new school year approached, I was ready to give up my baggy overalls, JNCO jeans, and leftover plaid skirts in an attempt to fit in with the Moraga girls, but the aspects of my personality I had cultivated in Concord would make it virtually impossible to blend entirely. For one thing, I had perfected my shameless flirting skills and honed my ability to be the hot Girl Next Door in a room full of Beauties. I was a little bit louder than the rest of the girls. I used dirtier language and showed more skin. And going into school, I had no idea that I had to ease gently into the minds of my new naïve and untouched classmates or how different these purebred psyches actually were. I couldn't begin to understand the cultural chasm I'd crossed by exiting 24 West and turning left down Moraga Road.

On the first day of school at Campolindo, I wasn't met with one Isabella but fifty. They were adorned in the finest from Abercrombie and J.Crew, their haircuts were professional, and they lacked the black liquid eyeliner that had run rampant in my middle school. In place of fist-size hoop earrings, there were delicate pearls and freckle-size diamonds. Instead of curled and hair-sprayed bangs, there were soft wavy tendrils falling over cashmere-shrouded shoulders. Rather than spend their mornings flirting and smoking weed behind Burger King, like Mel and I had, these girls played sports and went running in packs of fifteen and twenty. On any given afternoon, the cross-country or soccer teams could be found jogging the loop around town: young, determined women glistening with clean sweat. At the same time, I could be found stealing cigarettes from my closet-smoker mom while babysitting James and Lyss.

I had only two real girlfriends in the beginning of my Moraga Campo career: Kelli and Cynth. Because Cynth had rollover popularity with the guys from middle school, I bounced my get-popular-quick schemes off Kelli, which was awesome, because when I had launched my look-like-a-mini-stripper scheme back in Concord, I had no savvy friends with whom to discuss the potential outcomes of such a drastic wardrobe change. Kelli was popular but not *popular*. She was a cross-country runner, but had a rack that barely fit in a sports bra. She was a mismatch of possibilities, perhaps because her warm, tough, say-it-like-it-is pops had married an ultra-chilly woman after Kelli's real mom died, and the juxtaposition of parental influences created the contradiction that was Kelli.

We were in her bedroom one afternoon as she inspected her gargantuan tits in the mirror when I told her that I'd fallen in love with the spiky-haired boy who served as the assistant to my French teacher, Madame Branchard.

His name was Logan, although I didn't even know his name when I first fell in love with him in my French language lab. His hair was so perfectly spiked that it never moved. It looked as if it could impale my heart if he so chose. He sat next to Madame at the front of the lab, and I could see his big butterfly eyelashes from seven rows back, where I could also see him roll his eyes at her lame jokes. I even caught him sleeping a few times, unbeknownst to her. When those lashes fluttered open, I imagined being nose to nose with him. When I confessed all of this to Kelli, she just laughed.

"So? What do you want me to do about it?" Kelli asked.

"I don't know, dude, help me find a way to get close to him so I can, like, pass him a note or something," I said.

"What the fuck are you going to write?" she asked.

"Jesus, I don't know!" I said. "Does it matter? I can't even get close to him!"

"Well, why the fuck does anybody go to the front of the lab?" she asked, heading into the bathroom.

"'Cuz they get in trouble," I said.

I stood in the doorway as she opened the bathroom cupboard and grabbed a digital scale, placing it between the his-and-hers bathroom sinks.

"So get in trouble," she said. "Then give him your stupid note."

She glanced at me while she pressed on the scale and waited a moment to activate the sensor, then brought it toward her chest instead of placing it on the floor. I eyed her topless torso nervously.

"What are you doing?" I asked.

"I'm weighing my tits," she said. "What the fuck does it look like I'm doing?"

She placed each of her giant boobs on the scale, one at a time, and then both at once.

"Oh," I said. "What do I write?"

"Tell him that you like his hair?" she said. "Ask what product he uses? I don't fucking know; I'm not good at this shit."

She looked up at me, pleased with the readout on the scale.

"Five pounds each," she said. "These things are fucking heavy!"

She proudly spun her giant rack in my direction and pushed through the doorway, back down the hallway to her bedroom.

"Passing notes," she said. "You're fucking hilarious."

MADAME BRANCHARD HAD terrible asthma, so when kids wore cologne or perfume or bathed with Ivory soap, which had an unusually strong, lingering scent, Madame Branchard called them to the front of the room, humiliated them for the smell-good attempt, and then sent them to the bathroom to rinse off. Though I sat seven rows back in the lab, and we were separated by cubicle-like desks with plastic walls around them, I thought if I wore enough Calvin Klein Obsession she would notice, and humiliate me, thus allowing me to get close to Logan and pass the note. Taking Kelli's advice, I wrote two lines:

"Dear Lab Assistant, I know I don't know you, but I totally love your hair. Wanna hang out maybe? xo Jennie."

Before walking into class, I doused myself with an uncomfortably bold amount of perfume. There was nothing to do then but sit down and wait. The girl next to me leaned into my cubicle.

"She's gonna get pissed," she said, noting my bait.

I shrugged my shoulders like a badass and, with a queasy stomach, refolded my note into perfect triangles.

"Who is wearing all that perfume?" Madame said.

It had only taken six and a half minutes for the perfume particles to waft seven rows forward. She stood and started the classroom inspection, her sharp nose leading. When she finally came to my row, she took a deep breath. Her eyes watered and she began hacking and coughing as she returned to the front of the room.

"Mademoiselle Ketcham, would you please come here?" she said.

Just as I'd planned, I walked to the front of the room, adding a little extra bounce to my step so that Logan would notice my approach.

"Mademoiselle Ketcham, is this the first time you've come to class? Are you unaware of my perfume policy? Are you intentionally trying to kill me?"

As she stood there berating my scent choices, I felt as if I were in a dream. It was an underwater dream where the world moved in slow motion, her words sounded like "Blerhp blerhp blerhp," and the small triangular note in my hand began to float mysteriously toward Logan's seat. As her tirade continued, I turned in his direction and rolled my eyes. I mimicked her mouth with my own and he smiled approvingly.

"Please go to the restroom and wash that obnoxious scent from your body and then return," Madame said. "Education is neither meant to smell horrible, Mademoiselle Ketcham, nor is it meant to kill your professors."

Shoulders back and tits out, I nodded to her and gracefully slipped the note onto Logan's desk. When I had returned from my midday "bath," I disappointingly saw my note still sitting on his desk. While we listened through headphones to the irregular conjugation of *vouloir,* I watched him intently, waiting for the moment when he'd notice my secret message. In fact, I watched him so intently that I failed to notice the small triangular note on *my* desk until it was time to pack it all in and leave class for the day. He'd already written me back and, having free range of movement in the lab, he'd hand-delivered his note while I was in the bathroom.

His note read: "Thanks. It's blue Elmer's glue, you know, that makes it not move. What do you want to do? I'm Logan."

Three months later, we were head over heels in love.

WHEN IT CAME to family, Logan had the same lack of paternal relationships as I did, which I found appealing, because he never asked questions about my home life. The few times I did open up about hating my dad, he took the anti-dad sentiment even further.

"Dads are totally pointless," he said. "Mine just donated sperm."

"Really?" I said. "Your mom had a sperm donor?"

"No, not really," he said, touching his treacherously sharp hair spikes. "But pretty much. I never see him."

I had brought up the dad conversation because, the preceding week, I had had an appointment with a court-appointed therapist. When asked earlier on the stand where I wanted to live during my parents' divorce trial, I made it clear that I did not consider my dad an option.

"I'm not living with that asshole," I said. "He's scary, and dangerous, and I should not be forced to be anywhere near him."

"You seem a bit angry, young woman," the judge said. "I think it may help to talk to someone."

I guess that depended on his definition of "help." When the court-appointed therapist later asked why I'd come to therapy, I wasn't exactly sunshine and kittens.

"I know why you chose this job and why you help people," I provoked.

He braced himself against the polyester chairs that had seen so many broken families and angry kids before me.

"You're here because, at some point, you fucked your own family up so bad that now you have to fix other people's," I said. "There is no fixing mine. So we can stop pretending."

I never had to see him again. But I did have some fairly substantial resentment toward any sort of therapy or help in the years that followed. What counseling I did receive came from Kelli and Cynth: Kelli with her big boobs and even bigger attitude, and Cynth with her subtle and sweet demeanor and her love for peeing in public.

Kelli lived up the road from Logan, and so she and I would sneak out of her house and go over to his, every chance we got, especially on nights when he had his friend Jacob over. Jacob was a BMX-loving athlete who loved seeing Kelli's rack. When we tapped on Logan's bedroom window, the boys came out front, and we rode BMX bikes through the dark streets.

Logan had seen my rack plenty. I'd even given him a blow job once (or five times), but I hadn't had sex with him, because he was a virgin, a sensitive artistic-type guy, and I knew it would take finesse. One evening Kelli didn't come to Logan's house with me, and when I snuck into his bedroom, I told Jacob to wait in the living room. It was like a sexual demon possessed my young body, and I had to have Logan immediately.

He giggled nervously as I put my hands down his pants.

"Shhhh, you'll wake up my mom," he whispered.

"Whatever, let her listen," I said.

I pulled his pants down and then went for mine too.

"Oh my God, you're gonna get us all in trouble," he said, more stone-faced than I had thought he'd be at the prospect of losing his virginity.

"Seriously?" I said. "Just be quiet. I'll do the work."

I kissed him gently on the mouth and worked my way down to his piece, then back up to his mouth.

"Let's just see if it fits," I said.

Matt had said the same thing to me the first time we had sex—doggy style on the carpet of my bedroom—the summer before eighth grade. I had thought the line was good then, and I wanted to see if it worked on men like it had worked on me.

"Of course it will fit," he said. "What a ridiculous thing to . . . oh . . . umm . . ."

With Logan inside of me, I rode him in the moonlight streaming through his open window with my hand over his mouth so he'd shut the fuck up. I heard the tiniest squeak and turned to see the door cracked open, with Jacob's small face peeking in.

I smiled at him and continued my business. Logan came fairly quickly, and afterwards we cleaned up and climbed outside to ride bikes around the neighborhood. As I pedaled through the shadows, I thought of Logan knowing what I felt like inside. I thought of Jacob knowing what I looked like naked. I thought how these little things gave me an edge over them, like Matt and Alex had had the edge over me when they'd had sex with me. I decided that, as long as I was the one initiating sex, I was the one with the power.

Only, as I pedaled, Logan made a confession that shattered my thoughts.

"I wasn't ready to have sex, you know," he said. "I don't see why we couldn't have waited."

Jacob bounded alongside of us, riding onto low curbs and attempting handlebar spins.

I hit my bike's brakes, stopping under a huge pine.

"Are you serious?" I said.

Logan kept riding, but I could see his Elmer's-glued head bob up and down as he nodded.

I abandoned the bike I had borrowed from Logan and walked back to Kelli's house, leaving Logan and Jacob to play BMX in the dark. It had never occurred to me that a guy would want to wait to have sex—that waiting was an *option*. Or that there was something worth waiting for.

I felt utterly and completely alone as I walked the few blocks back through the starlit neighborhood before sneaking in through the sliding glass door of Kelli's house. Even though I'd given myself to Logan, I didn't know if he still wanted me. I didn't know if he could forgive me for taking something from him that could never be returned. The feeling was empty and sad and it reminded me of something.

I bet Mom feels like this.

AFTER HIS CONFESSION on the shadowy street, Logan never again mentioned his unreadiness when it came to sex. In fact, he became an enthusiastic participant, the guy I had wanted him to be that first night. I regularly snuck out of Kelli's house, which was my favorite sleepover spot on the weekends, and jogged down the street to see him and bang him. Then I snuck back into her house, all within an hour's time.

As I made my way into Kelli's dimly lit bedroom after one such tryst, I quietly hissed at her so I wouldn't wake her parents.

"I need a pack of frozen peas," I said.

"What the fuck do you want frozen peas for?" she asked, cocking her head back like the hammer of a gun.

"My vajayjay is sore!" I said. "Seriously, he's *huge*."

Kelli was having her own sexual adventures with a guy from a different high school. She always seemed to date guys who were older, drove cars, and enjoyed kinky butt sex, something I declined.

"Oh my God, you're such a dork," she laughed.

She went to the kitchen for the peas and threw them at me like a softball player as she returned.

Although I was excited to be having all the sex I wanted with Logan, I still thought about our midnight conversation and wondered what it meant to be *ready* to have sex. But because we were having sex so often, the logic of *being ready* or *waiting* faded in all the excitement of sneaking out and having secret, his-mom-doesn't-know-I'm-here sex. Once our parents did realize we were having sex, my mom worried more about the potential of me getting pregnant or marrying than catching STDs or anything else. One afternoon, after she came home early and found Logan and me visibly shaken by her surprise arrival, she sat me down to have a talk.

"I just see you throwing your life away for this guy," she said. "He isn't worth it."

"Mom, it's not a big deal," I said. "It's not like I'm gonna marry him or something retarded."

"Yes, Jennifer, it is," she said. "It *is* like you are going to marry him. Just like I married your father. It'll be a mistake, and you'll be throwing your life away for some guy way before you're ready."

"You're insane, Mom," I said as I got up to leave the room. "I'm not marrying him. He's just my boyfriend, and we're using protection. Chill out."

Again, the abstract idea of *being ready* for something was beyond my grasp. I didn't understand how anybody could ever *be ready* for anything, or how a person could *be ready* to throw her life away for someone else, as if *life* was something one could set down in a Dumpster and still exist without.

I couldn't help but think that if my mom's marriage to Dad had been a mistake, then all of the things that had followed were a mistake as well. And if she thought "throwing her life away" was equivalent to having three children and a twenty-something-year marriage, then I one day hoped to "throw my life away" too. But I would never regret it like she so obviously regretted us. There was no way that her marriage to Dad was comparable to my relationship with Logan. At any point Logan or I could walk away and it wouldn't ruin our lives, nor would it necessitate court or lawyers. But instead of talking to my mom about how I felt about any of this, I simply ignored her pleas for me to fly solo and kept sneaking out to see Logan.

After a few months, Logan and I started to drift apart naturally anyway. He started going to Golden Skate in San Ramon and flirting with a San Ramon girl. I stayed in Moraga, tried to act cool about him roller-skating with chicks I didn't know, and auditioned for the cheerleading team so I could wear impossibly short skirts in the name of school spirit. When Jacob, who lacked an internal empathetic filter, casually mentioned a dry-sex incident between Logan and some girl, I knew my relationship with Logan was officially over. Since I was already so committed to being cool about everything, I didn't show Logan or Jacob how heartbroken I was. I just brushed off any emotions I was feeling, a coping mechanism I had perfected during

my parents' divorce and would use for years to come, and committed myself to furthering my emotional detachment by dedicating
my high school years to collecting virginity cards—the metaphorical
cards on which people keep their virginity and subsequent fucks—
and heightening my levels of awesomeness.

I started with the concert choir. Since most of the cool guys sang in
choir, the pickings were delicious. I began with boys who were older
than me and then worked my way slowly into the guys my own age.
I picked players from the football, basketball, water polo, and swim
teams. I picked the bad boys who gathered at Jack in the Box, the
unchaperoned hangout in Moraga where we could sit in the parking
lot and drink beer from the keg in the bed of one boy's truck.

One night, I allegedly worked my way through an entire hot
tub filled with the Jack in the Box crew, a happening that I had no
memory of but heard about the following Monday at school. My
friend Dan and I were sitting in the quad, eating cheese zombies,
also known as fresh-baked bread buns filled with gooey cheese.

"Really, you don't remember at all?" he said incredulously.
"God, I feel kind of bad about it now."

"No," I said. "I mean, I remember making out with Frank, and
kind of Daniel, but then . . ."

"Then you got passed around the hot tub, and I'm pretty sure
you were with each guy in there," Dan said. "You fucking drove
home afterwards!"

I searched my memory for a glimpse of the drive home, for a
struggle with the keys when trying to get in the car—for any sign
that would suggest I'd had sexual relations with an entire hot tub
of young men—but came up blank, a fact that didn't bother me at
all—or at least that's how I acted.

"I got nothing," I said while secretly worrying about what else
I could forget in the course of being blackout drunk.

Once I had amassed a large collection of virginity cards, it was
time to heighten my levels of awesomeness even further. This
meant throwing, funding, and attending all the parties I could.

Mom, knowing what it took to be cool, let me have a party at our new condo. I invited every friend I had, and my friends' friends, and the condo was soon filled with high schoolers, drinking ice-cold Coronas and Mom's handmade margaritas while smoking joints or cigarettes. There were eventually so many kids in the house that they literally overflowed into the parking lot. By that point in the night, I was upstairs and in the process of seducing my classmate Mick and too busy to realize how out of control the party had become. Then I heard the kids outside scream.

"Cops!"

"Cops!"

I leapt from my bed, wriggled back into a T-shirt and jeans, and flew down the stairs.

"Out! Out! Out!" I screamed. "Everyone the fuck out!"

It was a mess. Outside, drunk teenagers were on the run, fleeing from the flashing red and blue lights of the cop cars in the parking lot. Inside, red Dixie cups littered the floor. When I went into the kitchen to tell Mom to hide, both she and the blender were missing.

I turned around and walked back through the house, still yelling.

"Fucking thieves!" I shouted. "Get the fuck out now!"

I went out the back door to the gate and met Officer Dickey, who stood with his hands on his cop belt in supercop fashion. Dickey had pulled me over twice before, once for doing forty-five in a twenty-five-mile-an-hour zone and another time for racing up the hill into town. I talked my way out of the first ticket, and since he hadn't been able to catch me on the radar during my race up the hill, I got out of the second one by sheer luck.

"Where's your mom, Jennie?" Dickey asked.

"She's not here, Officer," I said, sounding a little more buzzed than I wanted to. "She is out, out, out tonight."

"We received a call that she is here distributing alcohol to minors," he said. "Is she in there making margaritas, Jennie?"

"I don't know where you heard that, but it's a lie, Dickey," I said. "Officer. Officer Dickey."

I was horrified that one of the partygoers, one of my friends, had called the cops and ratted on my mom.

Officer Dickey arrested me, citing distribution of alcohol to minors, which befuddled me because *I* was a minor. He took me down to the puny Moraga jail, where I sat handcuffed to a rail inside the station while they tried to reach Mom. They questioned me until I was ready to pass out. Over and over, I said it was my party and my mess. Five hours after they arrested me, they finally let me go. I can't remember how I got home. Maybe a friend's parents picked me up, or maybe I walked the three blocks back to my house. Either way, I do remember that, when I got home, Mom was sound asleep in bed with the blender on her nightstand.

I FELT LIKE my mom's get-out-of-jail-free card that night gave me one too, and while I became more belligerent in my actions, she became less able to enforce any real consequences. I started coming home later and later—not that she really had a good idea what time I got home anyway. She had taken to drinking with our neighbors, Saint Mary's College boys, and after a night of drinking games and double shots, an elephant could have trumpeted through her bedroom and she wouldn't have budged. Usually she was coherent enough to clean the house and lock the sliding glass door before passing out, but that was it. I waitressed at the town's only Italian restaurant, and most nights after work and whatever partying I felt like doing, I would tiptoe stealthily into her room and kiss her good night.

One evening, I came home to an unlocked door and a disorganized kitchen table. I entered the living room carefully, afraid of robbers or my dad, a fear that had carried over from my mom's warning back at the Hillside Inn.

"Mom?" I whispered.

All was silent, except for the faint whoosh of the living room ceiling fan and the *click click click* of its metal pull string. I walked into my mom's dark room. She wasn't in her bed. I turned on the light.

"Mom, are you here?" I said.

The bed was perfectly made, but her purse, which normally sat on her nightstand, was on the floor. I started to panic. Then I heard labored breathing. I looked to the far side of the bed and saw two feet, their soles facing the ceiling.

"Oh my God, Mom," I said.

I rushed to her side, rolled her over onto her back, and brushed hair from her moist face. When I did, I discovered matching black eyes and a swollen, broken nose. I ran back out to my purse for my cell phone and called her boss/boyfriend, Samuel.

As I waited for him to come over and help me, I sat down on the ground next to her and started to cry.

"Who did this to you?" I said. "Who fucking did this to you, Mom?"

"Just with the boys," she said in a slurred, garbled mutter.

I took that to mean the boys next door. When Sam showed up, he went directly to the next-door apartment, and I heard him screaming through the walls. Gradually, the screaming hushed to talking. I stood out on the patio, smoking and trying to listen to the now soft sound of Sam talking through his tears.

It soon became apparent that nobody had beat up my mom. She had been drinking with the boys next door, was carried home, and after being placed in bed—with her purse next to the nightstand—she'd simply fallen off the bed and landed face-first on the Tupperware containers she kept in her room for storage.

The next day, I ran into one of the guys who had helped her home. I felt awful about my initial accusations and apologized profusely.

"Don't worry about it," he said. "It's gotta be tough having a drunk for a mom."

That stopped me short.

I didn't think I had a drunk for a mom. My mom just got too drunk sometimes. And that was a good thing, mostly, because it meant that it didn't matter when I smoked weed or cigarettes. It didn't matter when I ate acid or ran through the woods on mushrooms, because she wasn't going to do anything about it. She was too drunk. She had no power over me, no motherly muscles to flex. She couldn't stop me from hanging out with rough kids, from coming home whenever I wanted to, or from dealing drugs. Just like I couldn't stop her from getting so wasted that she rolled off her bed and broke her nose on some plastic containers.

There was nothing she could say or do that would make me believe that she was worth the respect that other kids seemed to give their moms. Because she wasn't like other moms. Other moms were there for their children. They were dependable and accountable. They took responsibility for their actions. They could *remember* their actions. They could be mothers. My mother could only be drunk. And I couldn't relate to that at all.

AROUND THE SAME time my mom's alcohol abuse spiraled out of control, my weed smoking and drug usage started, and I fell in love with a new boy named Marc. Marc lived in an intimate quasi-town amongst the redwood trees near Moraga. Marc was exceptional. Solitary. He was an understated genius among overrated brats and did the tall, dark, and handsome thing too. His eyes made me think of endless cups of black coffee, and the bone structure of his face made me want to look only at him. He liked to read classic literature while chain-smoking cigarettes, and this intrigued me more than any other quality a man my age might possess.

When Marc and I really started hanging out, my thinking shifted. I had already accomplished a full file cabinet of virginity cards. The pastime didn't bring me any real pleasure anymore, except for the few occasions when I got to say to another girl: "Already fucked him. Don't bother."

I had already achieved a heightened level of cool, thanks to my cheerleading skirt and my Mustang trunk filled with marijuana, because drug dealers and cheerleaders are organically cool, especially if they are one and the same

Kelli had some douche boyfriend she was dating, so I never saw her. Cynth was away at boarding school. And my new girlfriend, a chick nicknamed Meme, was down with Marc's crew, ganja, mushrooms, and parties. She and I blasted through the small two-lane street in her green VW Bug, listening to the Dixie Chicks, smoking joint after joint. On the weekends we could be found in the forest with the boys, at the empty post office parking lot drinking, or on the fire trails off-roading. There was a barn at the top of the hill where we had room to party and freezers to chill our bong water. We had everything we needed.

I'd been flirting openly with Marc in front of Meme, who claimed to be madly in love with him but slept with his other friends. When he started to warm to my presence—a feat all the more impossible because he'd grown up running with wild guys and crazy dogs—I couldn't believe it.

Then, one night, I had sex with Marc's friend Maddox in the back of Meme's car. Post-coitus, Maddox and I sat in a nearby barn's stairwell, talking about what a great guy Marc was.

"You know, he really cares about you," Maddox said. "And if you care about him, then you and me shouldn't ever fuck again."

I sipped my beer, tugged on the joint Maddox handed me, and passed it back.

"Yeah, I do," I said. "Care about him, I mean. I do."

Sitting in that stairwell, beers and joints and cigarettes and all, we decided I should go for exceptional and solitary Marc, the quiet genius, because he was "the good." He was a year older than me, and it was the summer before he left for college. In the fall he was going down to a small liberal arts college I knew I'd never be able to attend with a collection of young adults I knew I'd never be a part of.

When the relationship with Marc started, I don't think either of us was looking for anything serious. But one clear, sunny afternoon when his parents were gone and we were lazing about his bungalow-style home, drinking lemonade under the canopy of green trees, we started kissing a bit more sweetly than a nonserious relationship would entail. His hands touched my breasts, and the touch was a bit gentler than something casual. We ended up in his pullout futon bed with his red curtains drawn, casting the color of love all about the room. Nose to nose, he whispered a confession to me.

"I've never done this before," he said.

I fell in love with him that very moment.

All the other young men with whom I'd had sex—the twenty-plus-something guys that had gladly and eagerly acted as if they were old pros at the sex thing, when most were obviously virgins—were nothing but fluff. They had more swagger and flash than any fourteen- to seventeen-year-old boy should have had about his abilities in the bedroom. They acted as if they were hot shit and I should have been grateful to suck or fuck their cocks. Yet, Marc, tender Marc, apologetically slipped inside of me for the first time, recognizing my experience and not wishing to offend. Though the actual sex was short in time, the intensity of emotions that followed—the panting, caressing, heart-exploding, naked-body-melting, all-consuming love that was born on that sunny afternoon—turned into a hideous beast that crawled from my chest and into my throat and ears each time we touched. I couldn't control the way I felt for him. There was no manipulating my way into his bed, and the love for him that consumed me was so raw and uncensored that I had a difficult time breathing when he was near. I felt absolutely powerless.

After that day, he was the only person who existed in my world. Each glance he cast in my direction was the food I'd been searching for my entire life. Each kiss was the drops of life's water that I'd fucked man after boy after man to find. At night, I rested my head on his slim tummy and he read to me from Tolkien or the poetry of Rumi, my two favorite authors at the time aside from Jack Kerouac and Bill Burroughs, until I fell asleep thinking of Middle-earth or a friendship so profound, it caused one to spend one's life writing of it.

The summer I spent in love with Marc eclipsed all other memories: my siblings growing up, my mom being drunk, all of the other boys I had fucked. People ceased to exist except for Marc, and all other reality couldn't touch me except for the reality that existed within my love for him.

IN THE FALL, when it was time for Marc to leave for college and for me to stay behind for my senior year, we decided to continue our relationship. He bought a vibrator for me—my very first vibrator—and gave it to me with a special request.

"Please don't cheat on me while I'm away, Kitty," he begged, perhaps hoping that the use of his nickname for me would inspire faithfulness.

Even though I couldn't figure out how to orgasm using that funny purple vibrator—and was not entirely sure that I'd ever orgasmed with any of the guys I'd slept with, including him—I did manage to stay true. During that first year, I was his and his alone.

It helped that I was more concerned with dealing weed, making money, and moving out of Mom's house than seducing boys. It also helped that I'd already been with the majority of the boys in town. Still, Marc was in my every waking thought, his name always on the tip of my tongue, his dorm room phone number the only one I knew by heart. I went to visit him at school once or twice, and upon seeing his newfound collegiate freedom, I became terrified that he would fall in love with life outside of our small town—and fall out of love with me.

Senior year in high school felt incredibly common. I ditched class, smoked weed, ran through the woods on mushrooms, and was required by the vice principal, Mr. Mak, to attend every single one of the last ninety-eight days of school in order to graduate.

The week after I spoke with Mr. Mak about my attendance, I ate a few hits of acid and took to the streets for an adventure. When I came home later that night, still out of my mind on acid, I saw that my mom's car was in the driveway and the lights were on in our home. I quietly unlatched the gate to our back patio and slithered across the stones to the sliding glass door. My mom was likely in her bedroom, and if I could just make it inside and upstairs to my room undetected, there was a chance she would not notice my sweat-covered face and the fact that my pupils were bugging out of my head. But when I cracked open the door, she was waiting in the living room to confront me.

"You erased a call from Mr. Mak?" she screamed. "Jennifer, what drugs are you on now? Ecstasy? You'll never graduate high school. You won't get into college. You are throwing away your entire fucking life to go hang out with those people!"

"They are good people, Mom," I said. "And I'm on acid. I will graduate high school. I will graduate college. And I'm fucking out of here. So stop screaming."

I managed to remain calm even as her face melted like makeup on a clown who'd spent a drunken night driving around in a miniature car.

"I'm sure you're scaring the kids," I said. "You're scaring the fuck out of me."

"Oh, you're leaving?" she yelled. "Let me get your bags for you, then."

As I ran upstairs to my bedroom, she went to her closet to grab two suitcases. While Lyss sat on her bed next to mine, covers pulled over her head, crying softly into her pillow, Mom brought the suitcases to me and threw them on the ground.

"Get out!" she yelled. "Just get the fuck out. I'm done with you."

She spun on her heels and slammed my bedroom door behind her.

I went to Lyss, wrapped my arms around her, and whispered to her through the covers.

"It's okay," I said. "I'll be back during the day when she isn't here. This just means you get your own room."

It was early March, a week or two after my eighteenth birthday, and I had no place to go. So I parked in the woods and slept in my car. On lucky rainy nights, one of my best friends, Kurt, would convince his mom to let me sleep over, and she became a surrogate mother to me. And when the weather warmed up, I thanked her and slept back among the trees, going to school every day to prove my own mom wrong.

The whole time, I was waiting for Marc to come home. When he returned, I ran to the safety and comfort of his arms. I had stayed true to him that whole long year, from the moment our bodies had first united on that bright, sunny summer day. In spite of my mom's fears, I had gotten into San Diego State University and would be headed there in the fall. I thought it'd be easy to be Marc's girl once I left for school as well, and if I could continue loving him through college, we could be happily in love forever.

That fall, Marc and I drove down I-5 to Southern California. We holed up in an E-Z 8 Motel off Hotel Circle Drive in San Diego and I memorized every inch of his body before I left him at San Diego International Airport to catch his flight to school. We talked every night on the phone, cooing sweetly into the receiver but growing increasingly frustrated at how our surging hormones raged within us, with no outlet other than a hand or a battery-operated device. As I became more familiar with the noisy, crowded dorm that was now my home, with the tan-faced freshmen gaining their notorious fifteen pounds, I reestablished myself as a pot smoker and a drug dealer. When three weeks had passed, and the high from loving and being loved by Marc had worn off, I found a new guy and gave in to a bunch of old thinking, like *Where can I get more herb and who is gonna act like they love me most?*

5

"THE DUST HAS ONLY JUST BEGUN TO FALL."
—IMOGEN HEAP, "HIDE AND SEEK"

Two days before we checked out of sex rehab, Production organized a bonfire in the hills of Malibu, the kind of dramatic cleansing ritual the world of reality TV loves. They informed us, the sex addict patients, that we could pick whatever items we wanted for the burning. Because I'd gathered up all of my porn paraphernalia during my trip home with Jill, my most burnable belongings had already been tightly packed away into large plastic tubs, and I knew exactly what I would throw onto the fire. They didn't, however, give anyone a chance to look through their belongings to decide what would be burnt before we left the facility. I figured we would do so once we reached the bonfire, and so I made no mention of my concerns about this to Production, Dr. Drew, or Jill.

The patients packed into a white van, which was our regular transportation while in rehab. As we drove the two hours from Pasadena to Malibu Hills, we were all laughing and joking, excited to be exiting the Pasadena Recovery Center within forty-eight hours. I laughed along with everyone else, but I had a major worry weighing on my mind: the bleak state of my post-rehab finances, now that I wouldn't be returning to porn. Financial managers and porn paraphernalia eBay sales would provide the necessary tools to live a porn-free life. But I was still terrified and spoke with Duncan about money and the future the whole ride out.

Duncan and I had agreed to move into the same apartment complex in Hollywood, where the rent would be a thousand dollars less than what I paid for my house in Sherman Oaks. Even though I wasn't compensated much to do the show, if I planned it right, the money I had could last long enough for me to find a job.

"You'd be a lovely waitress," Duncan said. "Or a writer. I really do think you should pursue your writing, Jen."

He leaned forward in the van to grab a cigarette.

"Yeah. I think I need to go back to school or something first, though," I said. "Nobody will take me seriously as a writer. Not unless I have an education."

We grew quiet as the van slowly pulled through the low-slung, rolling hills that separated the ocean from the valley. I knew that the cast as a whole was tired, and we were all ready to return to our comfortable homes and the privacy we had there. Kendra was missing her husband time. Phil was missing his penis playtime. And I missed Saucy and Kitty. It had been the longest nineteen days of my life.

As we reached our bonfire destination, I could see Jill and Dr. Drew standing near the fire, along with a giant pile of objects that were unrecognizable from the distance. Duncan opened the doors of the van for us, and we began walking as a group toward the fire. As we drew closer, I realized the majority of things in the pile weren't mere things. Someone had taken all of the bins from my home and overturned thousands of dollars' worth of stripper clothes, heels, DVDs, and photographs into the dirt patch that Production had cleared in the middle of a grassy field. The entirety of my career had been thrown to the ground. Though I'd made the decision to give up my life as an adult-film star, I had been count-ing on selling these things so I wouldn't have to sell my *thing*.

"Who the fuck did this?" I screamed, tears rushing down my face, my throat closing, making it hard to breathe. "Who the fuck threw my entire life in the dirt? Do you know what this means to me? All this stuff? This is my fucking livelihood! This is all I have!"

I stalked toward Jill and Dr. Drew, who tried very hard to stand still and stay firm.

"Fuck you, fuck you both, you both fucking lied to me!" I screamed. "You don't want to help me! This is what you think of me, of my chances at getting better, of being normal. You think I belong in the fucking dirt, don't you?"

My eyes blurred from the crying and I was panting from the screaming as the sun set quietly into the mountains behind me and the fire glowed hot and angry.

No one said anything. So I kept going.

"Is this what you want?" I screamed into the cameras, which never missed a beat.

I started throwing things into the fire: a beer trophy I'd won in a drinking contest with Porno Dan, DVDs I had wanted to sell, eight-by-ten photographs that exposed my naked body to everyone at the bonfire.

"Is this what you fucking want from me?" I shouted.

I turned toward the production crew, a group of men and women we'd been instructed to ignore.

"Fuck you all!" I shouted. "Fuck this and fuck every single one of you."

Finally, Jill broke the standoff and came to me. Putting her hands on my shoulders, she turned me away from my dirtied career.

"I'm so sorry," she said. "This shouldn't have happened like this. I didn't know what was happening. We can leave if you want."

But her words were too little, too late.

"I don't trust you," I said. "I can't fucking trust you after this."

I ran back to the van, followed by a cameraman. I pleaded for him to stop filming me. "I'm sorry, I have to," he whispered.

Kendra and Duncan ran after me, and the three of us stood in the open field.

"Don't let them win," Duncan said. "If they see you like this, this is exactly what they want."

I didn't want them to win, but I was shaken to my core, and I didn't think I could have responded in any other way. I held on to Kendra and cried into her hair. She finally calmed me and we returned to the bonfire. The other patients were throwing objects into the fire that appeared to have absolutely no meaning to them. I watched in silence. For the rest of the night, I said nothing to Dr. Drew or Jill. I said nothing to Production or the other patients. When we returned to rehab, I began packing my clothes to go home.

I was heartbroken. I felt as if the entire show had been a lie, as if none of it meant anything to anyone. Late that same evening, John Irwin, the founder of Irwin Entertainment, the company that produced the show, came onto the rehab floor to apologize. We sat in my room and I wept and threatened to leave rehab two days before graduation. He spent two hours consoling me and promising me that they would withhold my mental breakdown from the editing bay and the show, and when I finally understood that they hadn't meant to hurt me in the name of quality reality television, I agreed to stay. By the end of our conversation, I could do nothing but cry. I was finally and officially broken.

I did undergo one positive change as the result of our Malibu bonfire: I got very clear on my place in the world and how I planned to live my life from then on. I understood that once I left the safety of the Pasadena Recovery Center, I would be on my own. I would have to fend for myself again. I would have to find a job—a real job in which I would remain clothed. Being a celebrity—a disposable celebrity whose entire career could be thrown into the dirt for a metaphorical and ritualistic cleansing—would not suffice.

ON THE LAST day of rehab, we made "circle plans," which provided a detailed reminder of what sexual sobriety meant. Because drug and alcohol sobriety were easy to define, and abstaining from sex for the remainder of my life seemed unlikely, I had a difficult time comprehending the point of sexual sobriety. I told Jill this as she gently worked her way through our final session together.

"So, what, we just don't have sex again?" I said. "I don't feel like that will work."

"No, you will have sex again, just in the confines of a healthy relationship," she said. "We can make a circle plan that will help you stay sober so you can build esteem, and you build esteem by doing esteemable acts. It's like your sexual sobriety blueprint. We can do your inner circle first."

"Sweet, inner circle, check," I said. "This looks like a bull's-eye."

I held my circle plan up in the air for her to see.

"Yes, it does," Jill said. "Now, your inner circle will contain things that you wish to consider a relapse. Put anything unhealthy in your inner circle—all the stuff that you would count as a relapse."

"Okay. Selling sex for money. Being emotionally unavailable. Lying. Using pseudonyms. Using sexual innuendos to dominate a room, group, or person. Manipulating people for my pleasure. Alcohol and drugs. Compulsive masturbation and sexualization to deal with feelings."

As I said them out loud, I wrote all of these things in the inner circle, using a bright red pen to emphasize their importance.

"Now, your middle circle is a slippery-territory area," Jill said. "That's where we'd put 'hungry,' 'angry,' 'lonely,' and 'tired,' because those things all lead to acting out. Some things that are in your inner circle will be in your middle circle as well. What else are you going to put in there?"

"'Sexual innuendos,' because sometimes it's okay. 'Flirting.'

'Lying'—you know, like white lying. 'Manipulation,' because everyone manipulates on some level. 'Masturbation.' 'Failing to keep my commitments.' 'Sexualizing people, places, and things because I feel uncomfortable.'" I wrote these in orange, to illustrate the correlation between dangerous and unhealthy behavior, and behavior that leads to dangerous and unhealthy behavior.

"Good," she said. "Now the fun stuff. What can you do to stay safe? We'll put that in the outer circle."

"'Yoga,' 'meetings,' 'hiking,' 'dancing,' 'writing,' 'walking,' and 'snuggling Saucy.' 'Hanging out with friends.' 'Reading books.' 'Going to the beach,' 'napping,' 'working out.'"

I wrote these in blue, my favorite calming color, a color that reminded me to stay cool.

"Look at you, darlin'!" she said. "This is a good plan. Now we just gotta stick with it and take it one day at a time."

"One day at a time," I repeated, rubbing my hands together with nervous excitement. I thought, *This is something I can handle. Just stick with this bull's-eye thingie and don't get in stupid or dangerous situations. Don't be the old you.* I worried a little bit about the no-sex thing, but because I hadn't been in a committed relationship for so long, and had no intention of entering one soon, I didn't give it much thought. Frankly, I was horrified at the thought of being seen naked anyway. I felt way too naked already.

Angel was picking me up in less than four hours and taking me to my old house in Sherman Oaks, where I would pack up my belongings and move to my new life in Hollywood. I missed my friend. But beyond that, I had no idea how to feel or what to expect.

FIVE DAYS AFTER I came home from rehab, I masturbated. Because masturbation was in my middle circle—and compulsive masturbation in my inner—I didn't consider the quickie a relapse because it didn't send me into a five-hour, compulsive, Magic Wand–versus-Jennie spree. And when it was over—less than three minutes of action and maybe five to ten seconds of titillating orgasm—I was grateful for the clarity the quickie brought, although I wasn't exactly pleased with what it meant. It was the first time in twenty-five days, and the letdown was huge. It felt like doing a line of cocaine, where I wanted more but knew that it would only satisfy the temporary craving and not the underlying hunger within. I knew how to make myself feel good. I could have sat on my couch masturbating all afternoon. But when I came, I felt empty and sad. The orgasm wasn't what I wanted. What I wanted was to feel loved, to be held, to be cared for. My Magic Wand may have been waiting for me when I got out of rehab, but it hadn't grown arms or a heart during that time, so it would give me no love, no hugs, no caring. I finally threw it in a Dumpster behind a grocery store. I knew that if I put it in my own garbage can, there would be nothing to stop me from retrieving it. I had successfully completed rehab. I had quit porn. But I was still an addict.

As part of the aftercare provided by Dr. Drew and the people at Irwin Entertainment, I saw Jill once a week, as well as Dr. Reef Karim. He was a psychiatrist, who functioned only as my mentor and advisor, and he was working out of Beverly Hills, and in the process of building a comprehensive treatment program, the Control Center. Although I never became his patient, he agreed to advise me pro bono and serve as a mentor. Jill said I needed a structured day plan to keep my mind busy, and Reef made suggestions about being more attentive to my thoughts, experiences, and the motives that drive me from day to day. What I felt when I first met him was nervousness. I shifted in my seat uncomfortably.

"Do you think the rehab experience was authentic?" he asked.

"Yeah, totally authentic," I said. "I mean, as authentic as I know. I think. Yeah. Why?"

"Just think about it," he said.

As I soon discovered from talking with him, he often asked a question I couldn't answer, leaving it open-ended and ambiguous so that I would continue thinking about it and often reconsider my initial answer.

Weeks later, I came back and revised my response to this early question.

"Yeah, I guess parts of rehab weren't that authentic," I said. "The therapy stuff was authentic. But the bonfire? My reaction was, but our reason for being there was super-contrived."

Reef wrote notes while maintaining eye contact with me, and I wondered how he didn't scribble all over the page.

Such revelations didn't happen on their own. A week after my release from rehab, I started a blog called Becoming Jennie to document the struggles of leaving my porn identity behind. My first post began: "My name is Jennie, and I'm an Addict. (Hello, Jennie.)." At that moment, I didn't feel as if I had a voice with which to write, so I wrote about my decision to be Jennie and not Penny Flame. I wrote about how I found it comforting that Penny Flame would never die, she would never be a day over twenty-six, she would never face the loneliness of growing old in an industry that lusts after youth. Mostly the post was about how excited and nervous I was to try living again as only Jennie. When I got everything out, I pressed PUBLISH and went about the rest of my intentionally super-structured day.

THREE DAYS AFTER publishing my first post, I returned to write another post, and there were more than ten thousand hits. Somehow, the Web address had leaked into the porn world. I was nervous about what the reaction would be, but there were hundreds of comments from wildly supportive strangers encouraging me to continue the battle of becoming Jennie. I sat at my desk, crying. Up until that moment, I had been convinced that the people who existed on the other end of the Internet only wanted to see me get fucked. It warmed my heart that someone would write something as simple and promising as "You can do it Jennie. I believe in you."

Those words were enough to solidify my decision to leave porn.

Meanwhile, Duncan and I settled into a château-style building off Franklin Boulevard that we had finally found after searching high and low for the ideal apartment complex in Hollywood where we could be neighbors. He had to leave the cliff side home he owned in Malibu because once he had driven up that big beautiful hill and was safe in his home overlooking the Pacific Ocean, he was isolated from the world—and, more specifically, the world of recovery. I had signed a lease on a one-bedroom, $1,400-a-month rental, which was still way too expensive for me; but because Duncan had said he wanted to live there, I let my pride interfere with my good judgment. Once again. On the day we decided to move in, we walked down the star-spangled Hollywood Boulevard, looking over the famous names and talking with interesting street people and bums. The whole time, I challenged Duncan's ability to see the positive.

"You just have to trust that things will work out fine," he said. "And if they don't work out fine, they aren't finished working out yet."

I grumbled in response, but he would not be dissuaded.

"You must write a gratitude list each morning, to remind yourself of all that you have to be grateful for," he said.

Duncan was a major part of my super-structured days. Early in the mornings, we went to meetings and hiked Runyon, a dog- and dog-shit-friendly hillside near the top of La Brea, with his dogs and my Saucy, who got along wonderfully. Early in the evenings, we drank coffee and smoked cigarettes. And the whole time Duncan dreamed of how great our future could be.

"I think we should get a publicist, because we want to have the best opportunities once the show airs," Duncan said.

"You should start writing your memoir now," he continued. "Once the show airs, your story will be very valuable."

One afternoon, as he wandered about my apartment, he asked, "Why don't you sell your paintings?"

"I don't know. I don't think anyone will buy them," I said.

Our post-rehab romance continued to blossom and bloom. Another meeting friend, E-Deez, moved into the building as well, and what had been a twosome of healthy living turned into a trifecta of super-crazy healthy living.

I stood in the kitchen one day, smoking and painting, while talking on the phone with my dad, whom I had reconnected with after my paternal grandfather had asked me to do so on his deathbed.

"It's pretty awesome, having all these sober and healthy people surrounding me," I said.

"Well, kid, next step is to get some girlfriends, and then you'll be super-duper healthy!" he said.

He was totally right, and I knew it. Although Angel was still my best friend, I didn't have any other girls in my life at all. I hadn't spoken with Kelli or Cynth since Kelli's wedding, over a year before. I had cut off all of my porn girlfriends, except for Vee and Fran, who worked at the old agency. But, as it was, I was just happy to have the five to seven friends that I did have.

"The girlfriends will come in time," I said to my dad.

When I spoke to Duncan and Jill, the therapist, about my dad's suggestion, they both had the same response: "Well, make some girlfriends at the meetings! That's what they are great for: you'll meet plenty of girls. Go to girl meetings!"

However, I found myself going to predominantly male-oriented meetings. I didn't want to go to all-female meetings because I felt lonely and vulnerable among other women. Jill said it had something to do with not trusting my mom, which made sense because I did not trust Mom. At all. I didn't trust any women. But especially not her.

EACH MORNING WHEN I woke up, the first thing I did was send Duncan my daily gratitude list. But while there was much that I was grateful for, money problems danced through my dreams, and I could not seem to shake my financial anxiety. Perhaps it was because I wasn't actively looking for a job. I knew I should have been, but I couldn't imagine any employer who'd be willing to hire me. I couldn't imagine explaining to someone where I'd been for eight years. I couldn't imagine someone willing to forgive me for nearly a decade of cocksuckery. My fears of rejection, being shamed, being laughed at and treated with contempt, led me to inaction. I didn't look for a job. I didn't make new friends. And soon I was so paralyzed with fear that I quit spontaneous living altogether, committing my life and my time to Anonymous meeting after Anonymous meeting.

One evening I agreed to meet up for a sushi dinner with Camilla Bangs, who was one point on the Angel-Penny-Camilla triangle. She was in town shooting for her new company, Camilla Bangs Entertainment, a company that she'd formed with the help of her semi-longtime dude, Brad.

When I got to the restaurant, a small sushi joint off Santa Monica Boulevard, Camilla greeted me warmly.

"Penny. Fuck. *Jennie,* dude, I'm so proud of you," she said. "Are you okay?"

Camilla rarely drank, and when she did, she usually drank too much. I could tell it wasn't going to be one of those nights.

Camilla led me back to our table. She'd invited a few different porn-oriented people to dinner, and one of my favorite performers, Katja Kassin, was there as well. Katja was a German porn star who had worked for my webcam company before I went to rehab. Because the webcam company was just finding its legs, the site wasn't fully functional when we worked together, and they had yet to build a button that could kick off abusive customers. One customer continued to write the most vile, racist, and hateful things to Katja about her fiancé, who happened to be black. Finally, when it became clear that we couldn't do anything about the comments, Katja walked out of the studio. I hadn't seen her since. I was a little nervous when I first sat down, but sitting across the table from her, sharing a small tray of spicy tuna rolls, and laughing at the studio's demise, I could tell that she knew I had done my best. And I was glad to feel like our fences were mended.

"You know, that blog you write about losing your identity to porn, it's really true," she said, holding my gaze with her strong, serious eyes. "It's all the things you wish you could say but can't because it will kill your career."

I smiled and nodded at her. The table was quiet for a long moment.

"Jennie, you're really done?" Camilla said from the end of the table, awkwardly shoveling sushi into her mouth with training chopsticks for little kids. "Like, *done* done? That's great, dude."

"Seriously?" I said, eyeing the ridiculous utensils. "You're gonna fuckin' use those? Jesus, C!"

"What?" she said. "I hate chopsticks."

"Many times I've thought I'd like to quit, but all the financial things I've committed to, I can't up and leave them," Katja said. "We just bought a house. It's very hard, the money. I wish I could quit at least once a day."

She spoke nearly under her breath, as if the younger generation of porn stars at the table would be best left to learn this lesson on their own.

"Well, you can give it all back—the cars, the house, everything—and say fuck it all," I said.

"You know I can't do that," Katja said. "That's why I read your blog. It is amazing, what you've given up. It makes me hope."

Katja's words lit a fire under me to continue, and the encouragement I had worried would be lacking from my friendships with porn girls was displayed so succinctly in her approval that I felt silly about hesitating to call any of them to hang out. But I also thought, *If I fail now, then every woman in the business who has ever wanted to leave will believe it's impossible.* I became convinced the hopes of every unhappy porn girl rested on my shoulders.

After dinner, I drove my Mercedes back to Hollywood. A few miles from the restaurant, somewhere along Beverly Boulevard, small, chunky tears began to well up in my eyes. Just then a call came through the car's Bluetooth and the screen on the dash flashed Duncan's name and phone number. As I pressed the ACCEPT button on the steering wheel, my tears began to overflow. He could immediately hear that I was upset.

"Darling, what's wrong?" he asked.

That was so Duncan. He never asked questions. He only demanded answers.

"I don't know if I can do it," I said. "I don't know how to live without porn money. I just saw some girlfriends. And I don't have any girlfriends, but not because I don't. It's because I can't. It reminded me of why I stayed in all those years. Duncan, nobody will take me seriously now."

"Listen to me, Jen," he said. "You will be fine. You *are* fine. You will continue living, and you will continue being sober, and happy, and joyous, and free. It will not be easy. But life isn't easy."

"Duncan, I really don't know if I can do it," I said. "I don't know how to make money."

"Once you quit crying, you'll get a job," he said. "The job will pay you, and it won't matter what you've done with your life, because you will go to work and do what you were hired to do. Your life is changing for the better, Jen, even if you can't see it now, even if you don't believe it. It is truly getting better all the time."

I could barely see the road through my blurry, tear-soaked eyes. I felt as if all I'd done since I checked into rehab was cry, cry, cry . . . and I hated the way it made me feel like a little fucking crybaby.

"You are surrounding yourself with people who can help you instead of people who don't even know your real name!" Duncan continued. "You just have to keep chugging along on this bright new path. And I know it's scary and intense, and I know it's terrifying, but it's *your* path. And you've chosen to walk it, to run it. And you attract wonderful things everywhere you go, so why wouldn't you in this wonderful new life?"

At that moment, Saucy farted in the backseat of the car. I didn't know whether to laugh, cry harder, or throw up. I was forced to open the windows, and as I did, I not only freed Duncan's words into the early evening Hollywood air, I was also forced to break that seal of safety that exists inside our vehicles with us. As the cool air and the noise of the night street rushed in around me, I came into contact with the outer world, and with it came a realization: my car was my biggest expense. This streamlined European luxury car that took me from place to place was also a monstrosity, the payment and insurance for which were equivalent to my rent each month.

I parked on Franklin in front of my complex and sat in the car. I touched its soft leather seats. I ran my hands along the wood-grain center console, the smooth lines of the German-designed panels. I brushed my fingertips along the radio buttons, the GPS, each part of the car I'd taken for granted over the two and a half years I'd driven it.

And then it hit me: *It's time to get rid of the car.*

THE NEXT MORNING, I called Noah, a porn director and sort-of-sort-of-not boyfriend whom I'd been seeing for four years, and asked him about the Mercedes dealership from which I'd leased the car. His longtime friend Owen had been a salesman at the dealership, and I'd leased the car through him. Even though he was a friend of a friend, on the day I signed my lease with him, he questioned my decision.

"Are you sure you can handle this payment?" he asked. "It's intense."

"Oh, yeah, I got it," I said. "It's like a day and a half of work. Easy peasy."

"If you want to trade it in after a few years for something more affordable, you can," he said. "Just bring it back here, okay?"

That wasn't going to happen. After signing the papers, I drove my $55,000 car off the lot, thinking: *Fuck yeah. This shit is sexy.*

But within a year, it wasn't so sexy anymore, as the payment had become a nuisance. Within two years, the payment had become a burden. By the time I got on the phone with Noah, the payment had become impossible.

"I can't do it anymore," I said to him. "Do you think he'll let me out? Into something cheaper? Maybe a GLK?"

"Drive it down there and ask, babe," Noah said. "What will they do, say no?"

Noah was always very optimistic when it came to leasing new vehicles. He was a flavor-of-the-day type of guy, and he was in and out of new cars like he was in and out of lust with new, young porn stars.

When I pulled my car into the sales lot later that day, I asked for Owen. He wasn't on the premises, and I was directed to his associate, some dude named Tim, who came out and looked into and around my E350.

"You're looking to get out of your lease?" Tim asked.

"Yes," I said. "Maybe a downgrade? I can't afford a payment over five hundred."

"Let's go check out your contract and credit," Tim said.

My stomach dropped as I remembered what Owen had said about my credit when he had originally leased me the car: "I shouldn't lease this car to you, but I'm going to anyway because you're a friend. Please, fix your credit."

Tim wasn't a friend—not like Owen was—and he had no reason to help me out of my current bad deal and into another deal. As we sat down across from each other and he pulled up my contract, the look on his face said everything I needed to know.

"You still have another three years almost," he said.

"Yeah, well, I recently quit my job," I said. "Finances are a bit different."

"Unfortunately, I can't get you into a new GLK with this credit score," he said.

He clicked his mouse a few times and looked up at me from his desk.

"I might be able to get you into something else, though," he said. "Come with me."

Tim led me out to the lot and through a line of used Mercedes: CLKs, CLs, G-Wagens, E-Classes—car after car that I couldn't afford. Realistically, I not only couldn't afford the E350, I couldn't afford the gas that had gotten me there in it, either.

"Well, we have a beautiful SLK that would be somewhat of a downgrade, but it's for sale, not for lease," he said. "Perhaps you're interested in that?"

"Dude, this is a $50,000 car," I said.

I pressed my fists into my hips, angry that we'd walked all this way for nothing.

"Yes, but that's five thousand less than your E-Class, so it's downgrading," he said. "You would also be purchasing the vehicle, so you could sell it later."

I didn't have time for this. I needed money now. Something inside of me snapped.

"Seriously?" I shouted at him. "I mean, I heard car salesmen were cocksuckers, but really, guy? I tell you I can't afford this, and you give me something more expensive? I quit sucking dick for money. Which means I can't afford this shit. Period. Thanks for nothing, asshole."

I stormed off the lot and drove back to Hollywood, furious with myself that I'd been stupid enough to sign a contract with no back door and was therefore being punished financially for an ego-inflated decision that I had made at the height of being a whore.

Back home, in the safety of my apartment, with a cigarette in one hand and a paintbrush in the other, I tried to work away all of my self-directed anger and doubt, and the shame of having my ego so thoroughly squashed. When I had calmed down a bit, I called my dad, hoping to sidestep the vehicular burden I had once caused him in order to get some advice about my current mistake.

"Sounds like you're up shit creek, kid," he said.

"I can't be, though," I said. "There has to be a way out. What do people do if they can't afford their houses anymore?"

"The bank comes in and takes them back, because they borrowed money from the bank," he said. "Where did you get your loan?"

"Stupid Mercedes-Benz Financial."

He laughed into the phone. It was a familiar sound, the hearty Dad laugh I remembered from when I'd messed something up as a kid and wanted a redo.

"Yup, stupid Mercedes-Benz Financial for giving you a loan, and stupid kid for getting a loan," he said. "Call them and tell them you can't do it. Maybe they'll rework your payments."

I grumbled at the thought of this, but thanked him for the advice and promised to call Mercedes-Benz Financial the following day. I was willing to do whatever it took to get out of the car lease, to make money with my clothes on, and to not relapse on dick. But I still wanted an easy way out. I wanted someone to tell me how to do it. I didn't want to have to figure it out for myself.

What I did figure out, however, was how to set up a donation button on the Becoming Jennie blog with a link that read: "Whatever money you donate will go to food, shelter, school supplies and help me stay out of porn. Thank you from the bottom of my heart." Within the first twenty-four hours, someone had donated a hundred dollars. When I awoke to the generous donation notice, I sat crying and hugging Saucy, totally recommitted to this change in my lifestyle. I figured it was a sign.

MONEY WAS MY primary worry, and I worried constantly. It was my new vice. I had no issues over alcohol: not drinking was as easy as not smoking weed. Both required money, and without a bank account that overflowed, I had no desire to use. I did feel tempted to return to porn, though, each time I checked my bank statement and saw that it had dwindled even further. It was impossible not to be tempted.

If I do five scenes, it'll be before anybody knows I've quit, it'll be enough to last me until I find a job, it'll be the perfect amount of money to get me through the summer, I thought.

I managed to stay strong and keep myself from lining up a shoot, but my worry over my finances had morphed from a simple fear of being broke to total paralysis about spending three dollars on the delicious Vietnamese coconut cakes from the Hollywood Farmers' Market. Each Saturday, Duncan and I hit the market, along with our new apartment complex friend E-Deez. While Duncan bought extortionately priced Brussels sprouts, E-Deez and I shared a ten-dollar burrito and lusted after those heavenly three-dollar cakes. My solitary splurge each week was for a bunch of fragrant stargazer lilies that made my home smell delightful. It was the only luxury I allowed myself, along with the cartons of Parliaments I ordered from online vendors.

Deez worried like I did about money, while Duncan shook his head at us.

"It will come back to you," Duncan said. "You mustn't worry."

But Deez and I didn't have a mysterious income like Duncan did, and so we laughed at his words and continued to pinch pennies.

That spring, Deez and I created healthy ways to stay out of fantastical financial catastrophe. We went on hikes through Runyon Canyon Park. We spent entire evenings eating ice cream and killing aliens on his Xbox. We even went so crazy as to talk about our financial worries, which seemed to take the power out of the fear. And then I suddenly had less reason to panic.

One afternoon, Deez, Duncan, and I were sitting curbside at Caffé Etc. on Selma and Cahuenga, smoking cigarettes and enjoying cappuccinos Duncan had bought for us, when I received an e-mail.

David Weintraub, who had gotten me a spot on *Sex Rehab with Dr. Drew,* had reached out to inform me that Irwin and Drew would be shooting *Sober House with Dr. Drew,* and the company was contemplating the idea of casting me again.

"Holy shit, they're doing another show!" I said.

I showed the e-mail to Duncan. He immediately drafted an e-mail to Bruce Toms, the head producer from our show, reading it aloud as he wrote: "Dear Bruce, Jen has just told me there will be a Sober House, and we both wish to live *in* the sober house. Sex addicts need sober living too!" Bruce soon responded warmly while also letting us know that he had very little decision-making power as to who would ultimately be cast.

"I suppose we just sit back and wait," Duncan said, pulling elegantly on his American Spirit.

Even though the new show would mean less money troubles, I was still worried. When I returned to my apartment, I called Fran, the accountant from my old agency and one of my best friends and confidantes. Because I had smoked too much weed as an adult-film star, I had a tendency to forget who all owed me money, and so I often called Fran to check on the status of late-arriving checks.

"Anything show up, my Franny?" I asked.

"Jesus, Pen. Fuck. Jen. No, nothing 'ere," Fran said in her awesome, tough-British-lady way. "Why the fuck, you feel like people still owe you money?"

"I sucked enough dick, Fran, someone better still owe me money!" I said.

As she laughed, I heard her shuffle through papers, open a drawer, and slam it shut.

"Listen, the only person that owes you any money is Del, an' you fuckin' know he ain't gonna pay!" she said.

Del owned the webcam studio I'd been managing when I quit porn.

"Isn't there something I can do?"

My carton of cigarettes had just arrived in the mail earlier that week, and I was very well aware that it was the very last carton I could buy before the shit hit the fan.

"Yeah, there is," she said. "You can go to the labor board, report 'em to the state of California! Ain't like you ever gonna work for 'em again. When you comin' by 'ere, Pen?"

"When you call me Jennie!"

"Bugger!" she said. "You'll always be Pen to me. But I'll try. Write 'em a letter, Del and those buggers, tell 'em ya want yer money."

"Thanks, Fran," I said.

With Fran's help, I wrote professional-looking letters to Del demanding the $1,500 his company still owed me from back before I went to rehab. They sent multiple responses saying I screwed them by quitting and they wouldn't pay me a thing. Finally, I went to California's Department of Industrial Relations' Division of Labor Standards Enforcement and reported the company for withholding my final check. It felt good to stand up for myself, and I knew without a doubt that I never would have gotten there if I hadn't quit porn.

IN THE WEEK that followed, I exchanged multiple e-mails with David Weintraub. Meanwhile, Duncan, unrepresented by any manager or agent, continued to send e-mails to Bruce Toms and Dr. Drew. As I started to feel like the deal was getting closer to being finalized, Duncan felt it all slipping away.

One evening in his apartment, over a meal of lamb and cauliflower he had cooked for us, Duncan expressed his fears to me.

"You're definitely going on the show," he affirmed. "You're going because they want a beautiful girl, and they won't cast me because I'm an old gay man."

I knew Duncan well enough to understand that there was no arguing with him, no reminding him that the VH1 audience might not be dealing with the problems he was, and so I kept silent. But as the minutes ticked away, his anger level rose.

And then one day near the end of June, as I slept peacefully, cuddling Saucy and Kitty, I awoke to Duncan at my front door, bellowing as I'd never heard him yell before.

"She's been hit, Jennie!" he shrieked. "Please, please come down!"

Each morning, Duncan woke up at five and took the Big Dog and the Li'l Dog for a walk around Hollywood. He very rarely leashed his two beloved pets. This particular morning, as I ran sleepy-eyed down the hallway, still barefoot and in warm pajamas, it became obvious that he had failed to leash them again. When I raced outside, Duncan dropped to his knees on the filthy Hollywood pavement where his beautiful white American pit lay bleeding under ragged, blood-drenched sheets.

"They didn't even stop, Jennie!" Duncan cried. "She saw a squirrel and ran for it, and the truck didn't even stop!"

I had never seen Duncan so demolished. And I had seen him in therapy sessions where he had discussed being molested. I had seen him let salty tears fall over his memory of being left at an orphanage for six weeks as a newborn. However, this was something different altogether. As I watched him crouch over his poor dog, who was in shock from the pain, and hold her face in his lap, I realized the two things Duncan truly loved had four legs and a wagging tail. And one of them did not seem like she was going to make it.

Passersby stopped and helped, finding a plywood board and moving her body from the pavement so we could take her to the vet. As they loaded her into the back of Duncan's truck bed, I reached out my hand to him.

"Give me the keys," I said. "Stay with her."

He did as he was told, climbing in alongside his dying dog and shutting the tailgate so I could take them to the nearest animal hospital. As I drove down the seemingly hundred-mile-long Ventura Boulevard, I kept glancing back at Duncan to make sure he was okay. Each time I looked, he was staring stoically into the cars that followed behind us, tears streaming steadily down his bristled cheeks.

We arrived at the vet and Duncan ran inside for a nurse. She followed him to the truck bed and he raised the sheet.

"Please save her, please put her back together," he begged.

The nurse looked as if she was going to vomit.

I still can't wash the image from my mind. The Big Dog's stomach had been ripped open and her intestinal tract and other vital organs were spilling out onto the board she was lying on. I couldn't believe she was still alive. As additional nurses came to carry her inside, I followed Duncan with a hand on his shoulder, wishing I could un-see what I'd witnessed.

Within ten minutes of our arrival at the animal hospital, Duncan made the difficult decision to euthanize his dog, and he sat holding her head gently as she fell into the deepest sleep. He agreed to come fetch her body the following day, and then there was nothing left to do, so I drove him home. Once he was in the solitude of his apartment, I could hear him crying from my own apartment, four doors down.

The next day we buried the Big Dog at the house Duncan owned in the Malibu hills, in a beautiful, well-tended garden overlooking the ocean. After we were done, the Li'l Dog sniffed around her grave site, burrowing his nose into the fresh ground. It was a clear summer morning without a cloud overhead. But inside Duncan, something that had once been very hopeful died along with the Big Dog that day.

WEINTRAUB CONTACTED ME again to say I'd been cast for *Sober House with Dr. Drew,* and I had to meet him to sign the paperwork. I hadn't seen or really spoken with him since right after my rehab release, when we fought on the phone and he said I'd been "brainwashed." I had been fueling my car a few days after being released from rehab when he called to talk about other potential reality television shows.

"Maybe some sort of love show?" he said over the phone. "Like *For the Love of Penny* or something? Are you upping your prices for scenes?"

He was ready to get me back into the reality world, to keep the money and quasi-stardom flowing. I felt way too raw and didn't want anything to do with Penny, but he had no reason to think I was serious about leaving her behind. He also had no idea that I wanted to quit porn.

"Seriously?" I said. "I don't want to do any shows. I don't want anything to do with porn or Penny, and I'm trying to stay sober and do this."

He responded quickly and aggressively.

"Look, I'm only trying to make you money, Penny, so don't yell at me," he said. "Besides, when you went in, you were on top of your shit. Now it's like you've turned into some kooky brainwashed Drewian. Fucking crazy."

I hung up on him before my gas tank was full and decided there would be no more Weintraubs in my new life.

But there I was a few months later, meeting him in Beverly Hills, at a Coffee Bean & Tea Leaf. I was sitting outside, drinking water with Saucy, when he pulled into the parking lot in his Range Rover, chirped the lock, and sat down next to me. Although I was still uncomfortable from that conversation, I was grateful and happy that I had money coming in. Some very conflicting emotions were coming up as he began speaking.

"You're still sober?" he asked.

"Yup, I'm taking this shit seriously, dude," I said.

I pushed my sunglasses back into my hair so we could look eye to eye and he could know how serious I was.

"I can tell," he said.

He sat back, relaxed in his chair, and pushed the contract forward.

"It's the same as last time," he said. "They'll send me my percentage directly."

I gazed over the contract and twirled the signing pen between two fingers.

"Sure," I said. "You realize we are only working on a show-by-show deal, right? You aren't my manager."

"Oh my God, Penny, yeah I know," he said. "I didn't know you were gonna take this shit so seriously, but yeah, I get it now, okay? Maybe you can be, like, Drew's success story or something. I never wanted to fuck you over, you know? I just wanted to make us both some money."

I remembered the front I'd presented to him to get on the first show: the heartless, cold girl who only wanted to be a porn star and increase her badassery by getting on some sex addict program. I thought about this new woman I was becoming, how drastically different I could be, how much happier I'd become in the past two months, even though I had new financial worries. I started to respond but opted instead to lower my sunglasses in case I began to cry. I had been doing a crap ton of crying lately, and I didn't want him to feel like he had gotten to me.

"Yeah, I know, dude," I said. "I just . . . Look, when you called me that day after I'd gotten out and shit was still super-fresh, and you started asking why I wasn't going back to porn and saying I'd been brainwashed, I was just a little bit raw, okay? I'm trying to live healthy and that doesn't mean I'm brainwashed. This whole thing has been really good for me."

I flipped through the pages and initialed with a "JK" instead of a "PF."

"I didn't mean to piss you off," he replied. "Seriously, I was a little confused because you went in like 'I'm gonna fuck everything.' And you came out like 'I'm never gonna fuck anything again.' Can we both make some money, please?"

He was right that my attitude had shifted dramatically. And given what I'd said on my way into *Sex Rehab*, it probably wasn't crazy for him to have made the reality-show suggestions he did. But that didn't make me any more thrilled to be working with him again. I smiled a fake and contrived smile, only real in the sense that we'd finally agreed on something—the financial nature of our relationship—and finished signing the contract, knowing he didn't care that this was the first contract I'd ever signed as Jennie Ketcham aside from tax forms. He didn't really care about my recovery or personal growth. He wanted his 15 percent.

I went back to the château complex in Hollywood, wanting nothing more than to sit and smoke cigarettes with Duncan. He'd been difficult to deal with since the Big Dog's death, but I wanted to be there for him as he'd been there for me, as a supportive friend. When I got home and checked my e-mail, there was a letter from him reading:

"I want the coffee table I've lent you returned, along with the three hundred dollars I figure you owe me for all the dinners I've cooked you. You'll never be a writer like Diablo Cody; you'll always be a white trash porn star."

I dragged the coffee table down the hall and left it in front of his door, returning to my home to smoke cigarettes and wait the remaining twenty-four hours until it was time for my *Sober House* intake. The death of Duncan's dog had really affected him. I wondered: *If he'd been cast for* Sober House, *would he still be reacting this way?* This wasn't the Duncan I'd come to depend on, the positive, unwavering, and strong Duncan that I knew and loved. This was a scary and angry Duncan. And in an instant, I felt as though this was a man whom I could no longer trust. And while I was sad that he wouldn't be visiting me at the *Sober House* set, I was more hurt when I considered what he truly thought of my future as a writer and a respectable woman. I thought about Dr. Reef's question regarding authenticity, and wondered how much of my relationship with Duncan was real and how much was for show. His letter was probably the best thing that could have happened before *Sober House,* because it shocked me into the *reality* of reality television, and I thought: *As I go into this, I will not be developing any more rehab romances with any person from any show, ever again. I'm doing this for me.*

6

"YOU HAVE BUT TO KNOW AN OBJECT BY ITS PROPER NAME
FOR IT TO LOSE ITS DANGEROUS MAGIC."
—ELIAS CANETTI, *AUTO-DA-FÉ*

Even though I barely graduated from high school, I had done well enough in the years before my main extracurricular activities became bong hits and mushrooms, and knew how to work the system well enough that I got accepted by two colleges: Chico State University and San Diego State University. Though I was no longer living at home, I still stopped by the house to grab the mail. When the Chico letter arrived, I was relieved that I had gotten in somewhere. But I wasn't sure about living in Chico. Mom summed it up best: "What is there to do in Chico besides drinking and cow tipping?" Nothing came to mind. When the San Diego letter arrived, I knew exactly what I could do there: everything. My brain was flooded with images of the roughly 266 days of sunshine that the city promised, beach-bound coolers, vats of sunscreen and yummy-smelling Banana Boat tanning oil, and sexified sand gods and goddesses playing volleyball until sunset. Additionally, my maternal grandfather, a recently retired statistics professor, had taught at San Diego State, and I thought it would be good to live near family. Even though I wasn't about to let anybody—especially my mom—tell me what to do, I wasn't ready to go out totally on my own yet.

Marc agreed to drive south with me, and after a blissful night in the E-Z 8 Motel and a tearful good-bye at the airport, my first task was to find a local weed dealer. It didn't cross my mind that I was trying to replace my boyfriend, father, or family with a drug dealer, nor did I worry about my second year of being geographically separated from Marc. I thought only of securing a man who would supply me, convinced that once I had this new, drug-dealing man, I wouldn't need to find affection from any others because marijuana would be enough to keep me faithful to Marc.

Classes started in mid-September, but I drove down two weeks early with two pounds of weed in my trunk. I had rationed out between 1.7 to 3.5 grams for my daily pot intake, depending on the day's activity schedule, and I knew this would last me a few weeks, but I was all about having the marijuana hookups I needed to keep me in ganja by the time I moved into the dorms. Until then, I stayed with my mom's parents in North County, and neither my grandma nor my grandpa had any idea how high I was getting because I was high from dawn to dusk, so there was barely any change in my demeanor. I made daily drives to Pacific Beach, thirty minutes south, to sit on the beach and suss out herb dealers. When my two precollege weeks passed by without any luck, I prayed that a weed dealer would fall from the sky and land in my dorm room with me.

I did my part to help the marijuana gods find me. The day I moved into Zura Hall, a dorm building shaped like an H to foster a sense of community, I posted a giant "Marijuana Girl" poster above my bed so it could be seen from outside the room. My roomie, a cute half-Portuguese, half-white baby from Santa Cruz whom I took to calling Pookie, was also an herb smoker. She could be a bit flighty when it came to street smarts, but she was studious and dedicated to the books that were constantly in her hands. I started out that way, too . . . well, for the most part.

Pookie's real name was Katrina. One afternoon during the first week, as we sucked down a toothpick-size joint, carefully blowing the smoke out the window, I shortened her name to Trina, then Trinookie.

"I'm not a Trinookie," she laughed. "I don't even know what that is!"

"I know, you're a Tookie Doo," I said. "A Tookie Tookie Too. Like 'Hey Tookie Tookie, the cat and the Pookie.'"

She sat there laughing at me through my burst of stoner inspiration.

"Oh my God, you're a Pookie!" I said. "A little Pookie Poo!"

"She is a Pookie!" yelled Burs, a kid from Northern California, who was our neighbor next door.

Our windows were near enough for us to hear what our neighbors were saying, and Burs sat in his room for hours, downloading songs from Napster, so he often joined in on our conversations.

Burs had walked into our room the first day of class, looked at the giant "Marijuana Girl" poster, and tapped his ten fingertips together like Mr. Burns from *The Simpsons*.

"Smoking?" he said. "Excellent."

A friendship was born and had been growing ever since.

Burs was not only a smoker but also sold me some of his stash. This suited me just fine for the first month of college. I was still smoking the two pounds I'd brought down from Moraga, but it was beneficial to my high to switch up the weed occasionally. So when I felt the need, I bought a dime bag from Burs and smoked something new in order to reset my levels of stoniness. When my two pounds ran out and I needed bigger bags, I went directly to Burs's dealer, Big Frank.

Big Frank lived down the street from the dorms in the "cool kids'" apartment complex, a shit hole called the Dorchester. He didn't attend SDSU but had moved to the area for the explicit purpose of selling weed to college kids. He always managed to know all of the weed smokers in the area within the first few weeks of school, and so, of course, he came to know me. Big Frank was from Los Angeles, which made him super-hip in my mind, and he had other super-hip friends from Los Angeles too. One of his friends whom I found particularly hip and intriguing was named Jeff.

When I first met Jeff, he seemed like he might very well be my marijuana intake counterpart, which instantly made me take notice. We were sitting together on Big Frank's couch one lazy afternoon when I didn't have class or had opted out of it. Jeff held up a joint in his long, thin fingers and examined it as I sat back and examined him holding my work.

"Who rolled this joint?" he asked, his short, dark brown hair hidden beneath a Los Angeles Dodgers ball cap.

"Me," I said, looking straight in his sexy and stoney milk chocolate eyes. He smirked like he had a secret, or like he just realized I had one, so I smiled back at him and raised my eyebrows as if to say, *I will rock your pothead world.*

Jeff nodded slyly and passed it back to me, revealing just the littlest bit of a snaggletooth. I loved the tiny imperfection.

"I'm impressed," he said.

I liked being the best at whatever I did, whether it was being the girl who'd taken the most boys' V-cards in high school or the biggest pothead in college. I beamed at him. Instantly, I imagined Jeff filling the role of "partner in crime" on the weed missions I embarked on all over town. Not long into the semester, I'd taken to going on smoke drives—to the beach, to Mount Helix, to anywhere that had a view—solely to smoke herb. Jeff was down with this. Plus, he had excellent taste in music. He introduced me to rad underground hip-hop artists, while I introduced him to more hard-core gangster rappers. He had sexy-ass lips and a sexy-ass truck with spine-vibrating boom, and smoked cigarettes like they were going out of style—all things I immediately liked about him.

He was also in San Diego, while my boyfriend Marc was far away. The first kiss with Jeff, standing on a balcony in my SDSU dorm, felt delightfully wrong, blissfully horrible, deliciously sinful.

With each new step in our connection, the wrongness of our affections began to fade, and I became more comfortable in being myself with him, with being honest and sincere—so much so that within a month and a half of knowing him, he knew everything about me, from the shitty relationship with my dad, to Marc, who faithfully slept alone, two states away from me. Jeff and I felt equally opposite; he was a bad boy with a good streak, and I thought of myself as a good girl with a bad streak. With Marc, I never felt deserving of his love. It was gratifying to have a man like Jeff, because I didn't have to try so hard. I simply got to *be*.

Jeff and I were soon sleeping together. We were virtually inseparable, save for the nightly calls I made to Marc. Jeff and I didn't talk too much about my situation with Marc, which was one of the things that I liked about him, since I certainly didn't like to talk about my feelings. But he brought it up one time when we were sitting at our favorite ocean outlook, a cliff side enclave past Ocean Beach we called Rock Spot.

"You're mine when you're here," Jeff said. "I'm fine with that."

"I know," I said. "Let's not talk about it anymore."

I tried to let the discomfort I felt about cheating get swept away by the crash of the waves before us and the joint we were smoking together.

Jeff eventually knew everything about Marc, but Marc didn't know anything about Jeff. He did suspect that *something* had changed. Since I'd started at SDSU, I'd gone from trusting, before Jeff . . . to suspicious, after Jeff; from being excited that Marc was going out on a Saturday night, before Jeff, to "Who the fuck is that in the background?" after Jeff.

Marc did his best to quell my guilty paranoia, but the more time I spent with Jeff, the more I convinced myself that Marc was spending time with an unknown girl.

The only solution I could find to my generalized anxiety was an increase in pot and exercise. I began smoking first thing in the morning before class and took maintenance bongloads throughout the day until I went to the gym late each night. Nevertheless, I made it to all my classes, from yawnfest Political Science to Music History, where we sat in a dark auditorium listening to the tonality of a gong, and I maintained excellent grades throughout, receiving nearly straight As my first and second semester. Sometimes I'd study in my dorm room with Pookie, sometimes I'd drive down to Rock Spot so I could get a sweet tan while building my new college brain, and sometimes I'd say screw studying and end up right back at Big Frank's house, smoking herb with the boys and pretending like I didn't have any work to do.

I spent more money than I should have procuring bigger bags of herb to keep up with my pot intake. The remnants of my own dealer lifestyle in high school had left me with only a thousand dollars, which was money I intended to use for new clothes, dining out with Pookie, and the sporadic bag of herb. Once my big two-pound bag of herb reserve was gone, all my money went to ganja, and it was soon time to get a job.

The *Daily Aztec,* the student newspaper, had a job section in its classifieds. I found a hostess gig listed at Osteria Panevino, a small, high-end Italian joint in the Gaslamp Quarter of San Diego. When I landed the job, I felt sure that I'd soon be earning enough to keep me in herbal heaven. But the wage of $8 an hour, plus a few tips, barely paid for the gas to go downtown. My first paycheck, a measly $250 for two weeks of hard work, had me rethinking outside-the-box options.

Pookie and I discussed the situation as we sat on my bed, Indian style, taking bongloads and blowing the smoke out the window. Our dorm was nonsmoking, especially when it came to weed.

"This will not do," I said as I considered ripping my stupid paycheck into small pieces and pressing the torn paper into my bong.

"Mmmm, maybe they will make you a waitress?" Pookie asked sweetly, innocence pouring from her every vein.

"No, that'll take too long," I said. "Weeks of training. Blech. I need money *now*."

I ripped the giant, two-and-a-half-foot glass bong.

"Mmmm, you still have a half eighth left," she cooed, her "Mmmm's" taking on a variety of meanings. "You are fine for a while, right?"

I was poring over the classified ads in between bong hits. I pointed to one for ovum sales.

"Maybe I could sell my eggs?" I said. "I mean, I plop one of 'em out every month and they are just going to waste anyway. I should sell this shit."

"Mmmm, I think you have to have surgery," Pookie said. "And a drug test."

She took another bong rip and began coughing, trying her best to cough out the window. We had taped our smoke detector earlier so it wouldn't detect our smoke, and shoved towels under the doors so the telltale smell wouldn't seep down the hall. Still, the place reeked of weed.

"Fuck, stoned eggs," I said. "Wait, what about this?"

I circled a small modeling ad that read: "Make 3k/mo, 18+ $$$$$, send pix."

"Does the plus sign by the '18' mean it's nude?" Pookie asked.

"Most likely," I said. "But I don't know *how* naked."

As she stared at me uneasily, her big almond eyes glazing over with the red of a good smoke session, I did my best to ease her gently into the idea of nude modeling. I'd always wanted to be a *Playboy* model, because I'd yet to see one *Playboy* layout with an ugly chick, and so I'd thought: *If I can get in* Playboy, *that would definitely solidify my hotness levels and chart-topping sex appeal.* I had known a chick who tried to submit pictures taken by her boyfriend at the time to *Playboy,* and although I don't know if they were ever accepted or not, the thought of doing something so confident and daring consumed and befuddled my brain. But I had never thought I was pretty enough to make it, and my fear of failing had stopped me from trying. This seemed like an easy way to get close to that goal.

"How naked can naked be?" I continued. "Naked is, like, naked, right? There is only one naked."

Her eyes, which were slowly squinting shut from the massive amounts of herb we had just smoked, tried one last time to open wide with alarm.

"I think there are varying stages of naked," I said. "Like, stage one: boobs out. Stage two: vulva. Stage three: butthole. I'm not going to get naked right away, anyway. I'll just see what's up."

"Mmmm," Pookie responded.

Her "Mmmm's" were generally a blend of a baby's coo and the angry/apathetic "Hmmm" of a teenager, used to relay a wide variety of emotions, from disappointment or frustration to happiness or surprise. It was up to me to translate this final murmur. I took it to mean that she didn't trust the situation. That wasn't the response I wanted, so I went next door to ask Burs what he thought. I found him in his customary spot at his computer.

"I'm thinking about sending pictures to this nude modeling ad," I said.

Burs nodded, barely turning his face away from his glowing computer screen.

"So, what do you think?" I asked.

Nothing. I poked his shoulder so he'd pay attention to me. His eyes flickered my way for a millisecond.

"What do *you* think?" he asked.

"You just repeated my question, Burs. You didn't answer." I sat down on his roommate's identical bed.

"If you think it's a good idea, then do it," he said. "If you don't, then don't."

End of discussion, as far as he was concerned.

I walked back to my room. Pookie was at her computer, searching for pictures of Brad Pitt.

"I'm gonna do it," I said.

She spun her chair around to look at me, her pack of smokes in hand.

"Are you gonna tell Marc?" she asked.

Immediate terror ran through my veins. There was no way that he'd be down with nudie pictures—no way.

"It's only pictures," I said. "I don't even know if this guy will want me. I'll tell Marc later if it turns into more."

That line of thinking was how I justified my decision not to tell Marc, but the truth was I didn't plan on telling anyone about my nude modeling, aside from Pookie and Burs, who were the only ones I trusted with this information. Not necessarily because I was ashamed of what I was planning on doing, but because I didn't know any of these new people well enough to gauge their reactions, or to measure how their opinions of me would or wouldn't change if they knew the truth. I felt maybe a nanosecond of guilt about withholding from Marc but managed to numb it with long runs and the StairMaster at the gym, along with pot and smiles from guys in the weight room.

I put a few of my junior prom pictures in an envelope with my phone number and a note that said: "I'm interested in working for you." Then I sat back and waited.

WHEN THE CALL came and the shoot was arranged, I held a meeting with Pookie and Burs on my bed. I did my best to deliver cool, unworried instructions, but I was worried. I wasn't worried about the nudity. I was concerned about everything else: worried about the sketchy location in some ghetto warehouse space off Morena Boulevard; worried about the gruff voice I'd spoken with on the other end of the phone; worried I might experience a horrific and terrifying death and never come back from the shoot. So I enlisted Burs and Pookie to help me.

"I'm gonna call you when I get there, before we start shooting, after we start shooting, and once when I'm in the car and leaving, okay?" I said.

"Okay, four calls," Pookie said. "Mmmm, are you calling the room or my cell?"

"I'll call until I get you on the phone," I said. "It doesn't matter what phone."

"What about me?" Burs asked, super-eager to be of help. "What can I do?"

"Just be ready to support Pookie if she has to call the cops," I said.

"Should we just come with you?" he asked as Pookie laid her head in his lap. "This feels scary."

"No, it's all good," I said, even though that was far from how I felt. "But if I'm not back in three hours, send the cops to Morena."

I planned the shoot for midday, so I could take the check straight to the bank afterwards. As I drove the 8-West to the 5-North, my four-call check-in plan seemed less and less ideal. But the closer I got to the studio, the less I felt I had a right to change my mind. For an increasingly bad girl who aimed to do what I wanted when I wanted, I still had a big good-girl streak that meant I also aimed to please others, a dichotomy that would play itself out fully in front of the camera.

I finally pulled into the parking lot, driving past empty-looking buildings and deserted parking spaces until I found the right address on a blacked-out glass-front warehouse. I parked and sat for an entire cigarette, wondering whether the plan I'd concocted would be enough to keep me alive. I contemplated calling Mr. Gruff, canceling the whole thing, and going back to Osteria Panevino to beg for my hostess gig again. Instead, I pulled it together and called Pookie.

"I'm going in, little Pookie," I said. "I love you."

"Mmmm . . . I love you too!" she said. It sounded as if she had, in that very moment, realized she did love me, no matter what I decided to do. The thought was comforting, but it did nothing to make me any less afraid as I walked across the parking lot.

I knocked on the door and waited as I heard what sounded like people inside shuffling and rearranging. My nerves twisted and jumped. I wanted a cigarette even though I'd just smoked one. It suddenly occurred to me that this might be more than a one-man operation. There could be five men or a hundred men inside this warehouse, waiting patiently for me to walk through the blacked-out doors, totally unaware and naïve. The warehouse could be a front for some crazy sex-trafficking ring where college girls who were young, sweet—and a tad bit greedy—were lured in with promises of the easy money that came with being a model and then kept imprisoned forever as prostitutes. My heart clawed its way into my throat as the door cracked open, and it stayed somewhere near my esophagus until the door swung wide. Behind the door was a large, frizzy-haired *woman* who stood smoking and looking at me as if I should have known enough to open the door for myself.

"You must be Jennifer," she said. "I'm Cissy. Come in."

Cissy led me past a beat-up desk with a laminate top that was peeling up at the edges, past racks of clothing that smelled as if they had been dying a slow, carcinogenic death for the past fifty years, and through an empty set area with big "soft boxes," which is what I soon learned they called the professional lighting equipment. Finally, our journey through the warehouse led us to a fully functioning set where an equally large man stood photographing a young lady. When I saw her, I nearly lost my cool as a wheelchair-bound man spun and welcomed me to work in a rush of words that could have been all one sentence:

"You made it, lovely, you're just lovely, did Cissy have you fill out paperwork? This is where you'll be. You'll be taking pictures over here, which is lovely. Have you modeled before? I think you'll be lovely."

He clasped his hands before putting them to his wheels, spinning again, and taking me back to the front of the warehouse. I looked over my shoulder as he led me away. I couldn't believe my eyes. But, yes, I had seen correctly. The young model who was being photographed was pregnant. She was also naked, spreading her vajayjay in front of Mr. Gruff's camera. Bleached blond hair and blue eyes, full, voluptuous breasts, soft facial features, and small thighs that complemented her perfectly tanned skin and giant, basketball belly.

"Is she pregnant?" I whispered, once we were out of earshot.

"Yes, yes, it's lovely, isn't it?" he said. "Pregnancy, the body, it's all just wonderful. There's quite the market for pregnant photos. Men seem to love it. Men seem to love women, though, so it makes sense, now, doesn't it?"

He laughed and wheeled on through the warehouse. I wasn't laughing, and I didn't know why the fuck Cissy had brought me to the back room just to walk back to the front.

"What paperwork do I need to fill out?" I asked.

"Oh, the standard release forms, you know, saying you grant us permission to use the photographs, and you are of the age of consent, et cetera, et cetera," he said. "You can read them if you like, but they are all fairly standard. I'm Rocky, by the way. I do Balboa Park Model Days. You should really come."

As Rocky spun around the desk in his chair, he handed me the paperwork. I read it over quickly, and while it was mostly legal jargon that I didn't understand, there were a few things I did comprehend and didn't like.

"Why am I filling out a tax form?" I asked. "Am I being taxed? I thought it was same-day pay."

Just then Mr. Gruff walked into the room and sat down at the desk next to Rocky.

"You are being paid same day," Mr. Gruff said. "If I pay you more than four hundred—that is, if you shoot more than once— I'll be reporting the payment to the IRS. Otherwise, it won't be taxed. Have you modeled before?"

Rocky wheeled back from the desk to move out of Mr. Gruff's way.

"No, I . . . What are the pictures going to be used for?" I asked.

"Oh, just my website; nothing, really," Mr. Gruff said.

The pregnant girl came to the front then, dressed in a robe.

"You should hire us for a girl/girl," she said, nodding in my direction. "She's so cute, and I only have a month left to work before I can't shoot."

Mr. Gruff lit a cigarette.

"She's new," he said. "Let's get some solos first, then maybe."

What the fuck is going on? I thought.

My stomach was in knots, and I knew if there was a time to leave, it was right now. As much as I wanted the quick money, I didn't want to have sex with a pregnant girl. But suddenly it was too late. Gruff put his cigarette out in a Dixie cup filled with water.

"You ready?" he said. "Hop up on the desk."

And instead of grabbing the paperwork with my Social Security number and home address, running out to the car, driving away, and finding some other way to make money, my thoughts froze up and I sat down on the desk as Mr. Gruff had requested, eyeing the ready camera in his hand.

"Now, turn sideways and smile like you've got a secret," he said.

Snap.

A secret?

"Sideways still, lift your shirt, and show me your belly."

Snap. Snap.

Dude, this is the awkward. Shouldn't have eaten those doughnuts this morning.

"Tits, hon, show me your tits now."

Snap. Snap. Snapsnapsnap.

Did I tell Pookie this was stage two naked? Or stage three?

"Great tits. Now unbutton your pants, fold the edges, and don't take them off. Just show me your panties."

Snapsnap.

This has to be three.

"Pants off, panties to the side."

Snap. Snap. Snap.

Stage four is probably equivalent to home base.

"Pink."

I don't know what the fuck pink is.

"Huh?" I said.

"Spread your little pussy with your little fingers and show me your pink little insides."

Duh.

I paused, thinking: *It's not like I can un-take the last fifty pictures. Might as well finish this bitch.*

Snapsnapsnap.

Mr. Gruff looked more annoyed at my inexperience than interested in my pink, so I continued to do as he said. I counted each snap of the camera: less than 150 pictures had been taken. I felt uncomfortable, but with each snap of his camera, the blankness that had first come over me when I was ordered to sit on the desk intensified, helping me to get through the rest of the shoot, as did the Simon Says feeling of the whole experience. I felt like a possum faking my own death. I changed my death position with each snap as I was ordered, and waited for the man and the camera to go away so I could come back to life.

"Now, put your fingers inside and then spread them apart," he said.

That nearly snapped me out of my possum death pose. I hesitated and almost yelled, *No, dude, I'm not gonna shove my fingers inside of my vagina and then spread them apart. I don't know what that looks like, and I don't want to be seen doing it! You shove your fingers inside your vagina!* But fear washed over me: fear of making Mr. Gruff mad, fear of not being paid.

"Okay," I said. "But be quick."

Snapsnapsnapsnap.

This was way past any stage of nakedness Pookie and I had discussed, and it made me feel like a total liar, a bigger liar than I already was.

After we were done with the shoot, I dressed as quickly as I could. Rocky continued his "lovely" spiel and gave me the Balboa

Park Model Days info while Gruff wrote out a check. As soon as I had my money in hand, I left. As I hopped in my car, the shit feeling transformed into a little high from having just earned the quickest $150 I'd ever made.

After going straight to the bank to cash my check, I went to see Big Frank and spent $140 of my earnings on weed. When I got back to my dorm, Pookie was waiting.

"You're alive!!! Yaaaay!" she exclaimed.

Promptly, her smile turned into a pouty frown.

"I was worried."

I had forgotten to call Pookie from the shoot, as we had arranged. I had been too paralyzed by the frozenness of my dead-possum body and too distracted by the excitement of counting the fast, easy money I was earning. She forgave me over bongloads.

"It was a bunch of boob shots," I lied. "Maybe one or two of my ass."

"Mmmm," she said.

I could tell that this was her "Mmmm" of doubt. Still, she smoked the bongloads I packed without asking me anything more. And I certainly wasn't going to tell her what had really happened inside that warehouse. So I smoked, too, and tried to forget.

FORTUNATELY, ROCKY'S BALBOA Park Model Days were on the weekends and didn't interfere with my classes, which I was still attending regularly, even if I had to get blazed first to do so. My first shoot with him happened on a beautiful afternoon in San Diego. It was a non-nude shoot and taken under the guise of building a portfolio, the necessity of which I believed important at the time. As Rocky and I sat in the Japanese Friendship Garden, beneath blossoming cherry trees overlooking a koi pond, he took infrequent pictures while graciously and generously helping me to define the terms of my modeling career.

"You can do, or not do, whatever you want," he said. "Nobody will tell you that, Jennifer, but I will. Girls all get a start with me in the porn business, and then they forget who I am."

"I won't forget you, Rocky, and I'm not getting into porn," I said. "I just want to do some modeling, some solo stuff, that's it."

As I smoked, Rocky snapped a shot here and there—nothing like the barrage of photos I'd experienced with Mr. Gruff.

"Girls generally get into the harder and harder stuff as the years go on," he said. "It's okay. You should just know that you can say no at any point."

I nodded my head, wishing I'd known that during the first shoot I'd done with Gruff because I now regretted my finger insertion photos. When I eventually saw them, something looked horribly slutty about them. There was no class, no sensuality, nothing especially sexy about the way I looked with a cunt full of fingers.

The Balboa Park Model Days were good for other reasons as well. Aside from a day spent in a beautiful park, being fawned over and looked after, they provided me access to a plethora of interested photographers with checkbooks, and there could be anywhere from three photographers to twenty. Most often, there were other girls there trying to make a few bucks, and the photographers would look over the small selection of photographable women and decide which they wanted to shoot. When they would follow me to a random bench to snap a few shots or down to a fountain for even more quick shots, I did my best to allude to further possible shoots. Balboa Park Model Days were never nude sessions, never inappropriate for the setting, and so I tried to show a bit of skin, knowing what my willingness could procure. While I never earned more than fifty bucks for the day—if that—the photographers and their checkbooks were always interested in shooting another day, in a less interesting setting and in more compromising positions. They also legitimized the modeling work I was doing, even providing some pictures I could give to the men in my life. After my first Balboa Park Model Day, I sent a few park shots off to Marc via snail mail, telling him that I'd started modeling for various up-and-coming San Diego photographers. It felt good to have a plausible lie to tell, even though it didn't feel great to deceive. Marc enjoyed the pictures and seemed relieved that there was some truth behind this new "modeling" career of mine. At least, that's how I understood it.

Mr. Gruff also helped me to define the terms of my modeling career, albeit in a skewed and much different way than Rocky. He wanted to get some sexy outdoorsy shots, so we set up a shoot at the Mission Trails Regional Park. After the forest living I'd done with Marc back in high school, I was fine with crawling around in the dirt naked. We climbed down the gorge, off the road, off the path, and past where signs suggested we stay. Gruff found some big rocks and pointed over at them.

"Why don't you undress now?" he said.

"Okay, but I will not be inserting any fingers today," I said, thinking about my conversation with Rocky and the fact that I could say no to whatever I wanted.

"Fine, that's just fine," Gruff said. "We can work around it."

When I heard his response, I felt relieved that we were in agreement and I didn't have to worry about doing anything I didn't want to do during that day's shoot. Only, as the shoot progressed, I felt myself shifting closer and closer to my earlier dead-possum position, with the frozenness of the first shoot always a few frames away. Maybe I was afraid of being caught by the park ranger. Maybe some uncomfortable feelings had rolled over from our first shoot. But the further we got into the shoot, the less capable I found myself of saying, *No.* He took the pink shots, which I didn't mind so much, because I now knew they were necessary for any good photo set.

And then he handed me a light blue plastic vibrator. I held it in my hand and looked at him. I didn't move. I didn't say anything.

"Don't worry," he said. "It's all cleaned."

I heard *No* in my head. But suddenly I was in full-blown possum mode.

"Put the tip in your pussy," he demanded, checking around to see if anyone else was watching.

I did exactly as he told me to do.

Snap snap.

"Deeper," he said. "Come on, deeper."

Gruff snapped away as I tried to insert the vibrator without inserting the vibrator and tried not to think about the fact that it ironically looked like the exact same vibrator Marc had given me when he left for college and asked me not to cheat on him. To which I had replied, "I won't."

Snap snap snap.

"You need to put it all the way inside of you," Gruff said. "We are almost done."

I did as he said. I was on my knees, under low-hanging leaves, with my ass in the air, my head cranked around as close to my ass as possible, trying to feign pleasure and delight. What I really felt was anger and distrust. I'd clearly told Gruff no finger insertions. He had agreed. Obviously, I should have said no insertions, period. But I doubted if it would have changed anything anyhow. I couldn't imagine saying no.

I finished the set, put on my clothes, and followed Gruff back to the car. As he waved to a park ranger, I promised myself never to work for Mr. Gruff again. The park ranger waved in return, and I felt confident in my decision and my ability to stick with it.

———

AT THE END of my freshman year of college, Jacob came to San Diego as soon as he finished high school. And that summer, when Pookie, Jeff, and I moved into a complex off Reservoir Drive, about a mile from SDSU, Jacob took up residence in an apartment off Alvarado Road, less than a quarter mile from us. We were soon as inseparable as we had ever been. We often drove down to Ocean Beach for a Rock Spot smoke session and then had hamburgers at

Hodad's, a super-delish burger joint on the main strip. One after-noon, as we drove back east, we started talking about the potential of my modeling career. Jacob, unlike Marc, knew the full extent of my career and often benefited from the monetary rewards. I'd bring beers, sandwiches, bags of pot—anything that I felt was nec-essary to enjoy his first year of college. This pleased him no end, and I assumed that approval of my largesse also meant approval of my life.

"You're shooting a lot, Bleeze," Jacob said, passing me a fully packed Swisher.

"Yeah, I know," I said. "Only till I'm, like, twenty-one, though. Maybe twenty-two. Gotta have a game plan."

I French-inhaled the smoke, breathing it from my mouth up through my nostrils.

"Gotta have a game plan," I said again.

"Okay, then, what's the plan?" he asked, taking the blunt from me and turning down the music. "You haven't told me shit about your plan. You haven't even told me your name."

"What name?"

"The name you use for the pictures! Every model has a name, Bleeze!"

"I don't know! I tell them to use whatever they want. I think they use Dolly sometimes. I saw Ariel once. So dumb."

I laughed and swooped the blunt back from his resin-tipped fingers.

"Bleeze!" he said. "You gotta pick one name and then stick with it! How else will they know where to go?"

"Fine," I said. "It has to rhyme with 'Jennie.'"

"Why?" he asked. "You could be something awesome, like Candy Molasses or Bleeze BaBlunt!"

"No way, dude, that's stripper and stoner shit," I said. "Besides, I get mad high and it's gotta rhyme with my real name in case I fuck up. What about 'Penny'? Like Kate Hudson in *Almost Famous*."

Jacob was laughing so hard, he choked on the blunt. I knew

it was because I was trying to use a nice girl's name for my nude modeling career.

"Like 'Penny Lane'?" he said. "What if the Beatles sue you, Bleeze?"

"I didn't say I would use 'Lane,'" I said. "But that's ill, huh, fools would masturbate and then sing Beatles songs about me. 'Penny' something else, then; something that rhymes with 'Lane.'"

"'Flame'! 'Cuz you're a bleeze! You always got a lighter and you're always blazed. 'Penny Flame'!"

"Penny Flame," I said.

I smiled and lit a cigarette. It felt like a good name.

ROCKY'S BALBOA PARK Model Days extended up into the Los Angeles area. Later that summer I arranged to stop by a model shoot on my way to San Francisco in order to earn some extra traveling cash. I was unfamiliar with L.A., besides the gas stations lining Interstate 5, which I sometimes stopped at on my drives north or south; but when I pulled off the Alameda exit near the east side of downtown L.A., I knew this was not an area where I would want to live.

When I arrived at the shoot house, the living room was overflowing with photographers fighting for a shot of one of the three models who had arrived. I pulled another girl aside.

"Where the fuck are we?" I asked.

She laughed.

"I hope you have enough gas to get outta here," she said. "We might as well have shot in Tent City. We probably can, if we stay here past dark."

Perturbed enough to debate hitting the open highway before I had done even a single shot, I set my bags down and freshened my makeup. Once made up, I decided to stay. I walked in front of thirty lenses, lenses that had been waiting patiently to snap topless shots of the next model. The photographers, anxious and crawling over one another to get "the shot," seemed to close in like walls on a claustrophobe, as if their zoom buttons didn't work and they had to be within licking distance to get a good picture. I excused myself and went out back to smoke. As I finished my cigarette and took a few deep, cleansing breaths in preparation for my return to the bright lights, a man with long gray hair and two ravishing twentysomething girls on his arms approached me.

"What are you doing here?" he asked. He brushed off the stunning women so he could fold his arms in front of his chest.

"Trying to make two hundred and get the fuck out," I said. "What are *you* doing here?"

I was confused and pissed, and I wanted to be safe on his arm instead of alone with the thirty wild animals and their faulty zoom buttons inside.

"I'm here to meet you and be your agent," he said. "You never need to do a shoot like this again."

I liked the sound of that. I gave him my contact information, and he ended up being totally right about his prediction. His name was John Stevens, and he turned out to be the most charismatic, charming, and spiritual scumbag I'd ever met. He started setting up shoots with professional photographers like J. Stephen Hicks and Holly Randall, the daughter of Suze Randall, one of the most talented photographers in the biz. With John as my agent, I shot for companies like Danni's Hard Drive, which was operated and owned by Danni Ashe, said to be the first porn girl on the Web with her own site, way back when the Internet first started. Within a month of becoming my agent, he had purchased the Penny Flame URL and many variations thereof. I didn't give it a second thought until years later when I tried to take control of my own life. It took seven years to locate him, another six months to convince him that giving me the domain was the "right" thing to do, and fifteen hundred dollars to seal the deal. Total scumbag move.

I WAS STARTING to feel like a legit model, and I was earning good money, five hundred a day and up. It got better. After a month of representation, John phoned me.

"I lined up a shoot with *Hustler,* with Clive McLean," he said. "Your call time is eight a.m. and you can stay with Matt Frackas from Matt's Models if you please. He's in Hollywood."

It wasn't *Playboy,* which had long been my dream, but I was getting close.

Excitedly, I drove to Hollywood, lugged my bags into Matt's Hollywood penthouse, and waited for the *Hustler* shoot. When morning came, I shaved more carefully than ever before, plucked my eyebrows, and arrived on set ten minutes early. Throughout the day, I threw everything I had into those photos. While I was bent over, I imagined having sex with Jeff. When I looked into the camera and made googly eyes, I imagined having sex with Marc. I sucked in my belly, which was by no means fat, and made sure that I knew what every inch of my body looked like in the photographs. I wanted to be remembered as a professional. Even more than that, I wanted that centerfold.

I drove back to San Diego, knowing that I looked perfect— breathtaking, even. I couldn't wait to see Jeff. I had yet to tell him how I made money, but now that I had done a real shoot and had the chance of being the centerfold, I felt proud enough to want him to know. When I arrived at Big Frank's that evening, I stepped out onto the balcony to smoke a cigarette with Jeff.

"Do you ever wonder how I buy so much weed?" I asked.

I exhaled smoke, pursing my expertly lined lips into a sultry pout.

"I figured you'd tell me if you wanted," he said.

He looked out over the Dorchester Apartments pool, which was littered with empty red and blue Dixie cups and a random floating yellow bikini bottom from some faceless bikini-bottomless girl.

"I'm a nude model," I said. "Actually, I'm a *Hustler* girl. I just shot for them today. Maybe a centerfold. I find out in a month."

A smile spread across his face. He quickly brought his smoke up to his lips, as if to stop himself from enjoying my confession.

"I figured it was something like that," he said.

A tiny flicker of lust flashed across his eyes as he looked at me, opening up an all-new world of sexual validation. Normally, I had to fuck someone to get that flicker, but now, with Jeff, all I had to do was mention taking off my clothes occupationally, and the deal was sealed. Suddenly, I was acutely aware that not only Jeff and Marc wanted me, but also all of America wanted me. Men across America wanted me enough for Larry Flynt to pay me for my body to appear in his magazine. Here was the power I had always craved, but on an even bigger scale than I had ever dreamed. And I liked how it felt.

Since Jeff and I had started living together, our relationship had taken a fairly serious turn. Our close quarters might have also been why I was honest with him about my career choices long before I was honest with Marc. I liked spending time with Jeff and felt comfortable with him. And the only time I put our relationship on hold was when I remembered that I already had a relationship on hold with a man because he lived two states away.

As the summer came to an end, I went home to visit Marc. One evening, as the sun sank behind the hills, we sat in my car at our spot in the forest—what we called the "35 spot" because of a little sign with a "3" and a "5"—and shared a joint. I was happy to be there with him, until the conversation took a turn for the serious. I had a tendency to lie and withhold, but I did not have a tendency—or ability—to be good at it.

"Are you sleeping with Jeff?" Marc asked.

I was stunned. I hadn't seen the question coming, although I probably should have, given Marc's super-distant behavior since I had gotten home from San Diego.

"No, I'm not sleeping with Jeff," I chided Marc. "He's, like, one of my best friends!"

I hoped the fake anger in my voice would hide the guilt that I was really feeling.

"No, it's more," Marc said.

"We may have kissed once, but it's really not more," I said. "I mean, there's really nothing." My heart started vibrating uncontrollably and I felt my throat closing down with each airy, unrealistic, and implausible untruth. Tears began their quick procession to my eyeballs, either because I felt so guilty for lying and cheating or so stupid for being caught.

"I know there's more, and I don't appreciate you lying to me," Marc said. "If you want this relationship to work, you better start being honest."

He turned to face me, offering me the half-smoked joint.

"There isn't more," I said. "We kissed, like, twice. That's it."

I couldn't look him in the eye, and that's probably what gave me away.

"No, that's not it," Marc said. "I can forgive you, Jennie. But you have to be honest with me."

Then he pulled a *Cheri* magazine out of his pocket. He'd somehow managed to hide it from me while it had been curled up in his back pocket, waiting to pounce, the entire time we'd been hanging out. My heart sank, but I didn't say anything to defend myself.

"Is this you?" he asked.

The page was already opened to one of my layouts, the one that had named me Ariel or Dolly. Even though the only words in my head contained four letters, I managed to string together a few words to come out of my mouth.

"I wanted to tell you so bad," I said. "I didn't know how. I'm so sorry, Marc."

I was sure that our relationship was over—that the only man I'd felt sure I could love was so disgusted by what I had done, and how I had lied to him about it, that he'd never be able to forgive me. But then, as we unrolled the windows to break the hotbox, smoke-sealed car, he surprised me.

"You look pretty sexy," he said. "Pretty fucking hot."

Stunned that we'd quickly moved from anger and distrust to hotness and potential sex, I regained my confidence. Maybe this could still be saved, and I thought I knew how.

"Maybe we should go back to your house and 'talk,'" I said seductively.

We fucked three times that day, four the day after, and twice the morning I left to drive home to San Diego. We didn't talk about Jeff or the photos again. As I made the drive back to my new life, I wanted to be a good girl for Marc, because I knew this kind of fluke—having his confrontation about my infidelity and lies be resolved with multiple orgasms—would only happen once. And I didn't want to lose him, as much as I knew I probably wasn't going to be able to stick to the kinds of life changes that would make him stay.

7

"IN THE SKY, THERE IS NO DISTINCTION OF EAST AND WEST;
PEOPLE CREATE DISTINCTIONS OUT OF THEIR OWN MINDS
AND THEN BELIEVE THEM TO BE TRUE."
—BUDDHA

I made it through my first sober Fourth of July. I had survived Duncan's poisonous e-mail that ended our friendship. All that was left were my final preparations before I left for Sober House. The morning of July 6, I drove Saucy to Noah's house—he had agreed to watch her while I was gone—and although I had taken his pet care kindness for granted in the past, I was appreciative of his generosity now that I had so few friends left.

Arriving at Noah's house was like stepping back into my old life. His gated driveway overlooked the entire San Fernando Valley—or Porn Valley, as it is sometimes known in Los Angeles—from Studio City in the south to Porter Ranch in the north. His over-size front doors always appeared dark from the outside because of the thick, black window film that covered the entryway's giant windows. Inside, beautiful women were often being photographed in compromising positions on the dramatic grand foyer stairwell. Each bedroom was a fully designed porn set whose decor changed from day to day, depending on the script. Some days the master bedroom looked like an office, other days it resembled a classroom. Noah lived in the shoot house full-time, which meant he didn't have to pay separate rent and made a crapload of money from the regular shoots.

I let myself in with the key Noah had given me. As I walked up the stairs, Saucy raced ahead of me to find her best friend, Noah's dog, Nutmeg.

"Babe!" Noah called from behind the closed bathroom door. As he stepped into the cool bedroom air, wearing only a towel, glistening water droplets still clung to his muscled chest. "Good morning, Jennifer."

He kissed me sweetly on the lips. It struck me that the growth of our relationship could be gauged by what name he used for me. When we first met, he called me "Penny," which was shortened to "PF," then became "JK," and settled on "J" as we became friends. After he introduced me to his mother as "Jennifer," he'd taken to calling me by my full name too. He also used "babe" when we were alone.

Noah's mother not only knew me as "Jennifer," but she also believed that I was a waitress. This was consistent with the fact that she thought Noah was a drug company rep and not a peddler of smut. Noah told me that it would kill her to know how he made his money, and so asked me to participate in his lie. I didn't care to lie about my occupation—to anyone—because it was so much effort to create an entirely fake job. I also secretly enjoyed the look on a man or woman's face when I revealed myself as a porn star; it gave me a tiny little ego boost. But there was a time when I would have done anything for Noah—even go against my conscience—and so I agreed. I loved him as much as I could love anyone in the business—or in the world, for that matter. I think Noah loved me too. The only catch was that, usually, Noah and I only loved each other when it suited us. But that seemed to be all that we were both capable of at that point in our lives.

Noah had a rotation of women with whom he spent his time. It generally varied from three to six. I was the only woman in his life who lasted for more than a few months and who was more than just a fuck buddy. But he kept me at a distance, too, and so there were times when I considered myself his number one, and times when I considered myself his number six.

I also had a rotation of men, but instead of rotating six men at once, I had one at a time who functioned as a singular boyfriend for however long he lasted. I didn't need to have multiple partners in the bedroom, because I had plenty of sex at work. What I *didn't* have—and wanted—were steady dinner dates, so I rotated men into my life for the affection they could offer. Whenever things became more "serious" with a new guy, I downshifted Noah to a weekly or biweekly dinner date. He could always tell when I was catching feelings for a guy, and would bring it up right away.

"Should we quit having sex, babe?"

My response was always accompanied by laughter.

"Yeah, for a while," I replied. "We will see how long this lasts."

It never lasted long. These relationships never developed into more than casual dating, and more often than not, I refused to call anyone my "boyfriend." Noah was the one constant in my life, and as far as I knew, I was the one constant in his.

On the morning of the day before I moved into the *Sober House* living quarters, I sat on Noah's bed and watched him apply Lubriderm to his perfect chest and abs.

Then I leaned down and addressed both dogs.

"Wanna go potty?" I asked.

They both ran down the stairwell to the backyard. As I sat down and lit a cigarette, Noah emerged and motioned to me with two fingers, his signal to give him the smoke for his ritual two puffs.

"I'm gonna miss you, babe," he said, awkwardly pulling on the Parliament.

"I'll come by and visit, don't worry!" I responded.

"Don't come if there are any cameras with you," he said. "You know I can't have my mother seeing me on TV. Especially since she's gonna know you're a porn star now."

He said the words "porn star" in a hushed voice, as if his mother were standing in the other room. For the first time, I realized that our relationship was about to change. Noah's mother didn't know that he was in porn. And having her believe that I was a good, wholesome girl was what kept my relationship with Noah solid and presentable, because it meant I was a girl whom he could bring home to her on holidays. Once she saw the show—which would be airing in a few months—and knew the truth, he would have to create a new lie about me: how we met and what our relationship meant. I'd previously been okay with our undefined arrangement, but his words about his mom suddenly jolted me into discontent. The relationship could never be more than it was. Even if we wanted it to be, there would always be lies.

Such lying was common in the adult business, and over the years I'd grown accustomed to the fact that the parents of many of those I worked with did not know about the source of their children's magical income. I'd also seen the polar opposite be true for porn stars, like Sunny Lane, whose parents knew way too much and even facilitated her participation in the business by acting as her managers.

My situation was a combination of the two extremes. I could never have maintained the kind of lies that Noah did. I smoked too much weed and would have forgotten what lie I'd told from one day to the next. My mother knew everything. She didn't particularly want me to be in porn, but she loved and accepted me as her daughter, which meant accepting my occupation. I had never explicitly told my father, mostly because I hadn't been on speaking terms with him for twelve years. The first I had ever mentioned it to him was after I left rehab and told him I was quitting the business. Even though I hadn't cared enough about what he thought to have him in my life for more than a decade, I was still pleased by his supportive and nonjudgmental response: "Good, Jen, you're better than that, anyway."

I left Noah's house, still simmering uncomfortably with the shame I thought he felt as a result of being my friend, and my inability to tell him how I really felt about him. I had yet to tell my agent, Derek Hay, that I was officially resigning from the industry, so I made a quick stop by my old agency, LA Direct Models. Derek was the fright of the biz. But once I started working for him, I realized this was just because he ran his agency with an iron fist, and many of his girls were in super-crazy porn-style party mode, which meant that responsible behavior was generally not in their vocabularies, and so they were always getting in trouble. Derek and I maintained a lovely business relationship, however, because neither of us ever forgot that we were there to make money, and so we were both pleased by our mutually beneficial relationship. I was an easy girl to represent, ever since I had gotten my cocaine problem in check a few years back. I showed up on time with a clean bill of health, paid him his fees, and rarely complained. In return, he treated me like the respectable porn star I was. Don't laugh: there is such a thing.

LA Direct Models shared the top floor of a building with Vivid Entertainment, and there was usually a constant stream of the plain to exceedingly stunning women who populate porn walking in and out of the elevator at all times. This particular day was quiet. As I rode the elevator in solitude, I reflected on the years I'd spent walking down these hallways on the heels of stunning, long-legged blondes, running into male performers whose curved penises I could recall but whose names I couldn't, or sitting on the counter in the women's restroom, talking to Fran through the stall. The LADM office sat behind a large, heavy door that opened onto a clinical waiting room where huge pictures of the best LADM girls hung on the walls. I had a picture on this wall, but I never looked at it as I walked past.

I stopped to thank Vee and Fran, and as I did, tears welled up in my eyes. Fran knew it was over the second she saw me, and she started to tear up too. Vee and Fran were strong-willed and tough enough to deal with Derek on a daily basis and keep the office running smoothly. Even more than that, Fran was like a mother and a sister to me. We both knew that my resignation meant we wouldn't see each other as often but that it would not mean that we loved each other any less.

I walked into Derek's office, shutting the door gently behind me, then sat in front of his clean, clutter-free desk and placed my hands in my lap.

"You've been an excellent agent and have taken my career further than I thought it would ever go," I said. "But it's time for me to do something new. I just want to thank you. For helping me and for understanding."

I began to cry. Even though I knew that I needed to leave porn for myself and for my future, my years at Derek's agency had actually been happy. I had met a lot of interesting people through him, some of whom had become good friends.

Derek smiled. This was big. Smiles only broke across his face on very special occasions.

"Miss Flame, normally I have girls in here crying because they've done something wrong and I've yelled at them," he said. "Never before has a girl cried in gratitude for the job I've done. So thank you. It's been my pleasure representing you."

And that was it. I had officially retired.

I hugged him and kept it together long enough to leave the office and the building. But once I reached the cool shadows of the parking garage, I sat in my Benz and wept. I felt lost, scared, grateful, and free, all at once. When my tears ran out, I reapplied my makeup and drove to Hollywood. It was time to start filming *Sober House with Dr. Drew*.

I MET MY trusty old producer Louie in a McDonald's parking lot, so his crew could mic me and place a cameraman inside my car to take the "reaction" shots during my arrival at Sober House. As I pulled into the bottom of a long, steep driveway and saw the mansion I'd call home for the next month, my reaction was: *Holy fuck.* It was magnificent, sitting high atop the Los Feliz hills, with panoramic views that stretched from downtown Los Angeles to Santa Monica.

The home seemed to have been carved into the cliff side. Fifty feet above the street, small faces hid behind cameras on a balcony off the home's patio, poised to film me walking up the giant hill. I carried a bouquet of my favorite stargazer lilies and one bag. The rest of my luggage would movie-magically appear in my room after the intro shots, so they didn't have to lose any time on awkward shots of me wrestling with a mountain of luggage. As I approached the front door, my heart began to beat harder. I rang the bell and waited while producers, cameramen, and the other patients took their places. The show was officially on.

The house "mom," Jennifer Gimenez, answered with a stern yet welcoming look. It was enough to tell me that this *Sober House* experience would not be the emotional roller coaster that *Sex Rehab* had been, which was a relief. I set my bouquet on the kitchen table and Jenn G. began her house tour and a rundown of our responsibilities and the rules:

1. We would be given mandatory drug tests each time we left the house.
2. We were responsible for cleaning up after ourselves.
3. I was not to go into the boys' rooms.

The house was a two-story marble-and-bronze-adorned palace with a heated pool and Jacuzzi, a kitchen overlooking a koi pond, four bedrooms, a pool table, and a Mac computer that would most likely go unused, because, as I had learned during my first stint, surfing the Internet does not make good reality television.

Jenn G. was curious about me, because she had never dealt with a sex addict before.

"Are there certain things you'll need for your stay?" she asked.

"Mostly things I don't need," I said. "Like sex. I can't have, allude to, or manipulate situations using sex."

She laughed.

"Well, there is no sex in the Champagne Room," she said. "There's not even champagne."

The intake shot was complete.

ALL THE WOMEN on *Sober House with Dr. Drew* shared a room except for Jenn G., who had her own private bedroom overlooking downtown. As I got settled in, Jenn G. and I decided that I would again be going by Jennie, as opposed to Jennifer or Jen, so as not to be confused with her. After a few minutes in my room, I followed her outside to the wraparound patio deck area to have my first Sober House cigarette. There, I met two other houseguests: actor Tom Sizemore and the former Alice in Chains bassist Mike Starr, who, by the looks of the overflowing ashtray, had both been chain-smoking since they arrived.

Tom was going on sixty days clean after having participated in *Celebrity Rehab with Dr. Drew;* he was then living in a clean facility between the shows. Mike had been on *Celebrity Rehab,* too, but he'd "gone out" since then, meaning that upon his release back into the world, where he'd faced thirty days without supervision between the shows, he'd gone out in Hollywood, found speed and heroin, and gotten high. Because the two men had spent a month together detoxing on the first show, there was an obvious sense of camaraderie between them. I immediately felt like the odd one out. As we sat smoking, we were joined by Heidi Fleiss, a former madam, ex-convict, and recovering meth user, who was also Tom's ex-girlfriend and had filed assault charges against him during the time they were together. She was wearing tattered sweatpants and an oversize man's T-shirt that had been fashioned into a tank top. She was frantically eating pistachios. As she munched and crunched the shells, she resembled one of the many parrots that I came to learn she lives with in her solitary Nevada home.

"Who are you?" Heidi asked me, smiling and chewing green nuts with an open mouth.

"Jennie," I replied, pulling on my smoke and trying to act like I had as much of a right to be there as she did.

Tom shifted uncomfortably in his seat.

"No, I mean, *who* are you," she said. "Are you famous? What are you famous for? This is a show for celebrities, right?"

Her tone was laced with insult, but Mike was apparently oblivious to the fine art of social snobbery, because he introduced us warmly.

"Hey, Heidi!" Mike said. "This is Jen!"

Tom leaned back in his seat nervously.

"Hey, Mike, thanks," she said.

Heidi turned to me again.

"So?" she asked.

"I guess I'm famous for being a whore?" I said. "I used to be a porn star."

As I confessed, I took a drag from my smoke and tried to keep my hand steady. This woman made me incredibly uneasy. Sure, I'd been used to working with Derek, who had been sort of like my pimp, and who was known for being tough. But Heidi went beyond that. If nervousness were a math problem, she was making me nervous squared, plus uncomfortable cubed.

"Oh," she said.

Just like that, it seemed that the standoff was over. She turned and shuffled off toward the glass door that separated the living area and the patio. When she reached the threshold, she pivoted and turned back to us.

"I know a lot of whores," she said, smiling wickedly at Tom. "What was your porn name?"

"Penny Flame," I said. "It *was* Penny Flame. Now Jennie will do just fine."

I stubbed out my cigarette. Immediately, I reached for another and lit it, trying to tamp down the feeling of regret that had surged through my body the moment I introduced the character of Penny Flame to Heidi Fleiss, the Hollywood Madam.

"Sweet. Nice to meet you, Penny," she said.

She walked back inside. When she was out of sight, Tom finally exhaled. It seemed he'd been holding his breath the entire time. I could sympathize.

WHEN DENNIS RODMAN showed up at the house later that day, it was like a real live Hollywood star had arrived.

Technically, to earn a place there, we were all celebrities of a sort. But I already knew Kendra Jade Rossi from *Sex Rehab,* so that was no biggie. Mike Starr was too insecure from years of drug abuse to have any starlike confidence or make much of an impression. Tom was still finding his footing in sobriety, and was quietly tiptoeing around the Heidi situation. And Heidi's focus on pissing Tom off—which she was very good at, no matter how much Tom tried to pretend everything was fine—detracted from her potential star quality. So none of my new roommates had that sensational magnetism and appeal of a real star.

But Dennis Rodman was a different story altogether. He started making demands while he was still in the driveway. He refused to sign the no-drinking contract, protested the location of the beds, and waved away suggestions that he should come into the house and settle down.

Holy fuck, this guy is famous, I thought.

Jenn finally convinced Dennis to come inside so she could give him the tour and rules breakdown. He then joined the other room-mates on the patio, just as the sun began to dip into the Pacific Ocean.

I summoned my courage and asked him about his star quality.

"Ahh, all drama for the camera, little one," he said.

Then he leaned back and tugged happily on a freshly lit cigar. I sat nearby, amazed to be watching the sunset in the reflection of Dennis Rodman's sunglasses. Apart from the scary Heidi encounter, my first day had gone better than I had hoped.

This is going to be an awesome month.

At the end of the first day, there were still two people yet to arrive: Kari Ann Peniche and Seth "Shifty Shellshock" Binzer, front man of the rap band Crazy Town. Kari Ann had been treated briefly on *Sex Rehab,* until she caused a tech to be fired and eventually quit the program. She was then re-treated on *Celebrity Rehab,* this time for meth, which was a bigger problem for her than the sex stuff. Seth had a crack problem and had been treated multiple times on different Dr. Drew shows. It now seemed to me like he might be developing an addiction to the cycle of seeking treatment and relapsing, though I never dared to tell him that directly.

When Kari Ann showed up, she pissed dirty for the drug test. But she claimed she hadn't been using, and by some fluke loophole she was allowed to stay in the home. When Seth arrived and tested positive for cocaine and marijuana, he admitted to using. He was asked to stay with Jenn's right-hand man, Big Will, until he got clean. That seemed unlikely to me. One of Seth's last filmed attempts at sobriety had included a segment where he climbed on the roof of the rehab center with a gerbil for his kid and some crack for himself—and was coaxed down only through the extreme efforts of a multitude of clinicians. It had become apparent that Seth didn't have many relapses left before he died of his addiction.

Seth wasn't the only person with only a few chances left. Gia, one of the field producers on the show, told us that before *Celebrity Rehab,* Mike and a relative were living in Seattle off his royalties from his Alice in Chains days and doing heroin and crack together. Mike was trying to erase some heavy memories. He felt responsible for the overdose death of Layne Staley, the original lead singer of Alice in Chains. It had been seven years since Layne died, and Mike lived the regret every day. Mike listened on repeat to the song "Man in the Box," which he and Layne had sung together, and tears filled his eyes when he described how it was the only time he got to hear his friend's voice anymore.

Tom Sizemore had been convicted of assaulting Heidi, and even though the conviction had been overturned, he had done some jail time and was now on probation. After prison, he failed drug test after drug test and couldn't seem to keep his life straight. By the time he ended up on *Celebrity Rehab,* there were no production companies willing to hire him, regardless of his super-excellent acting skills, because no insurance companies would insure him. He spent his days before rehab shacking up with hookers, doing speed, and rearranging the house furniture. At Sober House, he spent most days sitting at the patio table, smoking cigarettes and texting his girlfriend, who also happened to be in rehab. One day I sat down next to him.

"Hey, I saw that sex addiction pamphlet on the table in there," he said. "I think I might be a sex addict too. What do I do?"

"Work on getting off speed first, then worry about the other stuff," I said.

Out of everyone in there, it seemed like he had a real chance, because at least he was willing to face additional problems that he might have, like the sex stuff, and it felt like he might even be willing to work on staying sober.

Heidi had been living with twenty-five parrots in Pahrump, Nevada, a town of forty thousand residents in the middle of the desert. She had a difficult time connecting to women, which is probably why she made such a good madam. She couldn't look me in the eye for more than ten seconds. I could tell that there was a clever and enchanting woman hiding within her tough, drug-hardened exterior, but she didn't want anyone to see the soft, sensitive person beneath the open sores and foul language. I could totally understand this because I once wore the same drug-hardened and emotionally numb shell. I just called that exterior Penny Flame. Heidi did let some sensitivity show: she refused to eat animals. And she could be strong in flashes.

"I would never stick needles in my arms!" she said to me once. "Yuck."

Her tone carried such conviction.

If she could only channel that sureness into being healthy, she would definitely make it out of this lonely, isolated life she lives, I couldn't help thinking.

By the third or fourth day of filming, Kari Ann began to plummet into sobriety as the meth wore off and her feelings began to turn back on. The process made every opening of her recently plumped lips venomous. She leaned out the window of the girls' second-floor room, screaming at Jenn on the balcony below.

"You fat, ugly monster. Get the fuck out of my face. Stay the fuck out of my room!"

Kari Ann didn't last on *Sober House* much longer after that. Her departure came swiftly after she punched a cameraman, knocking his camera into his face and then his eye. The only problem was that with her went the drama. Production tried to bring her back the following evening for some good TV, but the remaining housemates were all getting along so well that we refused to allow her to return. I did agree with her about one thing, though: after she got kicked out, Kari Ann said, "I'm just doing it to make some drama. Jesus, guys."

It's true that reality television cannot get by on peace and harmony. But Kari Ann wasn't the only one who could create drama. With an eye toward making some riveting TV ourselves, Dennis, Mike, and I decided to go out to a club and create a tense scene that would leave the impression we were going to relapse. Being a former moviemaker myself, I was well versed in what made for a compelling scene. I figured that, as cocktail waitresses passed by, we'd give them some pensive, unsure looks. And then, even though we were never really in danger of relapsing, the commercials for the show could tease the episode by making it appear that we'd had a truly difficult time maintaining our sobriety.

I wasn't about to get in trouble just for ratings, though. So I secretly texted Jenn from the club: "We are going to intentionally break curfew tonight, just so you know. The show needs drama but we aren't willing to relapse to make it so."

Dr. Drew had no idea of our plot, nor did Production. I was totally surprised when girls began walking over to us with free vodka Red Bulls. Dennis was not impressed.

"They're gonna have to do way better than that to tempt me to drink," he said. "Look, it's all Production buying the drinks."

It seemed like it must be true. Toward the end of the night, we confronted the production crew about whether they'd tried to derail our sober evening, but nobody admitted to sending the cocktail girls our way. I never did find out if the waitresses were random or a setup. But we all went to bed sober, which was all that really mattered.

Another night, plans for a "Dennis Rodman in Las Vegas" party began to unfurl in the secret world behind Production's closed doors. Word reached Jill, whom I'd been seeing biweekly since *Sex Rehab*. She told me during one of our therapy sessions that she was willing to put her body in front of the bus they would have to rent to get us to Vegas for the party.

"There's no way any of my patients are going out there," she said.

She wasn't alone in her conviction that it was a bad idea. Dr. Drew had gotten wind of the Vegas party and put a stop to Production's plans. I'm not sure how that all went down, but the party never materialized, and we kept on chillin' at the Sober House. I found it reassuring that Drew and Jill didn't care about the kind of reality TV drama we wanted to create: they found enough drama in trying to help people stay sober.

Anytime we left the Sober House as a group, we packed into a giant white van and crept down the winding road from our mountain abode to Hollywood Boulevard. A few of the housemates decided an evening at Pimai It's Tai, a Thai place on Franklin Avenue in Hollywood, was much needed, so Kendra and Dennis, who had both been out for the day, opted to meet us there while Seth, Mike, and I loaded into the van with Gia. On our way down the hill, Seth said something that made me nervous.

"I'm good this time, I think," he said. "I'm gonna follow the rules."

"It's okay to break the rules," Gia said.

"You mean you're not," I said to Seth.

"No, I totally am, Penny," he said.

"Jennie," I told him coldly, squaring my jaw to Gia as if preparing for a knockout battle. This show was turning out to be nothing like *Sex Rehab,* and I didn't feel like I could trust the producers to have our best interests at heart like I had trusted the producers on the last show.

"Fuck, I'm sorry, Jennie," he said. "My bad. Don't worry, I won't smoke crack. Are you mad?"

Seth grabbed my knee like a dad grabs onto his kid.

"Don't be mad," he said.

I wasn't mad at Seth for his slip, because he slipped often, and I figured between my initial introduction as Penny and his Swiss cheese crack brain, it was probably difficult for him to keep it all straight. I was pissed at the producers who had been around the other times Seth had appeared on recovery shows, and yet with each appearance, had fallen further and further into addiction. I wondered if they subtly encouraged him to break the rules the entire time and if this had contributed to his chronic relapsing. If the crew had been whispering dirty little encouragements to him, it put the entire house at risk for relapsing; worse yet, it made the show feel like a farce. A joke of a show was not the experience I wanted. I wanted a repeat of *Sex Rehab.* I wanted authenticity, self-discovery, total breakdowns, and a safe place to rebuild. Production intentionally throwing obstacles at us to make good television was nothing more than just that: television.

Once we reached Pimai, I tried to let the spicy yellow curry and Thai iced tea wash away my resentment, but when the bill came and we'd been charged for a bottle of sake, I lost my cool. I looked directly into the camera.

"Who the fuck is drinking sake?" I said.

Production hated it when we looked directly into the camera, because it rendered the shot useless. While the cameraman and field producer, Patrick, listened through their ear walkie-talkies to whoever sat outside, overseeing the dinner, I looked around the restaurant for someone I recognized drinking booze.

"I think we bought it for another table," Patrick said.

Just then I saw Gia and her assistant toss back shots of Nigori sake. I continued to look directly into the camera as I spoke.

"No, Gia and her sidekick are drinking at that table," I said. "And they put the bottle on our tab? I cannot fucking believe this bitch."

I threw the bill and my money on the table and walked outside to smoke. As I paced furiously, Gia ran out to the parking lot and tried to explain what had happened.

"We weren't *actually* drinking sake, Jennie, okay?" she said.

I felt my face heating up with rage as I heard her deny what I had seen with my own eyes. She tried to stand close to me but I spun away from her.

"Listen, bitch, I'm not coming down off heroin or crack," I said. "I'm as sober and clear-eyed as I've ever been in my whole life, and I saw you and your little fucking buddy taking shots of sake. You really couldn't wait a few more hours until you were off work? Really?"

"I know, I shouldn't have been drinking," Gia said in a hushed voice as she looked around for witnesses to her admission of guilt.

"You shouldn't have been drinking?" I screamed. "I don't give a fuck what you do on your own time, but you have the nerve to get sauced while you film a show about staying sober? You've got a problem, lady. Get the fuck away from me."

Soon, Kendra and Seth were outside, trying to calm me down.

"You're gonna have to deal with people drinking out there in the real world," Kendra said.

I got that. The problem wasn't people drinking in the real world; the problem was this chick, who was supposed to be there to *help us,* putting her booze on our tab. It was a bullshit thing to do.

When we returned to the house, Gia resumed her "It didn't happen" stance and I called Bruce, the head producer. I was so upset that after I told him what had happened, our conversation blurred into anger and tears on my part until Bruce agreed to keep Gia away from me. I crawled helplessly into my bed and pulled the sheets over my head. The entire incident struck me as pathetic. It was pathetic that she needed to drink, pathetic that I cared about her drinking on set, pathetic that I felt I couldn't be near her and be safe. The only other time I'd felt this unsafe was when my dad asked that I check the house for cops when I was nine. I pressed my face into the pillow and cried, counting the days I had left.

My solitude didn't last for long.

"Listen, Jennie, I want to talk," Gia said from the foot of my bed. "I wasn't drinking down there. I'm sorry you saw something that you mistook for drinking, but I wasn't drinking."

I hadn't realized she was in the room until she started speaking. I kept the covers over my head, feeling like a child hiding from the monsters in her closet, and unable to behave like an adult.

"Liar, get away from me, you liar," I said. "Get away."

When she didn't leave and instead kept trying to convince me of her innocence, I ran into Jenn's room and dragged her into the bathroom with me, where I hid, sobbing and refusing to allow the cameras to follow us.

"She's on the other side of that door, I know it," I told Jenn as I opened the door and Gia nearly fell into the bathroom.

"Fucking leave, you psycho!" I screamed at Gia.

Finally, Patrick, whom I trusted the most apart from Louie, hurried into the bathroom and pushed Gia outside.

"Give us a while," he said. "Out."

Although the door was shut and Gia was on the other side, I was sure she kept the cameras rolling. I couldn't help but think of the wonderfully dramatic television I was providing: the break-down of Jennie Ketcham. I knew how this would all look on a fifteen-second VH1 commercial for the episode—how easily the situation could be twisted into a newly sober person lying and accusing a trustworthy production person of something she hadn't done. I was more than willing to make good dramatic television on my own terms, but this was something different: I felt totally out of control and super-vulnerable.

The next day in therapy with Drew, I angrily laid into him about Gia's bad behavior.

"Why is Production allowed to ruin our progress?" I said. "I want to be in a sober house, Dr. Drew. Not this fucking mess where the crew is allowed to violate everything I work to maintain."

Drew nodded and kept composed, although it was clear to me that he was not pleased with the story I had told him about Gia's behavior in the restaurant and then confronting me in bed and fol-lowing me to the bathroom.

"It won't happen again, I promise," he said. "And if I hear about Production causing any problems like this, there will be seri-ous issues. You are my patient. I have your back, Jennie."

"I just want to be done with this," I said. "I want to be done with the hard stuff, with trying to create boundaries. I didn't even know what boundaries were when I came to *Sex Rehab*; I didn't think I had a right to space, privacy, a right to be untouched. I just want to be better."

I grabbed a tissue and began folding it into the small comfort triangles that always helped to distract me.

"Jennie, I promise it's getting better," Drew said. "It's okay right now. You just have to keep working and I promise it will get easier. You're doing so well."

I didn't know if it was getting better or if it would get easier, but I trusted Dr. Drew because ever since I had met him, things in my life had started to evolve in a seemingly healthy way. I had started to experience feelings again, and though it was uncomfortable, he had given me some advice about dealing with them that really worked for me.

"Feelings aren't facts," Drew said. "They will pass with time."

And he was right. My feelings had already changed so much since they first started emerging during my time on *Sex Rehab*. My relationship with my dad, with the men and women around me, the way I saw myself—it was all changing. Sometimes this was terrifying, but it was inspiring too. I couldn't always see the changes when I looked in the mirror, but I could often see them through the eyes of another person, which was why I valued my sessions with Drew and Jill so much, and my relationships with the few people in my life who seemed to really see me and love me for who I was.

"I'll keep doing it, Drew," I said. "I'll do whatever you and Jill say. I'll do anything to get better."

And that was the truth. I was willing to do whatever he or Jill suggested if it meant my life got better. I would do it if it meant that the next time an uncomfortable situation arose, like the one with Gia, I would be able to handle it with grace and dignity instead of hiding under the sheets or crying hysterically in the bathroom.

Drew nodded and wrote something on his pad.

"Good, Jennie," he said. "I'm glad to hear that. That's really good news."

I WAS GETTING tired of living with crazy people. Tom Sizemore and Heidi were at each other's throats; Kendra and Seth had paired off into this strange codependency thing and spent nearly every waking moment together; Mike was great in the morning when we met on the patio for our watch-L.A.-wake-up coffee-and-smoke sessions, but come midafternoon, he was up and down from his de-heroin drug, Suboxone. Dennis kept to himself and worked out all the time. Aside from the house mother, Jennifer Gimenez, who turned into a wonderful friend and support system during the course of the show, Dennis was the only noncrazy person there. He was a total dad, even if he was a totally famous one. He said the craziest thing to me one day as I cleaned the granite countertops in the kitchen.

"You better wipe behind those knives, not just around them."

That made me laugh. I felt like he was going to dock my allowance if I didn't.

In the evenings we'd cook dinner or order in. After one meal toward the end of my time on the show, Kendra, Seth, Jenn, and I went for a late-night hot-tub session. We sat lazily in the chlorinated water, overlooking the city, puffing cigarettes, and drinking from our label-less water bottles.

"Have you ever played the Banana Slap Game?" Kendra asked. I shook my head no.

"What the fuck is that?" Seth asked.

Kendra sent Seth to the kitchen for bananas. When he came back, she stripped the bananas naked and kept the peels in her hand.

"My husband and I play this game all the time," she said.

Jenn was smiling as she watched this interaction, but she seemed a bit nervous.

"You just slap each other in the face with the peel," Kendra said. She laughed and moved closer to Seth, and then closer to me.

"I'm cool," I said. "Not really trying to get slapped in the face."

I lit another smoke while moving to the farthest point of the tub, again trying to exercise the boundary thing by putting physical space between my body and theirs. Dr. Drew had suggested this tactic when I didn't feel safe.

Kendra moved quick and slapped Seth in the face. They both laughed. She handed him the peel. He playfully swung it my way.

"No, really, I don't want to play this fucking game," I said.

"Awww, come on, Jen, it's harmless!" he said. "Why not?"

He took a swing and smacked Kendra in the face.

"I don't wanna play the fucking game," I said. "This is really fucking triggering, and I don't want to play."

I spoke sternly, trying to keep my cool. I had told Jenn about triggers, the things that made me feel unsafe and led me to want to act out or relapse.

Of course, Seth slapped me across the face with the peel anyhow.

As I climbed out of the tub, Kendra was snickering, but she pleaded that I stay.

"Come on, Penny, it was a joke," Seth said. "Don't be mad."

"My name isn't Penny!" I said. "It's Jennie, okay? It's fucking *Jennie*. Get it straight. Jen-fucking-ee."

I ran into the house to change, soaking wet and pissed off.

I stripped out of my damp bathing suit and caught a glimpse of my naked body in the mirror. As I did so, I realized that I'd been avoiding looking at myself naked since I got out of rehab and porn. I'd avoided looking at my face in the mirror or making eye contact with myself, and suddenly I realized *why* I'd quit spending hours in front of my reflection, as I'd once done when I was getting ready for porn shoots. I was so afraid that I wouldn't recognize the person looking back at me. But in the very moment that I finally dared to look at myself, I knew who the naked girl in the mirror was, with her emotions as much of a tangled and confusing mess as her hair was right now. Even if I didn't understand every part of that girl in the mirror, at least I knew her name. I knew what she stood for. I was starting to know her boundaries. I put my hands on the counter and pressed my nose to the mirror. When my breath fogged up the glass, I closed my eyes and whispered three words that were just for myself.

"I am Jennie," I said.

8

"THE LIAR'S PUNISHMENT IS NOT IN THE LEAST THAT HE IS NOT
BELIEVED, BUT THAT HE CANNOT BELIEVE ANYONE ELSE. . . ."
—GEORGE BERNARD SHAW, *THE QUINTESSENCE OF IBSENISM*

Even though I was smoking herb pretty much constantly throughout the day and driving up to L.A. most weekends for photo shoots, I still found my sophomore year at San Diego State interesting and academically inspiring. But I was also finding it more difficult to maintain the lies I told Marc. When he asked me about my future career plans, I responded: "I'm only going to do a few more shoots and then get a different job. This isn't where I want to spend my life. I want to be a travel writer or a secret hotel reviewer." I didn't even think this job existed, but I hoped that by making it up, I would shush him.

When Marc asked about my living circumstances, I said: "Oh, Jeff, Pookie, and me, well, it didn't work out. Pookie and I ended up moving into our own spot so we could be girls together. But it doesn't mean we don't all hang out."

The truth was I had no career plans, other than my pipe dreams of making enough money to finish school and magically jump into a career in which my employer would not mind my pornographic history. I was fairly sure that I could hide my past, and that whoever ended up hiring me would not suspect that by twenty years old I'd already graced the cover of multiple men's jerk-off mags. That's not to say I didn't want to be a travel writer or a secret hotel reviewer; it was simply that I didn't believe any of that was possible.

The truth about Jeff and me, well, that was more complicated. I came home from school one day to our two-bedroom apartment off Reservoir Drive dressed in low-slung, butt-crack-showing Bebe jeans, only to have Jeff confront me.

He pointed incredulously at the computer screen glowing on the desk.

"You're fucking old men now?" he yelled. "You're a fucking whore! You know that?"

"What are you even talking about?" I screamed back at him.

I actually was unsure what he was talking about. I looked at the glowing screen to see that Dirty Dave's website, or Dirty Dan, or some other old dirty guy, was advertising that he had Penny Flame content.

"Dude, I've never fucked this guy," I said. "You seriously think I'm fucking old guys?"

"Jennie, it says that he has Penny Flame content," Jeff said. "That's you. So that means you're fucking him. You fucking lied to me. I can't believe you're a whore. Ha! A fucking prostitute!"

He looked me square in the eyes and spoke in such a matter-of-fact tone, disbelieving me, even though he was the only man with whom I had been completely honest. I mustered all of my courage to stand up for myself.

"Wow, I don't know you at all, Jeff," I said. "You're the one I've been honest with. See what good that did me. Go ahead and join the site! See who's in there fucking him, 'cuz it ain't me."

I spoke the words as a quiet, sincere statement. But Jeff just laughed in my face. "You're a total prostitute," he repeated. "I can't believe it. I fucked a prostitute."

His words caused me to explode into screaming fury.

"Actually, get the fuck out of my house!" I yelled.

I flung my body at him, fists punching, nails scratching. When he spun on his heels to leave, I jumped on his back.

"I don't ever want to see you again, you fucking asshole!" I screamed. "Don't ever come back. Don't you dare show your fucking face to me or, I swear to God, I'll fucking kill you. You're dead to me. Get the fuck out!"

He didn't fight back. He simply tried to avoid the assault of my claws and my punches. When he left, I didn't notice that there was blood coming through his thin cotton T-shirt, and I didn't care to stop and think that his heart might be broken too. I felt utterly betrayed and I just wanted him gone.

After Jeff was out of my life and I had no penile distractions, my relationship with Marc began to disintegrate with alarming speed. I became convinced that Marc was cheating on me as I had cheated on him. I was furious when I heard girls' voices in the background at his home during our phone calls. I spent each and every dollar I had on flying him out to see me, or me to him. When I visited him, I death-stared every girl who came his way. In San Diego we holed up in my apartment and had sex for the whole visit. Those were the only moments that felt safe to me, like he still loved me and only me. I morphed into an uncool, jealous girlfriend as quickly as I'd become faithful. I was unbearable and the relationship was suffocating, but Marc hung in there. Still, when spring arrived and I decided to break up with him during one of our phone calls, the breakup seemingly came as no surprise to him. I cited various bipolar-esque reasons for my decision, but it was actually due to self-hatred. I hated that Marc could be trusted and I could not. As usual, Marc handled the situation with grace.

"I know you're fucking someone else," I said.

And then I did a complete one-eighty.

"It's not you, it's me," I said.

"I'll miss you," he said. "You *were* a good girl."

The past tense with which he spoke shattered my confidence. However, instead of picking up my broken heart and mending the wound with the love of girlfriends like Pookie, I called up Jeff and reignited our relationship, replacing one man with another. He quickly forgot that I'd attacked him once his cock was in my mouth. Or at least he quit talking about it. And the fire and lightning with which our relationship had begun—and ended—continued into the second round.

EVERY SUMMER, A group of my old friends packed up their camping gear and headed north for the annual Reggae on the River festival. I had gone the previous summer. But after the demolition of my relationship with Marc, I knew I'd be unwelcome in Humboldt County and chose to spend the weekend in San Francisco with Jeff instead. Besides, San Francisco was notoriously beautiful in the summertime, and hiding beneath a deliciously thick fog blanket, people were in motion everywhere. The trolleys rolled up and down the steep hills, and tourists covered every square inch of the wharf with prepurchased Alcatraz tickets and shit-eating grins, taking pictures of the seals smothering Pier 39's docks and eating sourdough bread bowls filled with clam chowder from Boudin. Jeff and I had been down at the pier, and then returned to our hotel for some super-satisfying daytime vacation hotel sex. We were reassembling our clothing when my phone rang. It was Marc. I hadn't spoken with him since I'd dumped him that spring.

"Hello?" I answered, cautiously.

For some reason, I was worried that he'd seen me in the city with Jeff, even though my fear had no logical basis, as he'd been in Humboldt County listening to reggae for the weekend and we were no longer even a couple.

"Kitty?" he said.

His voice sounded broken. And the nickname with which he

had once lovingly referred to me felt like a million dull knives in my already bloodied heart. I looked at Jeff and decided not to reveal who was on the phone.

"Hey," I awkwardly responded. "What's up?"

"Arianna is dead," Marc said. "She got in a car wreck on the way home from Reggae."

I couldn't comprehend what he was saying. Arianna was Marc's best friend Maddox's little sister, and over the course of their life together, she had become Marc's surrogate little sister. Arianna had been the glue that held the crew together. She was one of the few young women I knew who was disciplined enough to work hard and save money for a car instead of asking for help from Mommy or Daddy. She was one of the few people who could smile on her worst day and mean it. Her happiness and laughter were infectious, her optimism and drive inspiring. Her beauty unmatched. She was nineteen.

"They went off a cliff on the 101," Marc said. "She was in a coma, but they took her off life support today. I thought you should hear it from me. The funeral is next weekend."

Marc was obviously holding back tears, and his voice was no more than a whisper, barely audible through the phone. I wanted to reach out to Marc, to hug him, to love him, to hold him in my arms and tell him that everything would be okay. But I knew that all of it would be a lie, so I didn't say anything that was in my heart.

"Thank you," I muttered.

I hung up the phone and crumpled on the freshly fucked hotel bed. Jeff wrapped his arms around me.

"She's dead," I said.

He didn't ask who she was, just held me and kissed my head.

"I'm sorry," he said.

It was a crisp summer day in Northern California, a beautiful day to die, and from the look on my face Jeff knew our vacation was over.

We drove home the next day. I was shattered but my eyes were never wet. I wanted to save those tears for the funeral, for when I could stand in Marc's arms. He was the one person who knew every horrid and obsessive crack in my soul and loved me anyway. I fantasized about standing in the woods and crying with him. We would hold each other and make love under the giant redwood trees. I refused to share my pain with Jeff. *He didn't know her; how could he ever understand why I'd cry for her?* I thought. My response was totally irrational and illogical but perfectly aligned with my coping mechanisms. I don't know if it started with my parents' divorce or even before then, but I couldn't ever believe that my feelings would be valid to another person. And so I utterly refused to show any weakness or emotion when it came to Arianna's death.

The following Thursday, I drove back to the Bay Area for the funeral. When I pulled into the post office near where he grew up, I saw Maddox standing surrounded by others in the parking lot. I parked and hopped out of the car to offer my condolences. I hadn't seen or spoken to him since long before Marc and I broke up. Maddox and I made eye contact as I stepped out of my car and scanned the group for Marc.

Maddox stepped in front of his solemn friends.

"You lying whore!" he yelled. "Get the fuck outta my face. Get away from me, my sister, my best friend. You don't belong here."

My stomach was in my throat but I continued to approach him.

"What are you talking about?" I asked.

My tone was innocent but I was terrified that I knew what he meant. He stood inches from me, spitting saliva, tears, and grief-fueled hatred onto my face and into my eyes.

"You think Marc didn't tell me what you did to him?" Maddox said. "How you betrayed him? You're a cheating whore."

Venom oozed from his lips, and with each word I shrunk in size. I didn't say anything to defend myself.

"It wasn't enough to cheat, you had to become a whore too?" Maddox continued. "Leave now and don't come back. Don't come to Arianna's funeral. Don't breathe any of our names again."

Too shocked to respond, I muttered something closely resembling "I'm sorry." I ran to the safety of my car and drove quickly from the woods back to Moraga. Once at the Jack in the Box, I called Marc's house phone, praying he'd pick up, knowing I was shamefully incapable of speaking to either of his parents. After three rings, he answered.

"Yup," he said.

He sounded as if he'd been drinking. A lot. He sounded like he'd replaced his blood with alcohol. He sounded like he'd known I'd be calling.

Just hearing his voice was enough to make my finely polished exterior begin to crack and expose my grief over Arianna's death, my hatred of her brother, and my pain at the loss of Marc.

"Did you hear what he said to me?" I asked.

"Yeah, I don't think it's a good idea for you to come out here anymore," Marc said, speaking quietly, forming each word carefully. "He just needs some time."

The tears I'd forced myself to withhold from my eyes surged forth. I choked back the raw, ugly insides that were trying so hard to escape.

"Please, can I come see you?" I begged. "Please?"

"You can come now, this once, but after that . . ." His voice trailed off.

I can't remember if I wept while driving to his house. I can't remember parking on the pullout above his house, off the narrow and steep winding road that snaked through the neighborhood. I can't remember walking through his front door without knocking or searching the first floor of the log house for him. But I can remember taking the stairs to his parents' room, peeking over the ledge separating the bedroom and office. I can remember the look on his face as I approached him where he was lying in his parents' bed.

"What are you doing?" I asked, even though I knew where this was going.

"Come here," he said, patting the sheets beside him.

In his parents' bed, we explored one another's bodies as if it were the first time. Tears dripped to our lips as we kissed and devoured the salty skin of our bodies. I reached for him, brought my mouth to him, and, throbbing and out of control, he came. And just like that, we were through.

He put his feet to the ground, slumped over, elbows on his knees, and stared into his dirty hands.

"What are you doing?" he asked.

I stood and, for the first time, I witnessed the beautiful man I'd destroyed.

"I don't know anymore," I said.

I walked back to the stairs, praying he'd say, *Stop. Come be with me. Lie next to me until we don't feel anymore.*

But as I put my foot on that first step, he didn't say anything. I looked back across the ledge at him and he sighed the same heavy sigh I'd heard so many times before. He looked at me with his soulful dark brown eyes, beaten and hopeless, beneath heavy lashes.

"Good-bye," he said.

"Bye," I said, barely breathing the word.

I forced myself to smile and walked down the stairs, out the front door, and out of his life. I didn't cry. I didn't go to Arianna's funeral. And I didn't look back.

I HAD BEGUN doing girl/girl scenes during the previous school year, and by mid-September I had them booked weeks in advance. I was working so hard that when another friend died in a car accident in late August, I didn't have time to grieve him. His name was Drake, and we had met in college. This time the wreck happened in Santa Barbara. Because all of my college friends had gone separate directions for the summer, it was a month before any of us found out that Drake had died, so I didn't even know about his funeral. I never found out whether or not alcohol played a part, but given how all of us were living our college lives at the time, it wouldn't surprise me if it had.

And then, in late October, my high school bestie, Kelli, called to say her boyfriend Derek had died in yet another car wreck. There was no time to process my enormous amount of grief. Instead, I went on emotional autopilot as I drove back to the Bay to be a supportive friend.

Making one out of three funerals isn't too bad.

And because none of the friends who had died were old enough to drink liquor legally, I took it upon myself to drink for and in honor of them. It didn't seem like there was any point in doing much more than drinking anyhow.

Life is too short. It's really just a little blip. A meaningless little blip. I am taking it far too seriously, I thought.

All of this death, and my inability to process grief, led to an increase in my drug use, which led to a decrease in my academic abilities. Though I loved school—the environment, the ideas, the endless possibilities it seemed to present—when classes got under way that fall, I couldn't seem to move my body from the small leather couch in my living room. I'd already moved away from Pookie, who seemed much more goal-oriented than I could even pretend to be. Living in my own beach-town and bay-front apartment afforded me the luxury of privacy, so that even though I didn't shower for days and ate only blueberry mini-muffins from the vending machine in my complex, there was nobody to call me on my unhealthiness. I ignored Jeff's calls. I lay frozen on the couch when people knocked on the front door. I couldn't face anyone or anything they might ask of me. All I felt capable of doing was watching rerun after rerun on TNT.

The only days I felt anything close to being alive were those on which I was paid to drive north to Los Angeles to have sex with beautiful women. John, my first agent, whom I met on the Balboa Park Model Days in Los Angeles, and who had purchased the domain name PennyFlame.com for me and then promptly disappeared, never returned my phone calls. Eventually, I gave up on him entirely and found a new agent named Cam.

Cam represented a plethora of beautiful women who all had sex with other women on camera, and when he and I began our business involvement, it was obvious that I wouldn't be getting any work if I wasn't doing girls too. My first girl/girl scene was not the sensual, sexual experience I had hoped it would be. It was also not the first time I'd had sex with a girl. I'd had sex with Pookie on a drunken night in Mexico, and then, the sex only happened because we were both obliterated enough to go for it. But after that evening, we didn't speak of it, joke about it, reference it, or anything, which kind of made me sad because it was superhot and sensual.

The first time, on camera, was nothing like with Pookie: it was educational, a brief foray into the world of gay-for-pay women, which taught me that not all women—or men—who have same-sex intercourse *on* camera have a preference for same-sex intercourse *off* camera. The scene was with a beautiful blond Czech girl named Jana Cova. The bone structure of her face exemplified artistic renderings of the ideal beauty: famous ballerinas from eastern Europe and queens and princesses from places unknown. She spoke with a thick accent and had eyes that shone frostbitten blue like chunks of icebergs. Her cheekbones highlighted her perfect skin. She was flawless, from her soft blond hair, down to her quarter-size rose-colored nipples, and down farther to her French-manicured toenails. Her bright pink tongue tasted like strawberries. For real. She flicked it carefully across my clit, never making more than a second's contact, never placing her full mouth on my pussy, never performing in a way that would look unbecoming or cause her makeup to smear. When the camera stopped rolling, she gently floated from atop my body and stood patiently with her arms at her sides, as if between pictures or filming she ceased to exist except as a faultless mannequin.

I was quite nervous going into my first scene with Jana, and her apparent perfection didn't help matters at all. Next to her, I felt plain, mousy, and forgettable. As Jana and I moved through the sexual motions, our tongues millimeters from touching, we never fully engaged in what I would have considered sex. It was more like pretend play. And I learned that, when it came to girl/girl scenes, the most stunning women in the biz simply wanted to look stunning. They did not want to get fucked. They did not want to fuck. They wanted to be appreciated. Glorified. Captured like a deer in the headlights of the photographer's lens and then released back into the wild, untouched and unloved, except in the imaginations of the men who purchased their images. The stunners left the ugly sex, the hard-core, messy, sweaty, dripping, and adulterous stuff, to the real whores, the porn stars who did boy/girl scenes. Because I did not want to do boy/girl scenes, I took Jana's lead and primped and postured for the camera. I mimicked her movements, her inauthenticity—or perhaps it was complete authenticity, since none of it felt any more real to me than it seemed to feel to her.

On these mornings when I had girl/girl scenes booked in Los Angeles, I hopped in the shower, shaved my bits, and sat in my black Mustang, which I was literally driving to death. It felt entirely appropriate that my car was dying, too, since everything around me seemed to be dying just then. But soon I began to worry that it wouldn't get me to L.A. for work anymore, and then I'd have nothing.

So, in a moment of fear-laced hopefulness, I called Jeff to see if he'd accompany me to purchase a new car. Since our interrupted San Francisco getaway, and the distance I had created between us in its aftermath, he was unsure of how to be supportive, but he continued to try. He agreed to help me, and we drove to the Chevy dealership in his dad's Suburban.

"It's way better to drive onto the lot in a sweet ride," Jeff said.

I thought impressing the salesman with a sweet ride was pretty much all there was to the car-buying process, and that the paperwork would be no problem. I picked a sexy blacked-out Tahoe with cream-colored leather seats, pushed out my tits, and worked on convincing the sales clerk I didn't need a cosigner. But the clerk just eyed me suspiciously as he reviewed my credit report.

"Ma'am, you don't have enough credit to purchase this car," he said.

"But I can afford it!" I said.

I slithered up to his desk, glad Jeff was outside smoking, so I could try to flirt my way into the deal.

"You'll need a cosigner," he said. "What about a parent?"

Defeated, I nodded and grabbed my purse and phone. My first call went to Mom.

"Please?" I begged. "The Mustang is dying, Mom!"

"Jen, *I* can't even get a new car," she said. "Sorry, baby."

"I'm not asking you to pay for it."

"We don't have the credit, Jennifer," she said. "Why don't you call your father? He never does anything for you."

This statement was both a lie and the truth. It was a lie because my father had sent me Christmas presents for years, and would have been a large part of my life had I allowed him to be. And there was some truth to what she said because, after years of me returning his presents unopened, he had given up, and we hadn't even spoken since just after the divorce.

But that was before I had wanted something from him. So I called him. He surprised me by cosigning for the car. He sounded so stunned that I was calling, and so eager to help me, that the conversation was way easier than I'd expected. I laughed at this because I thought I'd pulled the proverbial wool over his eyes. Even though we were financially bound, I decided there would be no father-daughter bonding, no catching up about the years we had lost, no matter how much he might want it. There would only be an open door if I needed money. And because I was building my career as Penny Flame, doing at least four girl/girl scenes a month—which brought in at least twenty-eight hundred bucks—I didn't need money. I just needed his signature, and that only took ten minutes, which was as much of a relationship as I planned to have with him.

I SOON GOT very good at justifying and compartmentalizing pretty much every aspect of my life. I didn't find myself *attracted* to the women I pretended to fuck. It was all make-believe. So when I was hired by a guy named TJ to do a girl/girl scene at a Las Vegas bachelorette party for Carmen Electra and Dave Navarro, I imagined it as an all-new fantasy.

Having sex in front of real people will probably be much different from having sex in front of a camera, I thought.

I also considered how awesome it would be to fuck for Dave and Carmen, leaving a lasting impression on them premarriage. And it would be my friend Charlie whom I'd be fucking, who was really into women, and not gay-for-pay. But none of this seemed beyond what I could handle, since it was all pretend anyway.

When I arrived at the Hard Rock Hotel & Casino in Las Vegas, I met TJ in the lobby and greeted him with a smile. I'd purchased a few supercute outfits from Bebe and did my best to emulate the lovely Jana Cova. I kept my head held high and my spine straight. TJ approached and offered me his hand.

"Hey, hon, TJ. Let's go check out the room, huh?" he said.

As he spoke, he looked frantically around the hotel, as if he were being hunted. I followed his gaze with my own, but I couldn't see any cause for his alarm. After we tossed my bags into my room, we headed up to the suite that Carmen and Dave had reserved for the evening's event. TJ offered me a laminated pass on a lanyard. It looked something like a press pass, but it was printed with naked pictures of Carmen and Dave lying on a slab in the morgue, holding hands and looking cold and dead, and it read: "Till death do us part."

The suite was incredible. It had a bar, two bowling lanes, huge televisions, and flashing lights in a decadent collection of five different rooms that opened up together. As we walked through, TJ pointed at the hot-tub room.

"So you and Charlie are gonna fuck in here," he said.

I nodded and followed him, maintaining my inner Jana while nervously imagining how difficult it would be to convince viewers that a hovering tongue was as pleasurable as a tongue that really met and wet the skin. As I walked, I gently clasped my hands behind my back, swaying precariously in the new high heels I'd purchased specifically for this trip.

"Is it just us?" I asked.

"No, honey, we got a buncha girls here for the party," he said sweetly. "But you and Charlie might be the only ones having sex in the hot tub. I'm not sure yet. I'll let you know beforehand."

As we left the suite, he closed the door behind us and led me down the hall to my own room.

"Go ahead and get ready," he said. "Wear whatever you want and I'll swing back by to grab you for the party. You okay, hon?"

I nodded and he left me alone in my room. It was the first time I'd stayed at the Hard Rock in a beautiful hotel room, instead of some cheesy E-Z 8 Motel, and I suddenly felt like I imagined Jana felt: perfect and chosen. I went to the bathtub and slowly stripped off my new Bebe outfit, placing the clothes on the side of the tub and watching my body in the mirror. I wanted to know how I looked from every angle, to memorize the positions in which I looked best. I wanted my muscles to remember the feeling of perfection.

Charlie arrived and texted me from her room. She was equally as excited. When she came up to my room with TJ, she smiled at me with all of her pretty white teeth and her quiet eyes. She placed her small hand in my own, and we walked down the hallway to fuck for the crowd. The room was filled with guests. The large flat-screen televisions played Andrew Blake pornography:

images of my idol Jana, masturbating and smiling mysteriously, and Nikita Denise, fucking herself and another woman wildly, cursing in Russian or Czech or whatever language she could. The bartenders were all as beautiful as the guests, and stars and press whores drank cocktails together—including Jack Osbourne, who may have been sober and had fluffy big hair, and Brent Bolthouse, party thrower to the stars.

When the time came, TJ stole into the hot-tub room ahead of us. Charlie and I disrobed and climbed into the oversize bubbling tub and began to kiss—real, intimate, hungry kisses—as TJ opened the French doors to reveal our lovemaking to the party guests.

It was the first time I'd felt fire in a scene, the first time I'd thought: *Maybe this girl/girl stuff can be like real sex.* It was a comforting notion that it wasn't all smoke and mirrors, that there could be some real passion even though we both happened to cash checks after it was done. As we moved through the scene, taking turns devouring each other's body, displaying pussies and reddened round ass cheeks on the side of the tub while searching each other's skin with our tongues and each other's wet, pink cunts with one, then two, then three fingers, we came together and separately. We smiled and laughed, taking breaks only to sip cold champagne from tall glass flutes and shoot sultry glances at Carmen and Dave. When the scene was over, it didn't feel like it had been a scene as much as it had been a live performance. I was high from the attention, the orgasms, the fame, and the potential I felt in that moment.

We partied for the rest of the evening, drinking apple martinis and Grey Goose cocktails. Justine, another frighteningly stunning and wickedly sensual woman, came to the party and began whispering to Charlie and me. She introduced me to Brent Bolthouse and created enough intrigue that we all ended up in a separate room. I was with Brent, and Charlie was with Justine and Justine's boyfriend.

Brent and I fucked and watched as Charlie's freshly washed

body was laid back on an elongated couch and Justine ate her pussy while the boyfriend fucked Justine from behind. The champagne seemed to flow endlessly, like runoff water from snow-covered mountains. The harder we fucked, the more Charlie screamed with delight. The only words I can remember from that point in the night came from Justine's flushed and bitten lips and were laced with an accent she hadn't had earlier in the day.

"You are wasting your time in college, my dear," she said to me. "Most millionaires barely have a high school education. You must think wisely about this. You, too, can be an entrepreneur."

Her words sounded so sexy. And the more I mulled them over in my mind, the more they sounded so right to me too.

I am making a buttload of money, I thought. *Maybe all it will take is a few wise investments.*

The next morning, I met TJ for breakfast at Mr. Lucky's 24/7, a little food joint off the Hard Rock Hotel's casino floor. I was enjoying a Bloody Maria, like a Bloody Mary but with tequila.

"Hon?" he said. "I don't want you to be offended, but do you need to get paid for what happened last night with Brent?"

I nearly choked on the spicy tomato mix that was in my mouth.

"Get paid for fucking Brent?" I asked. "No. What a weird question. Why would you ask that?"

TJ sat back, looking relieved.

"Oh, I just wasn't sure if you expected, you know, compensation," he said. "Justine received compensation, you know, so I thought maybe you wanted . . ."

I suddenly felt ashamed and totally naïve.

"What the fuck do you mean, she received compensation?" I demanded. "Was I *pimped out*?"

"Well, I mean, I don't know, hon. I don't want to cause any problems. I just wanted to look out for you. I'm kinda glad you're not a hooker, though." He laughed. I didn't. I finally understood what Justine had meant by her decidedly seductive commentary on millionaires and entrepreneurs. She was a fucking hooker. Disgusted with myself for being so green, I took the elevator upstairs, with TJ following close behind, and stormed down Charlie's hallway and banged on her door.

Charlie answered, looking hungover and confused.

"Did you know she was a hooker?" I asked.

"No, I don't believe that," Charlie said. She shook her head and then sat on the floor, folding clothes and placing them in a bright pink suitcase. "She and her boyfriend are in love. She wouldn't be a hooker because he wouldn't love her if she were a hooker."

"*Love?*" TJ laughed. "Hon, you say you love your boyfriend, Taylor, and you threw him under the bus last night with no problems."

A bit surprised with TJ's boldness, but instantly in love with the expression "threw him under the bus," which I had never heard before, I had to agree with TJ.

"Yeah, you did kinda throw him under the bus, Charlie," I said.

"No, no I didn't," Charlie said. "I wouldn't have done any of that if you hadn't let me get so drunk, Penny."

She looked at me for a long moment, seemingly unsure if this excuse was going to fly. But TJ wasn't going to let her get away with it.

"No, hon, it doesn't work like that," he said. "You are a big girl now. Flame here isn't responsible for your drinking. You threw your man under the bus for some pussy. Love doesn't live here anymore."

TJ sang this last line, his voice cracking as he climbed the musical scale into a falsetto.

On my flight back to San Diego, I tried to shrug off my feelings of betrayal and promised myself that, no matter what I did in the business, I wouldn't become a hooker. The thought of the slippery, sticky, shady sensation of fucking someone for money felt like gliding down a Slip 'n Slide covered in fresh dog feces. I drew a distinct line between being paid to have sex with someone who was also being paid to have sex with me and being paid by someone to have sex with that same someone, which I would never do. As if there were a distinction, and somehow, porn scenes sat a few levels above prostitution in the caste system of sex work; at least for me it was true.

But regardless of the distinction I made between being a film star and being a high-price escort, my friendship with Charlie changed after that party. I wasn't exactly sure what she told her boyfriend about the weekend, but it seemed like she had thrown me under the bus too. A few weeks after the bachelorette party, I received a call from Taylor.

"I just need to know what happened out there," he said. "Why'd you ditch her?"

"Man, I'm not a snitch," I replied. "You should know that."

After that, Taylor, who had once been my good friend, quit talking to me entirely. Each time I spoke with Charlie, she glossed over the Justine issue completely. Right before Christmas, I learned that Justine's boyfriend hadn't known about her hooking, and that apparently Charlie had been playing with them ever since the bachelorette party. It seemed like most women in the business kept their men in the dark. Suddenly, I didn't feel like I was the biggest liar anymore. In fact, I felt like I was one of the few who had any honor.

DURING THE FIRST weekend of January each year, Las Vegas is overrun with porn stars, fans, and computer geeks when both the annual Adult Video News (or AVN) convention and the Consumer Electronics Show (or CES) are held. The tech guys with expensive passes "accidentally" wander into the porn convention, where people come from far and wide to walk around the show floor and gather autographs and semi-dirty pictures from the biggest, breastiest, and nastiest porn girls around. And at the end of each long, autograph- and picture-filled day, tired and scantily clad girls can be found walking back to their rooms, barefoot, through the Venetian hotel because they aren't used to standing in high heels all day. During a normal day's work, the heels they'd brought were generally pointed to the ceiling or removed as quickly as their underwear.

My first convention was rather uneventful, because I was so new to the business and I was still amassing fans. But I proudly stood at the booth of Matrix Content (a small company that provided adult content for various porn sites) and introduced myself to convention attendees by shaking my ass cheeks vigorously and leaning forward suggestively. I also quickly learned to bring slippers for the long stroll from the Sands Expo and Convention Center to the Venetian towers. There were far too few men with a foot fetish and desire to massage my tired dogs, which I would have gladly gone for just then. Thankfully, Jack Daniel's and Diet Coke numbed everything below my waist, and the time signing autographs for men who didn't know me passed quickly.

The final evening of the show, Matrix Content threw a party in the Palms' Real World Suite, and though Charlie and I had been at odds since the Vegas hooker mishap, I still managed to be friendly when I ran into her in a crowded room of near-naked women holding champagne flutes. I was avoiding Charlie's boyfriend, Taylor, though, because it had become increasingly undeniable that I was a terrible liar and I was afraid that, if I saw him in person, I would have no choice but to hemorrhage the details of that evening. When I did catch sight of him, sporting Adidas shell-toe kicks and an Oakland Raiders jersey with his black curls and green eyes, I thought that perhaps he wouldn't talk to me if I was hitting on the nearest seminude girl in the room, so I quickly turned to a gaggle of ladies.

"You girls want some more champagne?" I said.

The rapper Too Short, who seemed to have been in attendance at each party I'd been to that weekend, looked curiously at me. And then, looking at the girls, he shook his head no. Another girlfriend and Matrix model, Monique Alexander, leaned in and whispered an explanation to me.

"They're Too Short's hos, Penny," she said. "You're so funny. They don't talk unless he says!"

Defeated, I turned to Taylor, who continued to stand nearby.

"Hos, man, so difficult," I said. "She ever tell you what really happened, or do you still hate me?"

"I fucking know what happened," he said as he crushed out his cigarette on the floor, not caring that we were within arm's distance of an ashtray. "You left her high and dry, Flamer."

"Oh, okay, cool," I said.

I smiled at him, turned on my heels, and walked into the back room where two directors I'd worked for sat arranging lines of fluffy white cocaine. I'd seen only one person on cocaine before. That person was my father, and that memory was not one that I particularly cared to relive. I'd vowed, nearly eleven years before, never to touch that devastating, untrustworthy powder. But my resolve quickly melted in a puddle of drunken, bubbly anger. Anger at Charlie for lying to Taylor and making him hate me. Anger at Justine. Anger at myself for violating my own boundary within two years of getting in the biz: that I'd never do girls on camera, a rule I'd ignored the second solo-girl money decreased and my pot, drink, and need intake increased. I was also angry with Arianna, Drake, and Derek for dying, though I would have never admitted it then. I didn't think doing cocaine would make me less angry; I simply thought it would make me less *me*. And that was exactly what I wanted right then.

"Line?" one of the directors asked, barely looking up from the snorting frenzy.

"Yeah, sure," I said. "First-timer here. Let's go."

I sat down next to her, careful to keep my ashy cigarette away from the dander-filled table. One line turned into two, and the long string of words that were intended to be logical inevitably sounded more like a montage of thought snippets pieced together with sincerities, connected loosely by verbs and pronouns. After some unknown amount of time and a barrage of cigarette smoking, Charlie came over.

"What did you tell Taylor?" she asked, her words quick, without hesitation or pause.

"Ha! Nothing, I said fucking nothing," I said. "Know why?" I spoke like lightning and paused only to lean forward for an injection of courage powder. "Because *I* don't throw my friends under the bus when I fuck up. Ya like that? Ya. Because I'm a real fucking friend."

Ever since TJ had used the phrase about throwing people under the bus, I had done everything in my power to work it into any and all conversations.

"I wanna tell him," Charlie said. "Seriously, I do. I just can't. The words don't come out." As she confessed, I became acutely aware of her Midwest accent, which had always made me laugh.

"Well, it's not my job to tell him," I said. "He's *your* man. *You* fight for him. Love. Ha."

I grabbed my half-empty champagne glass and lit a smoke. Just then Taylor popped his head through the door, looking visibly uncomfortable with the plethora of strange pornographers and whores slithering about the cocaine-filled room, and even more uncomfortable with the larger room of pornographers and whores from which he'd come.

"Can I speak with you?" Taylor said.

"Me?" Charlie asked.

Keeping his eyes averted from hers, Taylor pointed to me.

"No, her," he said.

"WhatdidIdo?" I asked in a rush of words.

My blood was now fully coursing with cocaine, and as I stood to talk to Taylor, I was prepared to say more in ten seconds than I'd ever said in my entire lifetime. I stepped into the hallway and left Charlie in the room with the blow.

"What the fuck is going on with her?" Taylor asked. "Why

won't she tell me the truth? She's been acting weird since she saw you tonight, and now you two are in there talking and I just wanna know what is going on."

He pressed his body into the wall, leaning on it forcefully, as if he dared it to crumble under his weight. I noticed that he'd moved from bubbly to hard liquor.

"Look," I said. "I love you. I love her. I'm not gonna be the one to tell you shit she should tell you herself. Not my job."

My cigarette had somehow smoked itself, and I needed an entirely new one to continue existing.

"Go in there and tell her I'm going to break up with her ass if she doesn't tell me the truth," he said.

"Yup, yup," I said.

I pranced back into the smaller cocaine room, formed a line of coke, and spoke to Charlie only after snorting it.

"Truth time, sister," I said. "End time if you don't. Get it?"

Horrified, she looked to me for advice.

"What do I say?" she asked.

Snort.

"The truth, dude," I said. "Nothing but the truth."

Rail.

"I can't say it," she said. "Will you? I'll agree to everything you say."

She begged until I gathered a small pile of blow onto a hotel magazine, and the three of us carefully made our way into another bedroom. We spent the remainder of the evening there as I told Taylor the horrible truth about being pimped out, about TJ looking out for us and asking us if we were prostitutes, about Charlie's morning-after reaction of blame and quasi-denial. While I spoke, Charlie sat in silence, nodding as if her head were on a hinge.

At dawn, after all of the lies had been revealed, Taylor decided to stay in the relationship with Charlie, which I thought was total bullshit. As I wandered alone through the hotel corridors, heading back to my own room to try to sleep, I thought of Marc and how he'd given me so many chances, and I'd fucked them all. I wondered how damaged a relationship could be and survive. I wondered how many chances a person actually got in life and love.

I missed my flight and called Pookie, begging her to pick me up in Vegas, promising to pay for her gas home if she did. When she showed up in Sin City ten hours later, I was still drinking, smoking, and blowing lines. I forgot what day it was and knew only that checkout time was imminent. When we finally managed to extract ourselves from Las Vegas, we drove down Interstate 15 before dawn, with less than two grams of blow to last the five hours to San Diego and my soft, safe bed. Somewhere outside Temecula, I decided to take the semester off from college, so that when I turned twenty-one I wouldn't have to worry about missing class after partying at the bars all night.

THAT NIGHT IN Vegas kicked off a seven-month cocaine binge. I returned to Vegas for my birthday in February with all of Jeff's friends, but no Jeff. Allegedly, I had sex with more than one of these friends, a story that I later heard from an angry Jeff sometime after my birthday trip. But because my focus had shifted from Jeff to his best friend, Ted, by this time, I brushed off Jeff's accusations with a few rails and a drink. Ted, who looked like he walked straight out of Wales with his floppy hair and delicate blue eyes—who got lost in Vegas trying to find the perfect birthday present for me, and who wore sweaters and was clean and sweet and soft and everything I ruined—tried so hard to win me, unaware that I was dissolving into self-loathing and addiction, and there was nothing left to win.

In March, I applied for a scholarship given to daughters and granddaughters of professors, taking advantage of my late maternal grandfather's longtime position as a statistics professor at San Diego State. I wrote a brilliant essay about how Grandpa Oliver had always helped me with school, and what it would have meant to him if he were alive and still able to help me academically. When I was approved for the scholarship, I went out in Pacific Beach to celebrate, drank Grey Goose and blew lines until dawn, and missed the final interview that would have sealed the deal.

In April, I drove to San Francisco to re-up on the pounds of marijuana that I frequently sold to San Diego weed dealers. I brought down ten pounds with a friend named Sean. Half of the herb was mine and half was his. Because we got back late at night and I wanted to go drinking on Garnet Avenue, a mile and a half of college-oriented bars in San Diego, we agreed that we'd weigh the weed out in the morning, and I let him take all of it into his house. In the morning, he refused to give me the entire five pounds I'd bought, claiming that I was responsible because the hookup he'd purchased the weed from in the Bay had ripped him off. I took my two and a half pounds and tried to sell it off, because I owed my pot dealer girlfriend in Berkeley ten grand. While stressing about doubling my profits and trying to come down from my constant cocaine high, I also smoked a shit-ton of it. Though I paid her nearly all of the money I owed, the few thousand I had left to pay her with went to my cocaine use instead of the weed game. Cocaine is a helluva drug.

In May, Cam broke off our business relationship, saying he couldn't trust me to show up to shoots, which was definitely true, and a valid reason for him to end things. Over the previous four months he'd booked nearly $20,000 worth of work, and I'd made it to less than half of these shoots because I'd been up too late, doing blow and drinking, and couldn't make myself go to sleep in a timely fashion. I was usually in bed when 8:00 a.m. rolled around, eyes wide from the previous night, waiting for 8:01, when I felt it was reasonable to call and cancel the scene.

As a solution to my inability to drive to Los Angeles sober, and in an attempt to show Cam I was still capable of making shoots, I started taking the train. Then I only had to drive fifteen minutes north and could drink and drug the entire way to Los Angeles from the safety of an Amtrak car and, once in L.A., could be picked up and driven to work by my ever-patient Ted. I promised to make the two or three shoots that Cam had scheduled before severing our relationship, and I said that I understood his desire to end things. I thought about ending things all the time—the drugs, the biz—but I had nothing else to do.

In June, I took the train home to San Diego from one of Cam's final prearranged shoots. It was during this trip that I was raped by one of the conductors. I never breathed a word of what had happened to anyone who might have cared, because I was convinced that no such caring person existed in my life anymore—and because I was convinced that I had gotten myself raped and didn't deserve anyone to care about me anymore.

9

"IF ONE IS TO BE CALLED A LIAR, ONE MAY AS WELL
MAKE AN EFFORT TO DESERVE THE NAME."
—A. A. MILNE

It was sometime around June of 2004 when I quit answering my phone. I had been twenty-one for just over four months, and in the past six months I had lost more than thirty pounds. My mother, who had moved to San Diego shortly after I did, seemed to know something was going terribly wrong in my life, which was saying something, given how much she had let me get away with in the past. She had taken to arriving at my home in Pacific Beach unannounced with loaves of bread and Costco-size jars of peanut butter and jelly. I'd let her into my empty-cigarette-box-littered apartment and floated like a ghost back to the couch, where I covered myself with a red and blue knit high school blanket. This was where I spent all of my time when awake, except for the hours I spent at bars or doing cocaine.

My mom seemed to have a knack for knowing when the bread, peanut butter, and jelly—often the only food I had—would run out, and she appeared with more just in time. Some days she would stand at my door, knocking for an hour, calling my phone, and yelling my name. I always let her in eventually. But, toward the end of June, I couldn't bring myself to answer her calls or the door anymore. And soon she quit coming to visit.

I had stopped talking to Pookie after overdosing in her car while she was driving me and three other people to a party. I was embarrassed that I couldn't *hang*, but I was also angry at her that she hadn't taken me to a hospital. Her only intervention had been to gently suggest that I didn't need another line, as I thought I did. I don't know if I was embarrassed that I needed help or angry that she hadn't offered, but something changed that night, and I felt like she'd failed me as a friend.

I quit talking to Jacob and my other old friends after they expressed concern over my drug use. I cut off ties with Jeff, the guy I'd cheated on Marc with during my first year of college, after he and I had an explosive fight when he left a love letter balancing precariously on my balcony railing. Paranoid from all of the coke I was doing, I thought he'd scaled the tree near my apartment and attempted to break in.

In fact, I cut off ties with most of my friends in San Diego unless they did or sold drugs. The only person I spoke with who didn't abuse drugs as I did was Ted. This was the same Ted from my birthday in Vegas, who still wore soft sweaters and seemed to want nothing more than to help me. But he lived in L.A., and so there were times when his phone calls went unanswered as well.

Around mid-July, my coke dealer, Anthony, refused to sell me drugs. Instead, he started coming by my apartment to see if I was still alive. This actually got through to me.

Perhaps this cocaine thing is becoming a problem, I thought.

I had met Anthony in early 2004 at the Barnett Avenue Adult Superstore off Rosecrans Street in San Diego. This was perhaps a month or two after Marc had shown me my nude pictures in a dirty mag, and I had grown curious about what other publications displayed my body. It was comforting to walk into the giant room stocked with vibrating, colorful cocks; there was no one here to judge me. The store had girls doing mini-striptease shows in little peep show boxes in the back room, and I felt safe watching their bodies gyrate behind thick glass. As I scanned the shelves of the magazine rack, looking for my own picture staring back at me, I held my breath. When I found more than one of my covers, I felt victorious.

After a few visits, I made friends with the store clerk and through him I met Anthony. Four months later, my Adult Super-store visits stopped, because I was too fucked-up on most days to drive there. Anthony started coming by my house regularly, at first because I owed him money, and then because he grew concerned about what a wreck my apartment was. Empty blueberry mini-muffin bags and crunched cans of Sprite lined every table, along with a thick layer of cigarette ash. The only places not dusted with it were the couch and the carpet. The couch was ash-free because I lived on it, even though my bedroom was only steps away. The carpet was ash-free because every speck resembling cocaine found there was quickly and thoroughly inspected.

Some days, Anthony would come with cocaine; on others, he'd come with worried, fatherly advice. Some nights, he wouldn't answer my calls at all because he didn't want to sell me any more drugs but knew he couldn't say no to me.

For four nights in July, I stuffed my sinus cavity with whatever coke I could find, exhausting all of my resources, until I finally came full circle to the first dealer I'd phoned at the beginning of the binge: Anthony, whom I still owed $150 from the last bag I'd bought off him, but who I felt confident would help me in my time of need.

He waited five long rings before he answered my call.

"Hello?" he said.

"Please, Anthony, please come by with a gram or a half eighth and some vodka," I said. "My last gig didn't pay same day. Man, I'm so sorry. I'll have your money soon."

Lies were the only thing that came from my lips anymore. But I couldn't stop. I would have done anything to get more drugs.

"Okay, honey, I'm coming," he said, and hung up the phone.

As much as I never would have admitted it at the time, I appreciated Anthony's protective, fatherly treatment of me. I'd quit calling my own dad a week after I defaulted on a payment for the Tahoe he'd cosigned for, sometime in late April or early May of that year. At the time, it seemed like the $200 car payment was a huge interference with what I really needed: more cocaine and vodka. The most logical solution I could come up with was to spend the money on myself, quit calling Dad, and stick him with the bill. The car was in his name anyway. And Mom's statement that he had never done anything for me built an arrogance and sense of entitlement that had only been inflated by my drug use.

My plan seemed to work at first. However, as I began to fall apart, the Tahoe did as well. I was too ashamed to call my dad then and reveal how poorly I had cared for something I'd convinced him that I actually deserved. And I certainly wasn't going to reveal my inability to quit doing blow, or my need for help. The Tahoe had been undrivable for months, or so I'd been told by multiple mechanics, friends, and random drug acquaintances who had ridden in my car and experienced the frightening downshift, *chunk-chunk*-grind-to-a-stop that happened whenever I hit the brakes. So, by the time I reached rock bottom in July, I was stranded in my apartment with no way of getting to the store.

When I hung up the phone with Anthony, I immediately went to the front door and unlocked it. Otherwise, I was afraid that when he knocked, I'd be unable to leave the couch blanket cocoon, either because I didn't feel like I could stand up without a line or because I was afraid of who was there, having forgotten that I'd invited Anthony over.

Unknown door knockers weren't the only things I was hiding from. I also avoided clocks, unwashed dishes, and the fruit flies that lived in luxury in the filth of my kitchen. Plus, there were bills and stacks of paper that I'd arranged over and over again in my usual drugged state. My apartment was completely empty of anything resembling normal life.

At times like these, I'd think about Dad and Mom and how I'd left them both without any knowledge of whether I was dead or alive. I'd think of Jeff, Marc, and Logan, as well as the other countless men whose lives I'd ruined, and I'd think of Ted, the man whose life I was currently ruining. I'd write letters to Melanie, to Kelli and Cynth, to my little sister and brother, all of whom I had cut out of my life. I'd think about TJ's question in Vegas about whether or not I was a hooker, and make lists delineating the fundamental differences between porn stars and prostitutes.

When Anthony finally came through the door, he pulled up a chair, wiped off the ash-covered seat, and poked at my red-and-blue-blanketed head.

"Did you bring me a present?" I said.

I peeked out from under my safety cave, just enough to see his hands in his lap.

"Yeah, Penny, but I don't think you need it," he said.

I repeated my question as a statement: "So you *did* bring me a present."

"Why don't you come out from under the blanket and I'll make you a line?" he said.

I stayed under the blanket and listened to him move around plates in my kitchen, trying to find something clean on which to cut lines.

"Baby girl, you ain't done dishes in a long time, huh?" he said.

"I can't," I said.

For once, I wasn't lying. Although I had a perfectly functioning dishwasher next to my kitchen sink, it was stuffed with dirty dishes and I had no dish soap; hence my inability to do dishes. All my money was consumed by vodka, blow, Sprite, muffins, and cigarettes. Anthony knew this about me, and I couldn't figure out why he'd poke fun at my inability to move off my couch, do dishes, or be human.

"I think I'm depressed," I moaned.

He laughed.

"I bet!" he said. "The way you do coke? An' drink? That'd make anyone depressed! You ain't even been fuckin', an' that's fun, an' it's yo job. You ain't doing nothin' but laying here, right here on this couch. Shit. You covered in ash and all yo shit's nasty. I *bet* you depressed. I would be too."

I didn't verbally respond to him, but I peeked out from under the blanket again to see if he'd sorted out the line he'd promised. He had.

Once I did a few lines, I was off the couch, back to shuffling my papers and smoking cigarettes, all the while talking nonstop. I told Anthony how tight that club Moondoggies on Garnet was on Wednesday nights; how people looked at me like I was a swamp monster when I bought Grey Goose from the grocery store at 6:01 a.m. more than three days in a row; and how leftover cocaine particles sometimes fell from my nostrils onto the checkout stand, and when they did, I licked my finger, picked them up, and put them to my gums. Anthony stood at the door and shook his head as I explored the house like I had a ton of work to do and no time to do it.

"Pen, this is the last time I'm gonna help you out," he said. "Don' worry 'bout what you owe me. Just get outta here. You gon' die, girl."

I could barely hear him over the roar of drug-addled voices in my head shouting for more, more, more, along with the steady waves of need coursing through each vein, exploding at each synapse and crying as millions of my neurons shriveled.

Anthony left and, true to his word, never answered a phone call from me again. Soon after that, he went so far as to change his phone number. Whoever ended up with his old digits got really pissed that I didn't believe Anthony's number had changed and kept calling him around 4:00 a.m., when the blow and vodka usually ran low.

Two weeks after Anthony left my life forever, my landlord left a note on my front door that read: "You have three days to pay rent or vacate the premises."

Needless to say, I didn't have the money. And I didn't have any way to get it. Out of options, I called the one person who still had an active role in my life: Ted. He drove down from Los Angeles to help move my messy, ash-covered apartment into a storage unit. I did so without telling my family or friends that I was leaving San Diego for Los Angeles. Then he kindly allowed me to move into his apartment, where I continued doing cocaine while hidden under *his* blankets instead of mine.

I HAD BEEN staying with Ted for less than two weeks when I went on my last binge. Ted had been trying to level me out. He'd come into the room in the afternoon, bringing me sandwiches and coffee, and then he'd try to help me leave the bed. But the only way I found the strength to venture out of bed into his apartment—or out into the world at large—was if a bag of cocaine made its way into my possession. Ted didn't use, so he was no help on this front. But his roommate did. He was a kid whose stated goal in life was to be an actor but whose actions spoke more to what a complete mess he was. He attended acting classes when he could get his act together and get to them, and had small parts here and there, but for the most part he thought he was a lot cooler than he was. Had his father not been in the business, he would not have been given the multiple chances he'd received. He had an agent, and a driver to take him to auditions, and on the rare occasions that he was cast, he spent every dime he made on cocaine. He and I got on just fine, as our drug-oriented goals were aligned. It helped that Ted's house was a regular hangout for quite a few renegade Angelenos and coke-snorting hooligans. Big Frank, the pot dealer from my San Diego days, was still around. Plus, there was a kid named Brian, who rarely had any good ideas, and another kid named Sam, who seemed far too young to be as fucked up as he was. We'd stay up all night doing lines, telling stories that were both true and untrue, and walking in circles around the house, seeking even the smallest cocaine particles that had been overlooked.

Ted was a respectable young man with a job who always went to bed early, and he was quite upset with me for being such a coke whore. We'd be standing in the kitchen, staring at each other over a bottle of vodka, and his eyes would beg me to come to bed while he tried to play it cool.

"Okay, so you'll be up in a bit?" he'd say.

I'd smile uncertainly but go along with the game.

"Yeah, just another cigarette," I'd say.

Then, after he'd climb the stone stairway and creep into his dark, cavernous bedroom, I'd continue partying until sunrise. When I would finally sneak quietly into his room, only after the blow was gone, it would usually be around eight o'clock in the morning, the sun would be up, and he'd be awake. I could almost hear his heartbreak as he pushed PLAY on the DVD player so I could watch the only movie that could ever help me to sleep: *Finding Nemo*. Ted loved me, and it seemed like there was nothing he wouldn't do for me. In return, I abused him like any good drug addict abuses the people who love her.

By the time my last binge reached its climax, I'd spent nearly seven full days awake, doing cocaine and failing to eat or hydrate, except for the occasional blueberry mini-muffins and three-to-four-second swigs of vodka. Somewhere in the middle of this, I tried to go to sleep next to Ted, but I couldn't come down enough to crash. While counting the popcorn pockmarks on his ceiling, I decided an orgasm might do it. Only, all of my vibrators were locked up in the San Diego storage unit.

And then I had an idea: Ted's roommate's Oral-B vibrating toothbrush would do the trick nicely.

I slithered from Ted's room and into the bathroom. After

retrieving the toothbrush, I went into an empty, sun-drenched bedroom and set to work. After thirty minutes of trying, and failing, to come, I said fuck it and stayed up for day number eight.

At nine o'clock that morning, I phoned Ace, another Los Angeles friend who happened to do as much cocaine as I did. He also sold the drug, which of course, made our friendship one of convenience more than anything else.

"Up?" I asked him, knowing he'd either be on the same page or asleep.

Ace was like Ted in that he would do anything to help me. For reasons unknown, my life seemed to be filled with wonderful men who simply wished to love me. Since I couldn't understand what there was in me to love, I pushed each of them away and often used them against each other to do the pushing: I had pushed Marc away with Jeff, and Jeff away with Marc; I had pushed Ted away by running to Ace, and I later distanced myself from Ace by running back to Ted.

Ace and I hung out at Ace's house, doing lines until noon, which we figured to be a reasonable time to hit the bars. After a few hours of drinking, we were running low on coke, so we hit Ace's dealer's house. He bought an ounce, so that he could sell it off in pieces while feeding both of our habits. Instead of going home to stash the drugs, we hit one more bar. Ace had encountered some trouble with the police, while my record was clean, so I took the ounce of blow and rolled it up in the leg of my sweatpants. That way he wouldn't get caught with it on him if the cops stopped us.

" 'Fuck three strikes get the bitch to bat,' " I said, quoting a line from one of Mac Dre's songs.

We went into the dark bar and drank until closing time. But then, when we returned to the car, I realized my pants had unrolled at some point in our drink-a-thon.

"Holy fuck, Ace, it's gone," I said. "My fucking pants, man, look."

I rolled and unrolled the pants, freaking out, because at least a thousand dollars' worth of cocaine was sitting on the ground somewhere.

"Fuck," Ace said. "Back to the bar? Fuck."

He slapped his hands gently on the steering wheel but never lost his cool. He obviously seemed bummed, but he kept his temper in check—which was notable considering how much anger powder, also known as cocaine, we had running in our blood at that moment.

"Oh my God, I'm so sorry, we will find it, and what we don't, I'll replace, I swear, oh, fuck, I'm so sorry, fuck, fuck, fuck."

"Don't worry, Jen," he said. "We'll find it."

We returned to the bar and searched the parking lot. We searched the bar floor, around the barstools, and the bathroom. We searched the car and the parking lot again. Defeated, we headed back to his house. Once in Ace's room, I called Ted, who lived about fifteen minutes from Ace's house, and begged him to take me on a drug run.

"Please, Ted, I fucked up," I said. "Just come get me, please."

I intended to replace every lost rail. Somehow.

"Jen, just come to sleep," Ace said. "It's not a big deal."

But all I could think about was surprising Ace with a ton of new bags. When I saw Ted's car outside of Ace's house, I slipped away from Ace's bedroom and into the dusky Los Angeles night.

As I climbed into Ted's truck, he looked at me with concern.

"Have you slept yet?" he asked.

I shook my head no.

"I think I'm having an anxiety attack," I said. "I can't believe I lost that much blow, fuck, fuck, he's gonna kill me, please, let's go get more bags and then I'll replace it and then go back to your house and sleep." While I talked, I searched through my coin purse for the bar of Xanax I'd been saving for a special occasion, since Xanax was one of the only things that could put me out after a long binge. It was sectioned into four pieces, and although on some days a quarter of the bar would put me to sleep, after nearly nine days of drinking and drugging—and now, the missing-cocaine fiasco—I thought a full bar was necessary to calm me down enough to deal with the situation at hand. I popped it into my mouth.

"Easy, girl, easy," Ted said, patting my knee and unrolling the window so I could smoke. As we drove, the world began to swirl around me. His comfy truck seats felt like they were eating my body, and my eyelids felt as if they weighed a thousand pounds. Like the heavy luxuriance of early morning slumber, I slept hard.

I have only blips of memory of Ted carrying me into his apartment and up the stone stairs to his bedroom, where he placed my worn, skinny body in his bed. And I don't remember sleeping through the night next to him. I didn't really leave that bed much for the next two weeks. I begged Ted to get more Xanax so I could sleep until I felt human. I fell into a cycle of eating bits of Xanax bars with the Quiznos subs Ted would bring me and then sleeping for twelve hours, which is how I came to gain forty pounds over the next month and a half.

It was early September before I really woke up and realized I'd been asleep in Ted's bed for two full weeks. It hit me that I'd also been clean of blow that entire time. When I finally pulled my body out of bed and went downstairs to witness the wreckage that was Ted's hooligan-filled home, I couldn't face the world that had nearly sucked me under. I was scared of what I'd become. I crawled back into bed next to Ted.

"I can't do this anymore," I said. "I can't live like this."

He kissed me sweetly on the forehead.

"Good, we'll get outta here," he said.

A week later, we moved into our own apartment in Encino, a solid ten miles down the 405, and far enough away from the drugfest to start fresh. I never replaced the lost cocaine, never called Ace again. The first night in our new one-bedroom apartment, lying in Ted's soft, familiar bed, he made a confession to me.

"I've loved you from the first moment I met you, when I was still in high school and came to visit Jeff in Diego," he said. "I met you and decided if there were girls like you in Diego then I had to move there. But when I got there, all I wanted was you."

I didn't know how to respond to Ted's affection. He was a wonderful man, and I cared for him, but I knew I'd destroy every ounce of compassion and goodness that his heart held. I had lied to every man I'd ever been with, from Logan when I was fourteen, to Marc at twenty, to Jeff—not to mention my dad. Whether I was lying about who else I'd been sleeping with or how much I cared for them, I was a liar and unreliable to the core. I used every man who crossed my path, and I knew Ted would be no different.

It wasn't that I didn't want love. I did. Desperately. The problem was that I didn't believe that any of these men would still love me if they really *knew* me. As far as I was concerned, they loved what they saw: the tough, headstrong, weed-smoking, shit-talking, sexually open-minded girl who never required a commitment, never started drama, never got jealous, never acted like a punk. If they knew that I was really soft, scared, lost, and unsure—or if they saw the ugly things inside of me that weren't perfect and shiny—they would feel duped. And then they'd leave.

My best option was sabotage. That way, when they left, I knew they were leaving because of something I did, and not because of something I was.

AFTER I'D BEEN clean of cocaine for a month, Ted persuaded me to call my family. Because he worked a normal job, I found myself alone in the apartment all day, thinking of what I'd say to my mom, sister, and brother, all of whom I hadn't spoken with for three months. I didn't think about calling my dad because once the coke had left my blood, I found myself as mad at him as I had been at age fourteen, though I still couldn't exactly pinpoint the source of my anger. Weed helped the anger and hurt that seemed to bubble up inside, and I smoked as much of it as possible. Some days, Ted would leave his debit card and PIN so I could get money. Then I'd hit the pot store in Hollywood, a small yellow house off La Brea that sold the dankest of all dank. Though I didn't steal money from Ted, I did skim nuggets off the top of his weed bags to smoke on my own. I doubt Ted would have minded me smoking his nugs if I'd been honest and told him, but I never gave him the chance to decide for himself.

After we'd been living together in Encino for about a month, Ted offered to drive me to San Diego so I could reunite with my mom and sister. By this point I felt so guilty about all he had done for me, and all I had taken from him, that I could barely look him in the eye.

When we arrived at my mom's house in Rancho Bernardo, Ted waited patiently in his truck while I slipped in the back gate. My mom was outside gardening, and as I closed the gate, she looked up from her flower bed and began to cry.

"I thought you were dead," she said, wrapping her arms around me tightly. "How'd you get here?"

She knew from before I disappeared that the Tahoe was in no condition to drive.

"Ted brought me," I said.

As I hugged her in return, I tried to figure out if she was angry beneath her tears and gratitude.

"Go get him," she said.

I walked back to the parking lot and motioned for Ted to come in with me. When he closed the gate and approached us, Mom embraced him as she had done with me.

"Thank you for bringing my baby back," she said.

By the end of that brief visit, I felt more uncomfortable about Ted's inherent goodness than I had before; never had I met someone as selfless. As we drove home, I couldn't stop thinking that something needed to change.

I have to do something to pay him back, I thought. *I have to start contributing.*

I sat on the feeling all night, abhorring my dependency on Ted and the fact that I was guilty of nug thievery on top of everything he had been doing for me. It seemed to me that a woman who simply lived off another's hard work was not a woman at all. I had to start making my own money again.

The next day, I called a well-established agency, LA Direct Models, on the advice of one of my model friends and set up an interview with the head agent, Derek Hay. Though Derek generally represented girls who did boy/girl videos, or "hard-core," and I only wanted to do girl/girl videos, or "soft-core," I felt that the Penny Flame persona I'd built up pre–cocaine disaster had been successful enough in the girl/girl and solo mag layout world that there would be enough work to keep my idle hands occupied. I figured that Derek would be able to get me enough jobs to pay Ted back for the months he'd supported me, and to pay him back for the nugs I'd stolen. Plus, if Derek could get me more than a few jobs, I'd have the opportunity to show the world that I was done with the drugs and that my work ethic was back on track. If the world saw that I was all good, then Cam, my old girl/girl agent, would see that I was all good. Maybe then he would take me back.

The LA Direct Models office was off Ventura Boulevard in Studio City, above a City National Bank and around the corner from the CBS Studio Center lot on Radford Avenue. As I walked through the door and into the area that separated two small offices with big tinted windows, where two overworked secretaries tried to keep up with the constantly ringing phones, I instantly saw that this was an entirely different operation than the one Cam ran out of his small two-bedroom apartment in Hollywood. Derek's phones literally did not stop ringing; there were at least six different lines lighting up all at once. The walls were covered with long, taped-together papers—"call sheets"—with girls' names highlighted on them, printed next to the times they had to work, the people they were working with, and the deeds they would be doing. Other porn girls sat in the waiting area with their bright pink suitcases amid stacks of dirty magazines that had been strewn carelessly over the coffee and end tables, beneath big pictures of the agency's top clients. Suddenly, I was nervous as shit. My body no longer looked like it had in the magazines: it now carried an extra forty fucking pounds.

Vee, the twentysomething head secretary who managed what seemed like at least ten different phones at once, brushed her long black hair from her shoulders onto her back and waved me over to sit down with her. There was no way she was ever a porn girl, but not because she wasn't cute enough. She couldn't have been in porn because she just looked too damn nice.

"You Penny?" she said.

"Yeah, I'm, uh, here to see Derek?"

"Hold on, sweetheart," Vee said into the phone, scratching at the little bump on the bridge of her nose and squinting her dark brown eyes.

Then she held her hand over the receiver and addressed me.

"Come fill out this paperwork and just hold on a sec, okay?" she said.

She appeared to be doing a million things at once, accomplishing more than the other two secretaries combined seemed to do.

"Yeah, Dave is on his way to the house now to get you," Vee said into the phone. "You're doing a DP today, hon, the girls should have told you that when they called. Make sure you bring your test and IDs."

Vee shot a look to the other secretary and rolled her eyes, as if the girl on the phone was having a difficult time understanding what "ID" meant. I was still wondering about the abbreviation "DP."

"Yeah, I can have a driver bring them to you, honey," she continued. "But Derek doesn't like when we do that, so make sure you have 'em next time, okay?"

By the time Vee was off the phone, my nerves had calmed just enough for me to try to act cool, like the Penny Flame I'd been before my seven-month cocaine binge, instead of the slightly over-weight Penny Flame I was now, begging for a chance to be a work-ing porn girl again.

"Honey? Paperwork is right here," Vee said, bringing me back to earth with the papers in her hand. I stood and grabbed them, and on top of a naked Gina Lynn magazine cover, I filled out intro-ductory paperwork that looked like this:

Name: _____

Stage Name: _____

Age: _____

Breast Size: _____

Shoe Size: _____

Measurements:

Bust_____ Waist_____Hips_____

Circle All That Apply:

Solo Handjob Blowjob Girl/Girl Girl/Girl: Anal Boy/Girl
Boy/Boy/Girl   Anal   DP   Interracial   Swallow
Creampie   Squirt   Group   Bachelor Parties

Phone Number: (_____)_____-_____

Never before had I filled out a paper that looked anything like this, and since I didn't know what some of the terms meant, I had to wait for my meeting with Derek before circling anything other than "Solo" and "Girl/Girl." I also didn't have a cell phone any-more, although I did have a cell phone bill in collections, so I put down Ted's phone number as my contact number and made a men-tal promise to pay off my debt collectors with my first paycheck.

"He'll see you now, hon," Vee said.

She ushered me into the left-hand office and closed the heavy door behind me. I had never met Derek Hay before. I had only heard of him through the grapevine, and what I'd heard was that he was one of the toughest agents in the biz. He was the antithesis of Cam. Derek was not only an agent but also a performer, which made it super-difficult to lie to him. Because he doubled as porn star Ben English, Derek Hay knew exactly what a scene required and exactly what kind of effort should be exerted. And he could call a girl out on any time "mistakes" they might use as an excuse, because he'd driven to every single shoot house in the Valley, and he knew precisely how many minutes it took to get from North Hollywood to Northridge. Though I'd heard a wide variety of things about Derek's professional and personal life (true or not), from "He does gay scenes" to "He's a pimp," every gossip monger/director/producer/performer agreed about one thing: "He's a good agent." I'd also heard that he had, on occasion, broken bitches and made them cry when they tried to lie to him or give him attitude, so I was a teensy bit timid as I sat down with him.

"Hello," he said in his crisp British accent.

He breathed through his nostrils, looking me up and down with ice-blue eyes. His head, completely shaved and shining, was perfectly spherical. Every hair of his eyebrows sat firmly in place. His hands, with thick, sausage-like fingers, motioned to the seat across from him, and I noticed that he wore one silver ring, although not on either of his ring fingers. His clothes were formfitting, and when he stood to shake my hand, it was impossible not to notice the size of his cock, which was not very well hidden in his supertight pants. Now that I had met him, it was official: Derek scared the crap out of me.

"So you're looking for new representation, yes?" he said, sitting down.

"Yes, um, I've been in the business for a few years now and am looking for work," I said. "Also, I'm a month clean off cocaine."

I blurted out the last part as if it were somehow important that he know I'd recently stopped putting drugs up my nose, in case he had an ear to the ground and could hear what a wreck I'd made of my previous career. He absolutely did not care.

"I'll need you to undress," he said, motioning again with the ring hand. "Please."

This last word was tacked on, as if asking politely were an afterthought. He then looked back to his computer, giving the impression he'd seen enough of the female form to last him a lifetime. I undressed and set my clothes on a neat pile on the chair.

"Side," he said.

He barely glanced away from the screen as I turned to the side.

"Back."

Derek motioned again with a pen, and I swirled around on my toes, arching ever so slightly and trying to make my butt look cute.

"Fine," he said.

I sat down, naked, on top of my clothes, unsure of the next move.

"So, what does 'DP'—" I began to ask.

He cut me off.

"You can put your clothes back on, Miss Flame," he said.

Derek didn't mention a word about my body, good or bad. He said nothing about my perfect teardrop tits. He didn't ask to see my pussy. It felt like he hadn't looked up from his computer once, and I started to worry that he wouldn't hire me because I was fatter than I'd ever been. Though the majority of the weight I'd gained was necessary, as I had weighed eighty-five pounds at the time I lost Ace's coke, my clothes felt tight and didn't fit right.

"You haven't circled anything except 'Solo' and 'Girl/Girl,'" he said. "I can't get you that much work if this is all you're willing to do."

He finally put his pen down and looked directly into my eyes, which was more uncomfortable for me than when he had looked at my naked body. At least, when guys looked at me naked, I knew what they were thinking about.

"Well, I've been working for over three years now only doing what I've circled," I said.

As I talked, I felt more alive than I had during the entire previous year. He was giving me a chance to sell him Penny Flame.

"I've done plenty of magazine covers, Danni's, *Hustler,* even a bachelor party for Carmen Electra and Dave Navarro," I continued. "I have a solid following."

I was so eager to work again that I practically vomited this information onto his desk, while he sat back, twirling his pen.

"What about girl/girl anal and DP?" he asked, pinning me with his gaze.

"Oh, well, uh, I wanted to ask what 'DP' stood for before I said yes."

He smirked.

"DP is a double penetration," he said. "Either vaginally, anally, or, of course, one in each."

Of course! How could I be so fucking silly?

"Oh, no, um, no things in my butt," I said. "And no double things in my vagina. Just one. I mean, thing. I mean, toy. One toy in my vagina at a time. Single P."

He laughed. I leaned in closer to his desk.

"Is that okay?" I asked. "I mean, the one single P thing?"

He inhaled deeply through his nose.

"Is this your phone number?" he asked.

"No, it's my . . . boyfriend's. . . . Ted, he . . ."

Derek raised his eyebrows a fraction of a millimeter.

"Does Ted know you're here?" he asked. "I don't wish to deal with angry boyfriends."

Derek had obviously represented all sorts of girls who had connections with all sorts of men.

"Oh, yeah, he knows about my career and everything. . . . I mean, yeah, so just, uh, call if you're, you know, wanting to tell me stuff," I said. "Just ask for me."

Derek's eyes were already back on his computer, any effect that the revelation that I had a boyfriend had had on him already completely gone.

"Very well, Vee will call you and set up a photo day so we can put you on the website," Derek said. "Once we've done that, I'll send pictures to my contacts. You need to tan, trim your hair, and perhaps visit the gym as well. Toning would do you some good."

He spoke very matter-of-factly, as if he were giving me the recipe for a moist and delicious porn star cake. I was so excited that I nearly jumped out of my seat.

"You won't regret this. Thank you, Mr. Hay. Thank you so much. I'll be the best girl you have."

I stood and stuck out my hand for him to shake. He raised his eyebrows another fraction of a millimeter and handed me back the list of dos and don'ts.

"Give this to Vee on your way out, please."

I bounded through the door, handed the sheet to Vee, then went down the elevator and past the bank to my car in the garage. I was on my way home to tell Ted that I was back in business and that I planned to pay him back for all that he'd given me. Not that I really could. How does a girl pay someone back for saving her life, loving her unconditionally, and giving her a new start?

GIRL/GIRL WORK WITH Derek fell like rain in Seattle. It seemed there was an infinite amount of pussy to fuck, an infinite number of scenes to film, and an infinite amount of checks to cash. I fucked blond girls, brunette girls, white girls, Latino girls, and Asian girls.

I fucked a black beauty named Jada Fire, and in the middle of the scene I brought out some finger puppets that I kept in my purse, which had come in a gift set from my mom. I had a giraffe puppet, a little bear with a clown hat, an elephant, and a seal holding a ball. Each one of them made it into the final cut of the movie.

"Penny, you a crazy bitch!" Jada cried.

I took the puppets off my fingers and put my fingers inside of her.

"I'll show you crazy, you filthy little whore," I said.

I beat Harmony Rose, among others, for Kink.com in San Francisco, whipping her ass until it was bright red.

"You sure your arms are okay?" the director interjected, leaning in to Harmony as she lay hog-tied on her belly with her arms stretched back, her wrists bound tightly to her feet. Her fingers were bright red, like little sausages, and Kink directors always checked to make sure the bound people still had feeling in their joints.

When Harmony nodded and smiled up at me with those big beautiful eyes, I squatted down and helped her onto her side, sat on her face, and let her make me come while I held a heavy Hitachi vibrator against her clit. The vibrator was plugged into the wall and sounded like a lawn mower; it was a device that, after only one encounter, *had* to become a part of my personal vibrating arsenal.

I fucked girls whose names I forgot within ten minutes of fucking them. I used a strap-on and had a new respect for the work men have to do when it comes to sex. I filled at least four days a week with sex scenes, and not only was it a relief to be back at work, I thoroughly enjoyed fucking every single one of those girls. And at least three days a week I cashed a $700 check at the bank, hit the pot store to buy myself and Ted a present, and then went to Bed Bath & Beyond to get him a new duvet, new sheets, a new showerhead—anything I could think of to make his home look nice and, more importantly, show my gratitude. The more money I made, the more I felt it was *his* home—not mine—because he had paid every bill, while I had only consumed, consumed, consumed. Each night, as we climbed in bed, I imagined how lovely it would be to pay him back, to give him all that he had given me. But it wasn't possible, because what Ted gave me went far beyond the money or things I could ever give to him.

I paid off that cell phone collection agency, paid off the parking tickets on the Tahoe, and even had them remove the bright orange boot that had been placed on the front left wheel, which was a very joyous day indeed. I watched my bank account balance climb to a more reasonable number, and as the total funds in my account grew, so did my need for more. But in early December, two months after I'd climbed on board the Derek Hay and LA Direct Models train, the downpour of girl/girl work turned into a famine in the Sahara, and the four-times-a-week fuckfest became a once-a-week thing, and then none at all.

The rules of supply and demand, which I'd learned in my econ classes at SDSU, were finally clear to me in an applicable and poignant way. In just two months, I'd managed to shoot myself out entirely. I'd flooded the market with Penny Flame pussy, and by now every company had shot me having sex with nearly every single girl: the size of the porn business, in terms of the number of companies and people it contained, both being relatively small, there was no woman I hadn't fucked and no company I hadn't fucked for. It suddenly became a big problem that most of the money I had earned had gone to furnishing Ted's apartment, not because he asked me to, but because I felt guilty for not loving him more.

I realized that I had to make some changes. I had to move out and into my own place, and to do so, I had to go back to that sheet I'd filled out for Derek when I first started. I had to reconsider my options when it came to my career. Even more than that, I had to reconsider my career entirely if I wanted it to *be* a career, and not just a McJob. Supply meant me, and demand meant the world.

What did the world want Penny Flame to do?

I decided the world wanted Penny Flame to do boy/girl videos, and so did my bank account. However, I also decided the world would be a lot easier to face if Ted did not know about that decision.

10

"YOU KNOW THAT GUY IN YOUR BRAIN WHO WARNS ABOUT
BAD DECISIONS? HE WAS GETTING A CUP OF COFFEE."
—JERRY FROM *SEINFELD*

The more time Ted and I spent together, the more acutely aware I was of our differences:

He was kind. . . . I was cruel.

He had a legit job. . . . I was a porn girl.

He was compassionate and honest. . . . I was sneaky and had lied to every guy I ever dated, including him.

He would do anything for someone he loved. . . . I believed less and less that love was a real thing.

I knew I didn't deserve him, and I think that, subconsciously, the decision to do boy/girl movies was, in part, an attempt to show him my undeserving nature, although I didn't have the guts to tell him. Instead, I called Derek on Ted's phone and told him my plan. He insisted I go to the office immediately to discuss the matter.

An hour or two later, as I waited for Derek to summon me into his office, I hung out with his accountant, Fran. I had quickly come to love Fran, a mid-thirties, swearword-loving British lady with a positive outlook. She knew I was clean from coke and often said she was proud of me, even though we'd only known each other for a few months. She had a kid in high school, and I found myself wishing that she could have been my mom, too, because I looked up to her and asked her questions I didn't dare ask anyone else.

I put my hands on her desk and leaned across to see what she was working on.

"Is this a good idea?" I asked.

"Fuckin' 'ell, Pen, I don't fuckin' know," she said. "Is any of this a good idea?"

She shuffled the papers and swatted my hands, so her accounting details would stay private while we spoke. "Look, you're either okay suckin' cock for money, or you're not! Don't be askin' me or anyone else," she said. "It's on you, girl."

"I guess I'm gonna suck cock for money, then," I said.

"Well, good for you, then, you cocksucker. Ted know about this?"

"Well, yes . . . no," I said, averting my eyes.

"Which is it, then, girl. Speak up!" she said, nearly yelling at me. "'Yes . . . no' is not an answer."

I found myself forced into honesty, as if Fran had the power to eyeball and yell girls into telling the truth.

"No, he doesn't know," I said.

"Well, where the fuck did 'yes' come from, then?" she said, raising her superpower-mom eyebrows at me. "Y'ain't fuckin' told the guy you're fuckin' that you're gonna be fuckin' other guys? That's bad, Pen. You gotta tell him."

"I know, I know," I said. "I will. I don't want to. But I will."

"Look," she said. "He'll either be okay with it or not. You'll either continue to be his girl, or not. Not many outcomes, so that's good, eh?"

I nodded. Just then Derek summoned me into his office.

"So, Miss Flame, there are quite a few differences about doing boy/girl and girl/girl, aside from the . . . ," he said.

"Penis?" I interjected.

He smiled awkwardly.

"Yes, aside from the penis. For example, once you start doing boy/girl, you will cross the proverbial line into porn stardom. Girl/girl work never makes you a porn star. Once you start doing guys, you will be recognized. I want to make sure you are okay with that."

"I already get recognized, so that's all good," I said.

This was a lie, as I'd never once been recognized outside the Adult Superstore with Anthony and Jai. I don't know exactly what made me lie so much, but by this point the falsehoods seemed to be getting easier and easier to tell.

"Okay. . . . Well, you'll also be much more likely to get an STD doing boy/girl," he said.

He paused and waited for my reaction.

"Dude, I've been in the business for, like, three years now and never had any issues," I said. "The risk was always there. You just look, ya know?"

It was easy for me to be confident on this point, as I was sure that any STD I could catch would be so obvious, I'd see it pre-insertion and stop the scene before I got infected. Of course, that is totally not the reality.

"That's not necessarily how it works, Miss Flame," Derek said, as if he were reading my mind. "Some diseases will not be caught by the naked eye."

I realized I hadn't really thought things through to the STD part. I certainly hadn't expected Derek to warn me against it. And I didn't know how to react when he did. I was suddenly very confused about the entire boy/girl world of porn.

"Well, people have to be tested, right?" I asked.

"Yes, but—and I'm not trying to scare you; I just want you to know—the tests are done monthly, and you may work with someone whose test expires two days *after* you work, which means he may test positive for something after you've already done your scene," he said. "Guys generally do two scenes per day, so there is the possibility he has had sex with upwards of forty-five, fifty women by the time he gets to you."

Derek never dropped his gaze from mine this whole time. I doubted he gave this much information to brand-new girls. I didn't think anybody would still do boy/girl if he told them all he'd just told me. I wasn't sure what made me any different.

"Thank you, Derek, but my mind is made up," I said. "Risks are risks. Penis or vagina."

"Very good, then I'll send out a notice, and we will begin booking you," he said. "Still no anal?"

"No. Exit only. Sorry. Not. A. Chance," I said.

I had a smile on my face as I said this, but he was already back to his computer, finding some cock for me to suck and some money for us to make.

Three days later, I received a call on Ted's phone. My pay-as-you-go phone had died, and I didn't have any money to buy more minutes from 7-Eleven, the store that conveniently sold me a cell phone and cell phone minutes, so I had no choice but to use his phone to book my porn work. When his phone rang, and he handed it to me without answering, I felt excited that my plan seemed to be working.

I stepped outside to the balcony with cigarettes in hand and put the phone to my ear.

"So, Miss Flamer, you ready for this?" Vee asked.

My stomach jumped into my throat.

Am I ready for this? This is, like, no-turning-back shit. I cannot undo this.

I remembered back to what it had felt like to walk into the shady Morena warehouse and do my first photos with Mr. Gruff, and then my first girl/girl with Jana, which had seemed so fake to me.

There will be no faking with the cock, I reminded myself.

But at this point it also felt like the point of no return.

"Yeah, I think I'm ready, Vee," I said. "Give it to me."

"All right, lady, your first boy/girl will be a scene with Tyler Durden for the company American Hardcore," she said, reading from the long, taped-together call sheet I had seen in their office. "Your contact is TJ."

I almost choked on my smoke. TJ was the guy who had hired me to work Carmen Electra and Dave Navarro's bachelorette party. I had considered him a very close friend up to the point when he told me I was out of control. Then I quit talking to him.

"TJ? He's my contact?" I asked.

As I spoke, I tried to recall the last time I'd seen him. It came back in pieces.

I was on cocaine, naked, swimming in his communal pool, wearing flippers, a snorkel, and arm floaties. He was furious when I passed out, wearing the same swim gear, in front of his neighbor's house, right after I'd fucked his best friend by the pool.

When I woke up from my little misadventure, I learned that he had called every coke dealer in Los Angeles and cut me off. Ace was the only dealer that would still sell to me. And TJ had quit speaking with me after all of that. Understandably.

"Yeah, I think so," Vee said, snapping me out of my trip down memory lane. "I don't know for sure, though: it just says TJ's your contact. You sure you're okay with this, hon?"

"Yeah, I'm all good," I said. "Hey, Vee? If my phone is ever dead and you have to call Ted's, please just leave the time and place. No other details."

"He still doesn't know?" Vee asked, almost in a whisper.

"No, not yet," I said. "He will, though."

After I hung up, I finished smoking on the patio and went inside to take bongloads and cuddle Ted. Although my insides churned with fear when I thought of my upcoming "occupational change," as well as guilt for the lie now festering inside my soul, I managed to laugh at the appropriate times, cough when the Kush was too sticky, and smile like nothing was wrong. I don't think Ted noticed that our relationship was on the verge of a meltdown, or that I'd made a decision on my own that would affect us both.

THE SHOOT HOUSE was not extraordinary in any way, but my heart was doing irregular flip-flops as I tried to decide what to say to TJ when I first saw him. But as soon as I saw TJ's familiar face, his fluffy hair, and his protruding belly, all of my unease melted away. Our eyes locked immediately and we hugged with emotion.

"Hey, honey!" he said. "How ya been?"

His embrace was full-body. As he pulled me close, he kissed my forehead and buried his nose in my hair. I instantly remembered why I loved him so much. I recalled the sincerity with which he had asked me that now infamous "to be or not to be a hooker" question in Vegas, which was the very issue that had driven a wedge in many of my friends' relationships. He approached life in such a great, straightforward manner, and I knew that he would never throw anybody under the bus. TJ, like Fran, was the real-deal shit, and I was so glad that he was shooting my first boy/girl scene.

I thanked him warmly, hoping he could tell how grateful I was.

"Awwww, honey, I couldn't let anybody else shoot it," he said. "Besides, I heard that you were shooting your first only for a grand, and I couldn't let some asshole hire you and treat you like shit."

As we talked, he smoothed my hair down from its post-hug frizziness.

"So I got you Tyler," he continued. "He's kind of a pussy, but it'll be an easy fuck."

I laughed and hugged him again as he kept talking, no longer a million miles a minute, like so many of my memories of him. He was now calm, cool, collected, and very obviously not worrying about me anymore. It looked like TJ was all-new too.

"Shameless is shooting stills, so that'll be easy too," TJ said. "We just need thirty minutes of footage, hon. It'll be quick."

Shameless was a photographer friend of mine as well, and once I realized this first shoot had become more of a reunion than a work event, I relaxed and excused myself to go out back to smoke and stretch.

As I sat outside and puffed on my Parliament, TJ stuck his head out the sliding glass door.

"Whenever you're ready, hon," he said.

Again I felt so grateful to be working with him on that day of all days. There were a thousand things he could have harped on: my cocaine abuse, my absence from his life and the business, my weight gain, and my new foray into total porn whoredom.

Instead, all he said was: "Whenever you're ready."

I was so moved by his kindness that I vowed to make him proud.

I'm going to fuck like I've never fucked before; this will be the scene to end all scenes.

I trudged back inside the house, grabbed a Summer's Eve douche, and hit the bathroom for some pre-scene cleaning. I emptied out the packaged solution and refilled it with warm tap water, because using those things too much causes dryness, and obviously, for sex, dryness is the opposite of good. As I sat on the toilet with the douche inserted, I thought of dirty things I could say during the scene.

Yeah, fuck that pussy.

Take me, take me.

You like that?

I squished the warm water into me, and when it splashed back down into the toilet, I hoped that nobody could hear from the other room. A baby wipe and some lip gloss, and I was ready for the scene. I walked into the bedroom, where Tyler was already waiting.

"So, ready?" I said with a smile.

Tyler was sitting on a well-lit bed, and a guy holding a C light—a light that is predominantly aimed at a girl's cunt during the shooting of a scene—was waiting in the corner of the room.

"Hey, hon," Shameless said. "This isn't gonna be weird at all."

He laughed as he spoke because we both knew it'd be totally weird.

"So just come in, sexy style, and then walk to him and start making out, I guess?" Shameless said, attempting to direct the scene.

I wondered what TJ was doing. Tyler sat motionless on the bed, like he could only be brought to life if his dick were in a girl's orifice.

"Tyler will help you if you get confused, ha ha, though I know you know your way around a dick!" Shameless said.

I jokingly flashed him eyes that said: "Shut your shameless fucking mouth, bastard." That shut him up real quick.

I walked out of the room and waited for my cue.

"Action!"

I came back in, super-sexy like I'd been told, slinked right up to Tyler, and started kissing him. Like, real-kissing him. Then he kissed me back.

Whoa, this is not gonna be like Jana at all.

After a few minutes of kissing, petting, and rubbing, Tyler began to strip away my clothes. My skin heated up and his cock got hard. I actually felt turned on, and I was so excited to be doing something so naughty as Tyler started to go down on me that I almost forgot why we were really there. I didn't think about camera placement or shadows until the guy holding the cunt light stepped two feet away from my pussy with a light that could have landed airplanes.

Seriously? I mean, that light doesn't even match the color of the room before!

Then I realized that Tyler had his head awkwardly twisted to the side so that the camera could record his tongue flicking across my clit; the awkwardness of vagina licking was something that was a sort of nonissue in girl/girl work because, most of the time, we were too busy pretending.

Then, when he got his cock out for my sucking pleasure, it got superreal. I didn't know where to look, whether to focus on him, the camera, or down; and as I tried to slurp the excess spit from his throbbing member, I was struck by a new worry.

Oh, fuck, this is going to take all of my foundation off, and that huge fucking zit will be revealed and then, BAM, no more porn scene.

However, to my relief, my six minutes of cocksucking was not impacted by a slobbery face or a revealed zit, and we carried on into the sex.

The sex started with six minutes of cowgirl, during which my thighs cramped up and I felt like a heavy monster on top of Tyler as he tried to jackhammer my pussy.

"Hon, can you hold your ass open and look back at the action?" Shameless asked.

"Yeah, but I can't actually see the action," I replied.

"That's okay, just look that general way, like, 'Ohhh this action feels so good,'" he said. "And then hold your ass open so we can get more light in there."

This was so far beyond my early days of being upset over how I looked with a finger-filled cunt that I couldn't think about what was happening in any detail. I didn't even want to see how I looked holding an ass cheek open. But I did it, setting my lips in the shape of a sexy O and counting down until the second I could change position. I hated the thought of my asshole being exposed to the world. Finally, it was over.

Next was six minutes of reverse cowgirl, where I spun around and imagined I looked similar to a crab getting fucked. I thought of being a kid, and crab walking in my gymnastics class, and how fun and funny it was to have crab races across the mats. This was totally different, because there was now a smaller, jackhammer crab man beneath me, pummeling away at my soft-shell meaty parts. Also not a favorite position.

This has to be over soon.

Then we went into doggy style, and again I was told to hold my ass cheeks open for the camera's viewing pleasure. And then we were on to missionary.

"Flamer, can ya hold yourself up on your elbows and suck in your belly?" Shameless said.

That was embarrassing and my thoughts got dark.

Fucking fat stomach, you fat fucking girl, you disgusting fat fucking girl, time to get in shape, time to get that fat fucked off of you.

We paused so Shameless could take pictures of everything we'd just done, running through each position again.

"Wanna see some shots?" Shameless asked me when we were done.

I remembered Mr. Gruff showing me my first shots, and this time I knew better.

"No, thanks."

Finally, the grand finale: I assumed the frontal-knee position and waited patiently as Tyler jerked off. Shameless asked for him to nod at fifteen seconds, and once Tyler hit that fifteen-second nod, I started saying all the dirty things I'd rehearsed in my mind while douching, less than forty minutes earlier.

"You liked that, didn't you? You wanna come? I want you to come all over my face."

In actuality, I didn't want him to come on my face. I would have much preferred my tits, or ass, or someplace where there was no threat of losing an eye. But I didn't really have a say in the matter.

Tyler began to come, and it surprised me so much that, like a first-time fool, I tilted my head back and he came up my nose.

Awesome, just fucking awesome, smelling jizz for the rest of the night. Fucking perfect, I thought.

I managed to maintain a sexy face while trying to act like there wasn't cum in my sinus cavity. But once the camera shut off, Shameless started laughing and handed me another baby wipe.

"Guess it's official now, huh?" he asked, petting me on the head.

Then he offered me some sage advice.

"Don't put your head back next time. Let the guys aim and shoot, and you'll be fine."

I cleaned off, collected my belongings and thousand-dollar check, gave TJ a porno elbow-to-elbow high five—because nobody, not even another porn star, really wants to hug a porn star post-scene—and went home to the little apartment I shared with Ted.

As I walked through the front door, Ted looked up and smiled at me. I went past him and straight to the bathroom. As I stood under the nearly scalding hot water, he knocked on the door.

"Want a shower bongload?" he asked sweetly.

I closed my eyes and let the water run down my face, blowing my nose over and over, until there was nothing left to blow.

"I'm fine," I said. "Just fine."

A YEAR BEFORE I started sucking dick for a living, I did one of my best solo scenes ever for a company called Digital Playground, in which I played a woman with multiple personality disorder. It was entitled *Repo Man,* and the story went like this: my character was late on some payments, so the Repo Man, which happened to be a woman, showed up at my house to repossess my car. The script required that I dress up as three different women for the scene, and as a result of the stress caused by the repossession, the three different women got into a fight. Two of the women, one a horny slut wearing a furry jacket with penis buttons and the other an angry bitch who yelled and cursed profanely, both masturbated while the third, a prim and proper woman who wore a skintight, porned-out librarian's outfit, begged the masturbating women to stop.

The scene was awesome to film. It was fun, and it felt like everything that being a porn star should feel like. They actually let me act, and it was like I'd found my calling.

Yes, yes, this is why I've been put on earth: to act in big-money porn films like this, I thought.

A little over a year after the scene was shot, it was also the first one to land me a nomination for an award—Best Solo Video—at the annual convention held in Vegas by *AVN* (*Adult Video News*) magazine. As much as I had loved doing the video, I totally didn't think I'd win. But I'd also been hired to sign autographs for the third year in a row, and I was up for a good time at a convention that is all about gathering porn stars and porn lovers in Sin City for a week of decadent debauchery.

This year I was happy to be signing autographs for men that had seen my scenes, as opposed to the previous years, when I shook my ass and took near-naked pictures with guys who had no idea who I was. I was also glad to know the ins and outs of the convention. As I had learned the hard way, the worst part was not the semi- to super-creepy dudes who got a little too grabby with us girls on the show floor. It wasn't the smell of man sweat that transferred from their bodies onto ours while getting close for photo op after photo op throughout the day. It wasn't the long hours or the running makeup. No, the worst part of the convention was the walk from the Venetian towers, where we girls stayed, down to the Sands Expo and Convention Center floor. New girls never thought to bring tennis shoes or slippers for the seemingly five-mile trek through the hotel. But this year I had the walk down. And I was ready to sign for the whole day like a pro; also, mostly, because I got drunk.

By that year I had developed my very own porn convention routine: I woke up at 6:00 a.m., threw on the complimentary Venetian robe and slippers, tucked my outfit and shoes for the day in my purse, and hit the Oculus, also known as the "Circle Bar," on the Venetian casino floor. Generally, other porn performers were just straggling away to sleep after a long night of gambling and cocaine, so I got to high-five at least one of them before starting my day with a Bloody Maria, the breakfast of champions—at least porn champions. Then I smoked and drank as I made my way to the elevators. Once up in one of the hotel rooms that the porn companies rented to be used as makeup rooms, I sat patiently, being made up by the makeup artists. If it seemed like we were going to be there for a bit, I ordered a round of Marias for the room. Once out of makeup, I headed back down to the Circle Bar, where I got to enjoy the company of my male fans pre-signing.

"Penny, you look so good this early!" a fan shouted at me.

"Honey, it's only 'cuz you ain't been to sleep yet, and your eyes are all blurred!" I yelled back.

He laughed and offered me another drink. Knowing how filling Bloody mix is, I switched to Grey Goose and Red Bull, and began to make my way to the show floor.

AS I'VE ALREADY mentioned, the trek is nearly impossible to do without a good buzz, and thankfully, the Venetian had placed many satellite bars all along the arduous path. At the next bar, even though the drink in my hand was still full, I stopped and smoked two cigarettes.

"Penny, you gonna be at the booth today?" another fan shouted.

"Bet your sweet ass I'll be there, waiting for you!" I shouted back.

Meanwhile, I sucked down the last of my drink and headed on my way. After barely making it to the next bar, I refilled on another Goose and Bull and enjoyed myself another smoke or two. By the time I finally hit the show floor and made it through the long walk that awaited me there, while schmoozing passersby and pinching porn girls' bottoms, I'd had at least five or six drinks, and it was usually around noon. No matter what, though, I always arrived with a smile on my face, ready to sign.

THE EVENING OF the awards show, after three long days of signing autographs, I dressed myself in a see-through, skintight black and silver dress and the kind of six-inch stilettos that make newbies yearn for slippers. Once I was in my outfit and all made up, I went down to the casino floor and followed the velvet ropes to the award show room, where the tables had been piled with mints, vibrators, condoms, and the occasional ad, as well as a sprinkling of cock confetti. This was back when *AVN* was booming financially and only the performers were allowed into the award show—before they started selling tickets to porn fans to try to make the venture profitable. Knowing I was up for an award, I barely drank a thing, not wanting to fall on my face if I did happen to win. Still, I could hardly believe it when they actually called my name as the winner.

I was in shock as I walked to the podium, but I also felt powerful.

"Fuck yeah, me," I said as my acceptance speech. "Oh, and thanks!"

AFTER THE SHOW was over, I returned to the Circle Bar to make new friends. The girls who did girl/girl scenes didn't hang out with fans, and most of the girls who did boy/girl scenes didn't either. But I wanted to be a crowd-pleaser, so I decided to change that.

It's time to meet the masses, I thought.

I hit the bar like I was being paid to drink, hugging guys I'd never met.

"Oh, yeah, I'm gonna do this every year, believe that!" I said to a new friend.

When he bought me another drink, I flung my arm around him.

"What are you doin' later, sweet stuff?" I said. "Me, by chance?"

The power I had felt at the podium slowly melted into drunkenness. Soon my words were mushing and running together, and I don't remember how I ended up back in my room. Luckily, I got there safe, with all of my clothes on, but only one of my two shoes.

THE NEXT MORNING, brutally hungover, I missed my makeup appointment and had to order breakfast Bloody Marias sent to the room, just to get myself going. But I was still riding high from the previous night's excitement, and I vowed to win as many of these *AVN* award thingies as I could.

If I get a shit-ton of awards, then being a well-respected porn star will override the fact that I'm technically selling sex. But I'm pretty much an actress now, so I'm kind of not even selling sex anyway.

I threw on some foundation and tried to control my shaky hands enough to glue fake eyelashes onto my watery eyes. Finally, I gave up and surrendered to the nature of my beastly, hungover morning. Hitting the show floor with very little makeup on didn't frighten me as much as hitting the show floor with very little alcohol in me. As long as I was buzzed, I knew I looked *damn* good.

WHEN I GOT back to Los Angeles, and Ted, I knew I had to move out of his apartment as soon as possible before my whole elaborate lie came crashing down around me. As soon as he saw me, his eyes said that he had missed me, that he cared about me. His emotions, which I normally tried to deny, had become obvious to me, and absolutely terrifying, after our few days apart. The night I returned from Vegas, he made love to my body, but I was totally absent.

There was nothing he could do to fix the relationship or make me stay, because he already did everything right, so I finally forced myself to do the only decent thing. I began talking to him about moving into my own place. He even helped me with this, introducing me to a landlord who had a supercute little house in Woodland Hills, the southernmost end of Porn Valley.

When I moved out, I still kept a few things at Ted's apartment, as if those possessions meant our relationship was still okay. But I began to see Ted less and less, because each time I saw him, I actually felt guiltier than when we had lived together—like I wasn't going to be able to control myself any longer, and I was going to burst forth with all of the wrongs I'd done. I knew something really had to change.

If I can just disappear from his life, he won't question where I've gone, and it will hurt less than if he knows where I've been, I thought.

The day before my birthday, I asked Charlie to come with me to retrieve the last of the bongs that I had left at Ted's apartment. We dressed ourselves in camouflaged clothes and painted black on our faces like we were top-secret commandos, while I tried to make light of the fact that I was pulling the ultimate Houdini act on the sweetest man I'd ever met.

When Ted came home that day, he called me to see where I was. I didn't pick up.

"Noticed the bongs are gone," he said on his message. "And it kinda feels like that means you are gone too. I miss having you here."

The next day, which was my birthday, he phoned again and left me another message.

"I made dinner reservations for us at Firefly," he said. "Just letting you know when I'll pick you up."

I called him back, thinking this would be the perfect way to end things.

One last date, a final, lovely good-bye.

Only I didn't tell Ted any of this, and so he still thought that everything was normal between us. After a beautiful dinner, he drove me to my new home, parked, and started to get out of the car.

"I'm good," I said. "I can walk myself to the door."

I had tried to sound nice, but I knew I sounded like a cold-hearted bitch.

"You don't even want to invite me in?" he asked, clearly as hurt as I was frozen.

"No, it's my birthday," I said. "I kinda wanna sleep alone tonight, you know?"

I hopped out of his car.

"Wow," he said as I closed the door.

He tried to smile like my request was reasonable. But I felt like a total asshole. We'd been together for nearly a year, he'd seen me at my absolute worst, and yet he'd cared for and loved me through it all. He never asked me any questions, never judged me, never told me what a horrible person I already knew myself to be. I hoped that he would understand that my desire to be alone that night really meant that I wanted to be alone, period. But I didn't have the balls to end things outright by saying what I was thinking: *I am a bad girlfriend, and I don't want to see you anymore because I've done bad things that make me want to cry every time you touch me.*

Instead of saying anything more, I trotted up to my cute new house and went inside, locking the dead bolt behind me and praying that was the end of my relationship with Ted.

Less than a week later, Ted showed up at my front door and beat on the wood with his fists, crying and screaming at the top of his lungs.

"I know what you fucking did, and it's okay!" he shouted. "I never want to see you again. I just wanted to let you know I got into film school."

As Ted yelled and hit the door, I hid on the same old black leather couch from my San Diego drug days, beneath the same old, thick, red and blue blanket. But I had fresh tears in my eyes. I didn't know how to respond. I didn't know how to tell him the truth, or apologize, or congratulate him for getting into film school, even though I'd helped with his application, hoping it would give him a new, better life that allowed him to leave me behind. I didn't know how to say anything, so I opted for silence. I was becoming better at not talking about things than trying to express myself. As I listened to Ted's car door slam and heard the engine fade away into the Woodland Hills traffic, I thanked the heavens that I'd never have to face the hurt I'd caused him or the hate I was convinced lived in his eyes. As long as I didn't have to explain the truth to him, the truth didn't exist.

THE HOUSE IN Woodland Hills was perfect for me. It was a two-bedroom, one-bath duplex with a garage and a Zen garden in the backyard. It had beautiful wood floors and French doors that opened from my bedroom onto the patio, where two fountains gurgled peacefully throughout both the summer and winter months: this was Southern California, after all. I bought chairs and a table for the patio and would sit in the mellow space, reading, painting, and trying to pretend I hadn't broken the heart of an uncommonly sweet man. I was afraid that Ted might come back, but after his explosive last visit, and my implosive reaction, he did not return again.

Taylor, who was now Charlie's ex-boyfriend, needed a place to live, and so I opened my home to him, and he took over the second bedroom. He knew about the occupational shift I'd made—from vagina to cock—and because he was one of the few people outside the adult business who knew and approved, I trusted him immensely.

Each time I took a step deeper into the pornographic lifestyle, I tried to keep it secret, as if the Internet wouldn't reveal any choice or decision I'd made. Such denial was necessary in order for me to maintain my increasingly complicated double life. But the secret had a way of getting out.

One night, Jacob and I were hanging out at an industry party that was being held at a bar. Jacob had excused himself to the restroom when a random male performer started talking to me.

"So, how are the scenes going?" he asked, his Jack and Coke spilling on his hand as he attempted to maintain an air of non-FUBAR-ness—or Fucked Up Beyond All Repair–ness.

"They are going just fine," I said. "My thighs are a bit more sore, but what are you gonna do, right? It's a good workout."

I laughed as I attempted to straighten his drink from its near-sideways position.

I hadn't realized that Jacob was standing right behind me.

"What makes your thighs sore?" Jacob asked.

"Oh, ha, scenes; just telling him what a good workout they are," I said, recovering quickly.

I was about to make my escape, leading Jacob away to the other side of the bar, where male performers were not slithering about drunkenly, when this particular performer threw his arm around me.

"Squats on the cock will do that," he said. "Make ya sore."

He smiled, kissed my cheek, and moved on to the next available girl, pinching her barely clothed butt and causing her to turn around and smack his arm.

"Squats on the cock, Bleeze?" Jacob said. "Doing boys, Bleeze? Little liar!"

Jacob was laughing, but it wasn't a "ha-ha funny" laugh.

"Yeah, only a few, but, yeah, it's interesting," I said.

I made my way to the bar, feeling ashamed that I hadn't been forthcoming, and fearing what his real reaction would be. I knew that once the alcohol wore off, his mood might change from playful excitement to anger over the fact that I had lied to him.

"Two shots of Hornitas," I yelled to the bartender as Jacob leaned on the bar next to me.

"Bleeze, don't try to tequila your way outta this," he demanded. "How many?"

He playfully pinched my side and cocked his head with curiosity.

"Like, *five*?" I said.

"You definitely know exactly how many, Bleeze," he said. "Just be honest."

The shots arrived and we stayed and hung out longer, but I don't remember if I ever was honest with Jacob about how many scenes I'd done before he eventually found out on his own. But when we both sobered up the next morning, with the help of a giant, Kush-filled blunt, Jacob wasn't angry, as I had feared that he would be. Instead, he accepted that this was a part of my career and that I was on a path to porn stardom. Everything seemed totally normal as we sat in my perfect Woodland Hills house smoking with Taylor, except for the fact that Taylor kept shooting *I'll fucking kill you* glances at Jacob throughout the smoke session.

When Jacob finally left to drive back home to San Diego, I confronted Taylor about his behavior.

"What's up with the knife eyes, homie?" I asked. "I thought you were going to visually murder him the whole time we smoked!"

"I don't like that fool, and I don't like that you felt like you had to lie to him about doing scenes," Taylor said, looking directly into my eyes and putting his hand on my shoulder. "It don't look good on you, lies. Makes you ugly.

"You lied to Ted about shit," Taylor continued. "You lied to Jacob about shit. Maybe it's time you stop doin' shit you gotta lie about. Or stop kickin' it with dudes you think you gotta lie to."

While I had earnestly thought about and regretted the lies I told, I had never imagined a reality where I didn't have to tell them. I liked Taylor's way of thinking, because it suggested the guys I had lied to were part of the problem too.

It's them, the guys I choose, I thought. *I have to lie to them because they won't love me if they know the truth. Maybe I should choose different guys.*

Standing in our kitchen, with Taylor's hand on my shoulder, I decided that I would no longer date guys who weren't part of the business, because it always meant having too much to explain. If I only dated guys who already knew every bad thing I did, then I could be the biggest porn star in the world and I wouldn't ever have to lie again.

ALTHOUGH MY FIRST boy/girl scene had felt super-contrived, it didn't take long for me to really start enjoying the sex I had on camera. Similar to the girl/girl portion of my career, there were guys that were into the sex, too, as well as guys who seemed like the biggest fakers on earth. That may sound hard to believe, since it's way easier to fake it as a girl. But with the advances of modern medicines like Viagra and Cialis, along with an anabolic steroid called Caverject that can be injected directly into the cock to create a lasting erection, plenty of male performers could fuck well for the camera, even if they weren't necessarily good fucks. There were definitely some good fucks, though: some guys who could actually make me forget that a cameraman and a guy holding a C light were standing less than a foot away. And those amazing fucks made up for the lesser fucks, as did the money.

I was living the life. I worked no more than three days a week. And whether it was a workday or not, each morning that I woke up I started my day by rolling two blunts. Then I hopped in the used BMW I'd purchased with my new, glorious income—having gladly traded in the nearly worthless Tahoe to the dealership in exchange for a $600-a-month car payment—and went on a solo blunt drive up Mulholland Drive and around the Malibu hills. Sometimes I drove to a spot I called the Top of the World to sit and look out over the seemingly endless Pacific Ocean. While there, I liked to contemplate my life as a single, hot, young porn star and remind myself that at twenty-two years old, I had as much of my life in front of me as the vast blue water before me. I told myself that it didn't matter that I hadn't gotten out of the business when I'd originally intended to, that old plans were not new plans, and that one should not affect the other. My new plans were much more fruitful than the old anyhow. They included a life in which I didn't have to lie, men I didn't have to lie to, and a secure future with financial stability and total adoration.

Occasionally, as I sat in the hills on the back of my car, looking out into the world and feeling the world look back into me, I wondered if anyone would ever really be able to date a girl who

had sex with multiple partners for money; sometimes up to fifteen different people a month. I wondered if any of my potential dating prospects would be able to differentiate between sex
on camera and sex at home—if they would understand that one
was a paycheck and the other was, well, more than a paycheck.
I wondered if they would be doing the same thing as me: compartmentalizing people, events, emotions, and experiences so
that the results were manageable and seemed totally logical, no
matter how crazy they really were. I wasn't sure if a person like
me existed in the world, except for the one I saw in the mirror. I
figured I'd spend the rest of my life alone. While this made me
sad, it was also a relief that there would be no one else to disappoint or hurt.

AFTER I'D BEEN shooting boy/girl scenes for a few months, I
was booked to shoot a scene in San Diego with a company called
Naughty America. They prided themselves on shooting natural-
looking, college-type girls who seemed the most likely to live next
door to the fans. As I drove back into San Diego County, I realized
I hadn't been there since emptying my storage unit into a U-Haul
when I moved to Los Angeles with Ted, which was yet another
time I had run away from my lies.

I hadn't lied to anyone about anything since my conversation
with Taylor, but I still felt an overwhelming sense of generalized
anxiety about returning to the scene of the crime as I parked in the
Gaslamp Quarter, and gathered up the bag of girl-next-door attire
that my agency's secretary Vee had asked me to bring. I tried to
talk myself down.

Those days are gone, Jennie. No need to worry now. You're not a
liar anymore. Now you're just a porn star.

I threw the bag over my shoulder and made my way across the
street to the shoot's address. I was buzzed up to a fantastic loft,

with fifteen-foot ceilings and soft, natural light spilling in through the expansive windows. As I wandered in through the unlocked door, I called out the name of the contact Vee had given me.

"Noah?" I said, keeping my voice down while hoping that I was in the right place, and that if I was, I had not interrupted a shoot.

The man that came around the corner toward me was magnificent. His muscles were taut under a thin white T-shirt. His jeans were tight enough to show off his strong lower half, yet loose enough that they weren't sprayed onto his superthick thighs. He had spiky hair and wore torn black Converse sneakers.

"You must be Penny," he said with a smile.

I crossed my fingers that this was the guy I'd be fucking for the day.

"Hey. Yeah. Um. Hey," I mumbled.

"Okay, weirdo," he said. "I'm Noah. Come on in."

He laughed as he spoke, and for me it was love at first, awkward giggle.

Throughout the scene, I couldn't remember the name of the guy whom I was fucking. I was too busy watching Noah, who was the shoot's director, while he held the camera and got the close-up shots of my junk being penetrated. When Mr. Nameless came in for the fucking, opening his left shoulder and hip so Noah could film the action, I lay back in missionary on the couch. Noah held the camera with one hand and used his other hand to hold my foot so it wouldn't be in the way of his shot. That got my attention.

Will it be weird to have sex with someone who just filmed me getting fucked? I thought. *Because I'm going to fuck the fuck outta this guy.*

Later, after I had my cum facial for the day, Noah accompanied me up to the roof of what I had learned was his apartment building so I could smoke. We leaned on the railing and looked down at the sidewalk three stories below.

"Can I have a drag?" he said.

"Do you want your own?" I asked, ready to give him the entire pack of smokes if he wanted.

"No, I only take one or two puffs," he replied. "Never the whole thing."

I handed him my half-smoked cigarette, pleased that he was willing to put his lips to a place my lips had been, especially because he knew exactly where my lips had *really* just been.

"I can share," I said with a smile as he handed back my smoke.

I tried to flirt subtly, figuring that every porn girl who came to his loft must have tried to suck his dick.

"I used to live down here, you know, in Pacific Beach," I said. "I miss it sometimes."

"Oh, yeah?" he asked. "Why'd you move to L.A., PF?"

I beamed, secretly pleased that within two hours of meeting me, he'd already given me a nickname.

"Cocaine," I said. "I had to get my act straight. Not that there isn't coke in L.A., but L.A. isn't here."

I lit another cigarette and did a self-conscious swaying motion with my hips.

"Yeah, I get it," he said. "You're in the Valley now?"

He was referring to the San Fernando Valley, which was where Woodland Hills and all of the porn industry was located.

"Yeah. You ever make it up there?" I asked, hoping he'd make a special trip and spend the night in my bedroom.

"Not really, but they're talking about getting a shoot house up there," he said. "If they do, maybe we could get some sushi."

My stomach churned at the word, because I fucking hated fish, but for this guy I was willing to make it work.

"Yeah, that would be awesome," I said, giving him my number.

From that moment on, I prayed that he would call me; that he could be the first guy I dated without any lies; and that, somehow, I could get drunk enough to like sushi.

11

"I DON'T KNOW ANYONE WHO COULD GET THROUGH THE
DAY WITHOUT TWO OR THREE JUICY RATIONALIZATIONS.
THEY'RE MORE IMPORTANT THAN SEX."
—MICHAEL IN *THE BIG CHILL*

n early spring of my fourth year in pornography, and my twenty-second year on earth, Derek called me into his office for a one-on-one meeting. As much as Derek intimidated me, I had begun to consider the office a second home because of my close relationships with Vee and Fran, and so when I slid through the door, I pranced directly into Derek's office, as the door stood wide open.

"Hey, buddy!" I yelled, always eager to unsettle his brute toughness with niceness.

"Miss Flame, always so prompt," he said. "Have a seat, will you?"

Derek stood and closed the door behind me, then returned to his seat.

"Was I a bad Flame, Derek?" I asked with a fake British accent, getting straight to the point.

"Miss Flame, you aren't in any trouble," he said. "In fact, quite the opposite. Shane's World is interested in hiring you. I think the company may be precisely what your career needs."

"What my career needs?" I asked. "What does that even mean?"

"Miss Flame, you have great potential, and I think working for them could open some interesting doors for you," he said.

As Derek talked, I wondered if he had talks with any of the other girls about their futures. I doubted he did, and so I felt special, especially because, up to that point, the scenes in which I'd performed had been predominantly gonzo. That means they had no story line, like the first scene I ever shot for TJ, where the girl walks into the room, drops to her knees, and gets fucked. The only beginning, middle, and end to the scene were the blow job, four sexual positions, and then the pop to the face at the end. Rarely was there any room for "artistic expression" or "self-exploration." It was pornography for guys who don't have time to watch pornography and just want to get off. It had been a fine introduction to the business, but I was ready for something else.

"All right," I said. "What do I do?"

He gave me the booking info for Shane's World. Shane's World was a company originally owned by a porn girl named Shane who would take porn people on trips, during which they would fuck everywhere they could and give hand jobs to anyone with an available penis. The company became famous for its College Invasion series, where a group of porn people literally invaded a college and any frat that would take them. Shane's World, even after Shane left and sold the company to a sweet couple, was rumored to be the only shoot in porn that was as much a party as it was work. I was pleased to discover that my first shoot for them was a weekend trip to Mammoth Lakes, a combination snowboard-fuckfest that directly aligned with every fun trip I'd ever imagined wanting to take.

"You'll do one boy/girl, one girl/girl, and then up to ten hand jobs at $150 each," Derek said.

I WAS AMPED for the snow trip. My life in porn up until that point had always seemed fun enough to me: I'd wake up, smoke weed, go have sex, get paid, and come home. But I wanted more. I needed more excitement than my three scenes a week, with their blow job, four positions, and pop to the face. I longed for an adventure. The only interesting and potentially surprising part of being a gonzo-porn star was guesstimating the size and curvature of the man du jour; whether he would have a pinprick-size spot of blood on his boxers from injecting Caverject into his dick before the shoot; how red his face would get while we fucked; and if he'd be unable to orgasm because he'd taken too much Viagra. Shane's World sounded like the antidote to boring porn, and that seemed precisely what I needed just then. I packed my bags, sure to include an ounce of weed, and hopped into the shoot van the company had rented for our drive to the mountains.

I was warned that the weekend would entail constant filming, but I had thought we'd at least get some privacy on the way there. But when they turned the camera on in the van, I decided to go right for one of those $150 hand jobs. I began fishing around in one of my male cohorts' pants.

One of the cameramen, Smokey, quickly turned the camera lens to the ground.

"The hand job's gotta be on a stranger," he said. "Just so you don't think you're gonna get paid for this one. Sorry."

Holy fuckballs—strangers?! *But . . . how . . . Really?*

A big-breasted Chinese beauty named Lucy chimed in.

"Yeah, Flame, don't waste the guy's jizz now," she said. "We need him for the scene later."

She turned to him.

"Keep it in your pants," she growled to him playfully.

I quickly put his penis away and sat back for the rest of the ride to the snow- and stranger-filled land ahead.

What have I gotten myself into now? I wondered.

Once we got to Mammoth Lakes, I started filming a scene with a male performer, Chris something-or-other, just to get it out of the way. We fucked upstairs on one of the twin beds in our rental condo. But because I wanted to be able to focus on the hand jobs, which seemed the easiest way to secure an additional fifteen hundred dollars, my mind was elsewhere while we worked through the positions and the final pop to the face.

It seemed like it would be easy enough: guys loved hand jobs, right?

The next day on the slopes, I found out just how difficult this extra money would be to make.

We slept in that morning, having drunk and smoked weed for the majority of the previous night. I'd even had some superhot girl/girl sex, off the clock, with a brunette lesbian named Danni. She was rumored to be crazy, which was fine with me. Crazy chicks definitely make the best lovers, as she proved to me in her bed around 2:00 a.m. She definitely out-fucked that Chris something whom I'd banged earlier in the day, and even out-fucked most of the chicks I'd ever been with, save Charlie. While my enjoyment of girl/girl scenes had steadily been progressing to enjoyment of girls in the land of real sex, having sex with *her* put a sharp peak in the scale of real pleasure with another woman. It might have felt good, but it was, nevertheless, emotionally distant; at two a.m., filled with drink and herb, it wasn't exactly easy to stay present.

At noon the next day, as I slid up to the lift with my right foot secured to my snowboard, I reviewed with pleasure the way the weekend was progressing so far. I became especially pleased when I saw that I'd managed to hop on the lift next to a stranger. Smokey was in the chair ahead of me, camera in hand. And I was ready to earn my first easy $150.

In my head, I repeated possible propositions for the stranger:

How about a hand-me?

What's a hand-me? he would ask.

It's where you hand me your dick and I make you splooge!

Finally, I worked up my courage.

"So, uh, can I, um, you know, give you a hand job?" I asked.

The stranger looked at me in horror. Then he looked at Smokey, who was smiling back at us, camera in hand. Finally, the stranger looked back at me, his expression suggesting he wanted to jump off the lift to the mountain of snow below.

"It's free," I said.

The word "free" came out more like a question than an enticement.

He started laughing a hard, twitchy laugh that made *me* feel like jumping off the lift. Then his laughter stopped just as suddenly as it had started.

"No, no thanks," he said. "Funny, though, very funny."

Thankfully, by this point we'd reached the end of the ride. The stranger went right and I went left to Smokey, who still held the camera on me while making a puffer-fish face as he tried not to laugh.

"What a dick," I said into the camera. "Who doesn't want a hand job?"

Smokey busted up.

"You freaked him out, Flame!" Smokey said. "Poor guy looked traumatized. He probably thought he was getting punked. Or that he'd get arrested."

We stepped into our boards and flew down the hill together. Once we reached the lodge at the bottom of the hill, Smokey told the production manager about my lack of skills when it came to offering hand jobs.

"Yo, she was mad creepy," Smokey said. "She pretty much had a hunchback."

Suddenly, Lucy came flying out of the bar, thoroughly drunk on Jack Daniel's.

"I'm gonna fuckin' punch a guy if I go back in there," she said to Smokey, who immediately started filming.

"Lucy, how do you get guys to get hand jobs?" I asked, hoping that in her drunkenness she'd reveal a trick of her trade.

"Really, Flame? It's easy! Watch this."

She pointed at a nearby snowboarder.

"You, come here," she said to him.

The guy walked over to her like he was in a trance.

"I'm going to give you a hand job and you're gonna like it," she ordered.

He smiled at her.

"Where?" he asked.

Befuddled, I watched as she led him around to the back of the lodge, pulled out his dick, and started to jerk him off, right there in the open daylight. When Smokey saw what was happening, he ran to her and started filming.

I turned to the production manager, who was equally enthralled.

"Amazing, simply amazing," I said.

"Some girls got it, Flamer," she said. "Don't worry if you don't."

Once the guy came in her hand and the scene was done, she wiped her hand on the snow and pushed the guy away while his pants were still down.

"Get the fuck away from me, you nasty boy," she yelled, laughing. "Yuck!"

Then she walked back into the bar. A few hours later, after she had started two more fights, we were all asked to leave the mountain and never return. As we trudged out of the hokey, wannabe-Aspen lodge bar, I couldn't stop thinking about hand jobs.

I don't know if I want to give hand jobs to strangers if it means I have to be like that.

Suddenly, I felt perfectly content with the $1,700 I'd already made for having sex with Chris something and Danni, which was theoretically off the clock, but since it was filmed, we were both compensated anyway. When I thought back on these scenes, it really had been quite lovely to film sex that wasn't as contrived as the normal scenes I did. I'd gotten to enjoy having sex with someone, while that enjoyable sex just happened to be filmed, and I'd gotten paid for it all; not a bad day's work.

As we drove home the next day, cameras finally down in the van, signaling that they had gotten plenty of footage, I kept thinking about how fantastic it would be to work for this company all of the time.

This is how porn is supposed to be: fun, I decided. *Being a porn star is supposed to be fun, not boring.*

I vowed to shoot for Shane's World as much as I could, and that when I shot for them I'd be the best girl they'd hired, while having all of the fun there was to be had.

BESIDES SHOOTING ADVENTURE porn for Shane's World, at this time in my career I also began having the pleasure of shooting feature-length films for Vivid Entertainment. I had become friends with a Vivid director named Paul Thomas, who had an eye for translating all things sexual into something that was also beautiful and artistic. While I almost always found something to enjoy while shooting porn, Paul Thomas's flicks were fun in a different way. As in the award-winning multiple personality movie I had shot two years earlier, I was excited to have Paul give me the opportunity to act. And I was thrilled to participate in remakes of some classic, and classically awesome, skin flicks like *Debbie Does Dallas* and *The Devil in Miss Jones.* Paul even gave me leads in a few of his movies, although leads usually went to Vivid contract girls—who were contracted to work only for Vivid—and so being in Paul's good graces made me feel positive about where my career was at. I liked being appreciated for more than just my bedroom skills—not to mention that I felt more pro, as these were days with full makeup, twenty-person crews, one-hundred-page scripts, and deftly placed lighting that created the perfect shadows on our bodies as we fucked.

I usually found it easy to fuck and be fucked on film. But acting introduced an interesting new dynamic to the job, because it gave me a space to play with the truth, which was a relief after I'd vowed to stop lying to the men in my real life. The idea that truth was subjective was also helpful on the gonzo shoots I still sometimes did, when what I really wanted—instead of having a heavy body pounding away at me—was to go home, smoke herb, and watch television.

One day, after a particularly grueling afternoon of running dialogue for a new film I was shooting, I finally received the dream call I'd been anticipating for months.

Only, when I saw Noah's number come up on my phone, I freaked out and let it go straight to voice mail.

The message was exactly what I had hoped it would be:

"Hey, PF," Noah said. "They finally moved me up here. Got a big shoot house right in Woodland Hills. Just seeing if you wanted to grab some sushi. Okay, call me."

Still too nervous to call him, however, I texted him, letting him know that I'd be home in two hours.

He wrote back: "Maybe tomorrow? I don't like eating after eight p.m."

Weirdo specific-eating-hour-man, I thought.

"Sure," I wrote.

It was my first date as a boy/girl porn star, and I felt sure it would be a good one.

The following day, I shot a scene for a director named Van Styles, a totally hot, young, hip-hop-cool dude who worked for *Hustler.* He was Italian, with dark hair, dark eyes, and perfect white teeth to go with his shy smile. His shoes matched his hat, which matched his sweater and his watch, and I wondered where the man got his style, because he looked super-fly. He brought sexy clothes for me to wear and hired as my partner one of the finest fucks in the biz, this French-fucking-god, Manuel Ferrara. My porn girlfriend Camilla had actually warned me pre-shoot about the size of Manuel's man parts.

"I would use something to numb you down there, dude," she said. "Seriously, he is a fucking cock monster."

"You take him in the ass all the time!" I said. "What are you talking about?"

She snorted.

"Whatever, I stretch my ass out for five hours before I let him fuck it," she said. "No, really, Penny, five fucking hours of ass stretching to fit his cock. It's a goddamn event."

I didn't think she was being literal, but I brought some Vagisil anyway, knowing that it could easily numb everything down there if I used enough.

When I got to set, Van dressed me in a sexy pink and silver outfit, tied balloons to my ass, and filmed me crawling around this beautiful house in Encino like a sexy little doggy. When Manuel came out and I saw his giant dick, I was glad I was prepared.

Thank fucking God my whole vagina-ass region is numb, I thought. *Bring it on, Frenchman.*

"What a sexy, *petite* present you give me," he said to Van, who laughed from behind the camera as he filmed.

"Happy birthday, Manuel," Van said. "She's all yours."

Manuel scooped me up in his arms and gently tossed me onto the couch. I landed on my back with my legs in the air. He started kissing my heels and worked all the way down the back of my thighs until he came to my wet and ready pussy. Then he spread my legs, traced his fingers down along the curve of my ass, and dipped his tongue deep into my pussy. He licked and licked. Van walked behind the couch to film from my point of view, into Manuel's eyes. And then Van returned to the front of the couch and shot from Manuel's perspective, up to my face. I tenderly brushed Manuel's brown hair away from his brow, which then, suddenly, furrowed. His eyes shot up into mine as he whipped his head back, tongue hanging slack from his mouth.

"Ma mouf ith nub!" he gasped.

He scraped his tongue with his fingernails.

Fuck, the Vagisil, fuck, fuck, fuck, I thought.

"Ith nub!" Manuel said.

Van laughed so hard, he had to put the camera down and hold his belly.

"I'm so sorry," I said. "Camilla said you were huge, and I was so worried about it fitting in me. Fuck, I'm sorry!"

"Peddy, why ith ma tongue nub?" he asked.

"I put Vagisil down there," I cried, running to the bathroom. "I'm sorry! I'll go douche, sorry, sorry, sorry!"

"Douth! Douth a bunth!" he yelled.

Once in the bathroom, I squeezed bottle after bottle of warm tap water into my pussy until I was fairly sure that the cream no longer coated my inner walls. When I exited the bathroom and returned to the shoot area, Manuel was gone and the lights were dim. I walked slowly back into the makeup room, where I found Van talking to the makeup artist.

"Where'd he go?" I asked. "Is he pissed?"

"Ha, yeah . . . no," Van laughed. "I mean, he'll be back. He just went to get something to eat. You know, so that his mouth works again. I think he took it as a compliment. It was pretty hilarious."

Bright red with embarrassment, I turned to the window to watch for Manuel's car returning, when my phone rang. I turned it off without checking to see who was calling, put it back in my purse, and looked at Van.

"You're not mad?" I asked.

He laughed.

"No, it's fine," he said. "You like Murs?"

"Huh?" I asked, unsure why he was suddenly talking about one of my favorite underground hip-hop artists.

"Murs," Van said. "Your phone ringtone was Murs."

"Oh, ha, yeah, Murs is my pharmacist," I said, quoting one of my favorite songs.

"You know him?" Van asked, not getting the reference.

I immediately felt like a fool for having implied that I bought pharmaceutical drugs from a hip-hop rapper.

"Oh, no, I mean, I don't even take pills," I said. "Just weed. But. No. I *wish* I knew him."

"He's a homie of mine," Van said. "We should go to a concert sometime."

Suddenly, I didn't know what he was talking about.

"Like a hip-hop concert?" I asked, feeling like a third grader who flirted by kicking a boy in the shins and then running away. "A Murs show? That'd be supersweet."

As I saw Manuel pull into the parking lot, I wished he'd go away. I didn't want Van to have to film me getting fucked by the French guy anymore. I didn't want a repeat of the awkward moment when Noah had held my foot while I got plowed in missionary. At the same time, I didn't want to be distracted from the scene by my fantasies of a potential relationship with the director. I just wanted a chance to date a new guy—fresh, from scratch—with no lies or weirdness.

"Cool, I'll introduce you to him," Van said.

I wasn't sure anymore if he wanted to date me or set me up with Murs.

Confused about Van but with full feeling down below, I finished the scene with Manuel. At first he nervously put his tongue back into my pussy. But then he smiled with his eyes, relieved that I'd "douthed a bunth," as he had requested. We went on to have super-awesome, Cirque de Soleil–type sex. Whether it was the size of his massive piece of manhood or his unbearably delicious accent, I forgot I was being filmed—by Van, no less—and succumbed to the enjoyment of a good, hard fuck. Even though it was the same old, contrived blow-job/four-positions/pop-to-the-face routine, the intensity of Manuel's hotness, and the idea that I now had two mega-fine dudes who wanted to go on a date with me, overrode the mediocrity that usually accompanied a gonzo scene. When it was all over, I thanked Manuel politely for the amazing lay and slipped Van my phone number. As I drove home for my first date with Noah, I was a happy girl.

THANKFULLY, I NEVER had to find out how much sake it would take for me to eat fish with Noah on our first date. Instead of sushi, we decided to meet at Monty's Steak & Seafood Restaurant in the Valley, because of its close geographic proximity to my house. Noah looked exactly as he had the first day I met him, from his spiky hair to his Chuck Taylor All Stars, except in place of his thin white T-shirt he now wore a plaid Paul Frank shirt. Even though I lived around the corner from Monty's, Noah had offered to pick me up. I liked the feeling of sitting down in the luscious leather seats of his brand-new E350.

These are seats my ass could get used to, I thought.

"Hey, there," he said.

He leaned in to kiss me on the cheek, totally catching me by surprise and upping my hopes that he'd end up spending the night.

"You look goooooood," he continued, stretching out the word, as if the longer it went on for, the more serious I'd know him to be.

"Hi," I said shyly.

I crossed my legs daintily, as if I hadn't just been fucked by a French stallion a few hours before.

"Hungry?" he asked.

"Very," I replied.

With one turn and a three-block drive, we were at the restaurant.

ONCE INSIDE THE restaurant, Noah urged me to follow close behind the waiter, allowing me to lead the way, either so he could watch my ass or impress me with his gentle-manly-ness. I *was* impressed. He let me sit down first, asked what wine I wished to drink, and then ordered it for me from the waiter. I had never dated a guy like this. Of course, most of the guys I'd dated were under twenty-five, and Noah was in his late thirties. I wondered what it would be like to have an older man in my bed, and daydreamed through most of the beginning of our first real conversation.

"How was your day?" he asked, shocking me back into reality.

At first I scrambled to think of a lie I could tell, as I had always been forced to do with my dates and boyfriends in the past. But then I remembered why I had specifically wanted to date someone within the industry: I didn't have to make something up. I could tell him the whole truth and he wouldn't be shocked or disgusted. He wouldn't even be surprised. So, for the first time ever, I went for it: I told the truth.

"I put Vagisil on my pussy, because I was nervous that Manuel wouldn't fit," I said.

Noah started laughing his fantastic laugh, which I had loved from the moment I first met him in San Diego, and wine nearly squirted out of his nose.

"His mouth went numb," I said. "It was horrible."

"Who did you shoot for?" he asked when he finally stopped laughing.

"Van Styles," I said, pausing to sip the pinot noir. "Supercute," I added.

While pretending to be a sophisticated grown-up, I swilled my wine a little too hard, so that some escaped the glass and dribbled down my fingers. I hoped Noah didn't notice.

"You gonna go on a date with him?" he asked.

I wondered if he had super mind-reading powers. I paused before answering, then remembered that this date was all about telling the truth.

"Um, well, he asked me to a hip-hop show and, yeah, I think I'll probably go," I said.

Wow, that was easy.

I was starting to enjoy this 100 percent honesty thing. It made conversations a lot simpler. It also meant that I got to see if Noah would get jealous at the thought of me dating another man.

"Good, hon," he said. "I think that would be good for you."

Even though nothing had happened between us yet except for a kiss on the cheek, a glass of wine, and an ordered steak, my heart broke a little at the realization that he supported me dating someone else.

"Think he'd be a good boyfriend?" Noah asked.

"We just met today, so I don't really know what to say about that yet," I said. "So, yeah, I guess. . . . I mean, he handled things well: he wasn't, like, pissed or anything about the whole Vagisil thing."

As I talked, I wished more and more that Noah wouldn't be so cool about it.

Just say no, goddamn it. Say that you want me to date you, not someone else.

"I think you should go for it," Noah said. "I hear he's a good guy."

Noah sipped his wine, then looked around the restaurant for our fillets.

"Oh, yeah?" I asked, unsure how to react. "Maybe. We'll see."

Later, as we pulled up to my house, Noah leaned over and kissed my lips. As much as I had been looking forward to it, the kiss was oddly passionless and borderline superficial.

"Sushi next time?" he said.

I didn't know what the fuck had happened that day—from Manuel to Van to Noah—but I could tell that something strange was afoot, so I decided to continue being honest.

"Actually, I fucking hate fish," I said. "All of them. I hate them all equally."

Then I kissed Noah back, trying to manifest the passion that I had felt earlier in the day with Manuel, and failing miserably.

I had wanted to find a guy who didn't care if I fucked other guys, who could ask me on a date and not need me to date *only* him. But now that I had found such a guy—maybe two of them—I wasn't quite sure it was the right way to be after all. I was reminded of that old adage about the complications of getting what you wished for.

Shouldn't people be jealous? I thought as I shut my front door and listened to him drive away before going straight for my bong. *Shouldn't we want a person only for ourselves? Does it mean they care but they are accepting when they act like they don't care that I fuck other people? Or do these guys really not care? And am I okay with them not caring? Do I not care? Is that the deal now? Do I have to not care about them fucking other people too?*

A steady stream of such thoughts ran through my head as my face met my pillow. Before I passed out, high on confusion, wine, and pot, my final thought was: *If these guys can care about me and not about my occupation, then I'm going to do this porn thing, for real. I'm gonna make it a career. That way, nobody will get too attached, and we can all do our own thing, pain- and emotion-free. That way, I can make dumb money and never have to worry about a man taking care of me.*

The next morning, feeling more rested than I had in a long time, my decision to make pornography a lifelong career was reaffirmed when I received an offer from Shane's World. They wanted me to direct my own movies. As I said yes, I jumped up and down happily, thinking of a secure future, both financially and emotionally. I knew that my dreams were totally achievable as long as I kept sucking dick for a living.

SHANE'S WORLD OFFERED me two movie lines to direct. One was entitled *Girls Night Out,* and the other was *Blazed & Confused. Girls Night Out* involved a bunch of girls going out to the clubs to cause mayhem, give hand jobs—a task I'd already decided to relegate to the girls for hire—and have sex in random places. *Blazed & Confused* was more of a daytime shoot that focused on the hunt for marijuana, hand job recipients, and having stoned sex in random places. Shane's World was big on sex in random places.

While a bit more difficult than I'd imagined, the directing thing was super-rewarding, both in terms of my finances and my confidence level. Shane's World offered me a very lucrative deal, which even included a small percentage of money on the back end, meaning that I got a buck or two for every movie that they sold. Since they sold a good amount of movies, and I was already getting paid $700 per scene as a director's fee—with five scenes per movie standard—I made out like a bandit.

Directing meant more responsibility, but all of the business stuff that came along with it was surprisingly easy. It wasn't all that hard to manage the legalities of shooting a porn movie. Performers had to sign a waiver releasing the rights to their images, and a W-2 or W-4, depending on whether they wished to be paid as an individual or as a business, as well as a 2257 compliance form, in which they legally stated that they were of age and could participate in an adult film. They also had to provide proof of their age and citizenship. Once completed, all of the forms were stapled to a copy of an STD test taken within thirty days of our scene. These were done by the industry testing company AIM (Adult Industry Medical), and as long as the performers tested negative for gonorrhea, chlamydia, and HIV, they were good to go. It was suggested by AIM that performers get a full panel of tests done every six months, also checking for things like hep C and HPV. But very few girls or guys that I knew cared to do the full panel. The extra tests cost extra money, and no one wanted to hear any more bad news than was absolutely necessary.

THE MOST DIFFICULT part of directing a shoot always seemed to be the porn stars for hire. I soon found out that most girls, unlike me, didn't want to have the kind of adventure where they ran around town having sex in illegal public places like club bathrooms and parking garages or on brightly lit street corners. They wanted to show up for work, get fucked, get paid, and then go home. So I became more specific about whom I cast in my movies, preferring to know and be friends with the girls first, so that our friendship as well as our professional relationship was on the line when they showed up for the shoot. This made them much more likely to cooperate. Like me, most girls in the business didn't have a plethora of female friends, and so we didn't want to disappoint the few we did have.

The second movie line, *Blazed & Confused,* was much more my style than the *Girls Night Out* line was. Because I didn't normally go out and party with chicks, the *GNO* line always felt a little fake to me. I did, however, smoke a ton of pot, so *Blazed & Confused* made sense to me. It was a movie series that I could really *get*; I understood the audience and felt able to create what it would take to get them off.

The first *Blazed* movie took place during a road trip to Humboldt County in search of California's best pot. I hired my best friends in the biz at the time, including a cute little Brit named Roxy who lived with Fran and occasionally went on dates with my roommate Taylor. I also hired my friend Jack Venice, whom I got on with so well that I ended up hiring him for every *Blazed* movie I made. We stayed at a seedy little hotel in Santa Cruz on the way to Humboldt. I was excited to be directing my second film, but as we filmed Jack and me fucking in the hotel room, I felt dissatisfied.

This isn't going to do it, I thought. *I need more. We can do better.*

The next day, as we passed through the San Francisco Bay Area, I remembered a Grateful Dead poster that depicted skeletons sitting on a cliff side overlooking the Golden Gate Bridge and San Francisco Bay. I demanded we drive into the Marin Headlands to search for the spot.

"Stoners across America will fucking love this!" I told my production manager as we crossed the bridge and exited the freeway. "They will see the scene and feel like it's familiar. Stoners love familiarity."

I was pumped about my idea as we drove up the one-way road. But as we parked and trudged up the big lookout hill, I realized that the large number of health enthusiasts in the park and the

brisk wind on this chilly day in October would play a big part in
how well the scene went. As Jack and I walked to the bench overlooking the ocean and the city, he swooped me into his strong arms
and we kissed. He pulled our pants down to our ankles so that if
we were caught, we could pull them up quickly and run. Then, as I
lay back on the bench, he grabbed me by my bunched pants so that
I had no choice but to put my legs up in the air and he had some
support for fucking me.

Knowing that we could be interrupted at any moment was
invigorating, but whatever wetness this might have caused me
to achieve naturally was quickly dried by the violent winds now
sweeping over us.

"Let me spit on that, Penny," Jack said.

He moved down to manually lubricate my pussy.

"Just fuck it," I said.

He laughed.

"Okay, but it's not my fault if you get raw," he said.

But all I cared about was getting an awesome scene and ensur-
ing that I would get to film multiple *Blazed & Confused* movies in
the future.

Finally, Jack sat down on the bench to let me ride him. This
became even more awkward with my pants around my ankles,
because I couldn't spread my legs to mount him. I removed one
of my tennis shoes and pulled off my pants, because there was no
other way for us to see the action on camera. I rode him until he
was ready to come. And then, like the good little porn star and
director I was, I dropped to my knees, with views of my favorite
city nestled among the clouds behind us, and he came all over my
face. He laughed and apologized when some of his semen snuck
into my right eyeball. I'd become accustomed to men "misfiring"
and carried various "fix-it" tools, including eyedrops and neti
pots. But as we looked out across the rolling hills, we noticed a
random guy who had set up camp on another hill to watch our
scene.

No time for cleanup now, Penny, I thought.

"Get him," I said to Smokey, who quickly turned the camera on our voyeur. The guy clapped a few times to show his appreciation for our show and waved at us. Then we jumped back into our van and continued on our way.

The movie ended with a naked game of tag through the redwood trees, which was not only fun but the kind of showstopping scene that I hoped would make my directorial efforts stand out.

When we got back to Los Angeles, and I learned that I'd be allowed to continue the series, I called Noah to see if he wanted to celebrate.

"Sushi?" he asked.

I quickly hid my frustration that he'd forgotten what I told him on our first date.

"No, I hate fish," I said. "But dinner somewhere else, maybe?"

"Sure, PF," he said. "Hey, would you want to do a porn-stars-at-home thing? We'll pay you to let us into your house, like *MTV Cribs,* but of porn."

Business, business, business, I thought. *Maybe this is all just business?*

But I wasn't feeling as brave or as honest as I had on our first date, so I didn't ask him what his intentions were. Instead, I just went along with it.

"Okay," I said. "Um, how about next week?"

We set a date for him to come over with a camera. In preparation, I got my garage ready so I could display my artwork.

Two nights later, Van called.

"Yeah, uh, wanna grab some dinner?" he said. "There's a little Italian joint right by you: Paoli's."

Maybe I should go out with him, I thought. *Actually, yes, screw Noah. I'm gonna see what this Van is all about.*

"I'd love to," I agreed.

The day of my date with Van, I decided to go shopping for a cute new outfit to wear. I wanted something not too sexy that said:

"I'm cool, and comfortable, and I like guys that skateboard and listen to hip-hop."

Halfway through my shopping excursion, I got a text from Noah: a single question mark. I realized that I'd totally forgotten that we were supposed to shoot our porn star *Cribs* that day. I didn't respond, deciding that if he asked me about it later, I would say I had never gotten the text. When I got home later, there was a box of cornflakes on my front door. I knew exactly who had left it there because the word "flakes" was circled.

Yup, no more lies, Flame, I thought. *No more lies.*

Then I picked up the box of cereal and walked inside to get ready for my date with Van.

MY FRIENDSHIP WITH Noah remained just that. He was obviously not interested in having a girlfriend, and I was *too* interested in not being the uncool chick who wasn't okay with him not wanting a girlfriend. My friendship with Van, however, quickly morphed into a serious relationship: he was my boyfriend and I was his girlfriend. It was easy being with someone who understood the proverbial ins and outs of the business. He worked hard shooting girls getting fucked hard, and I worked hard getting fucked and shooting myself and other girls getting fucked. After we started dating, he never shot me again, and I was thankful that, even though he'd already seen me having sex with other men, he wouldn't have to see it again. This felt more intimate than any other relationship I'd had, primarily because there was nothing to lie to him about, except for the fact that I occasionally had sleepovers at Noah's house. But I didn't think of this as lying; I was just leaving out unnecessary parts of the story, because Noah and I had had sex only a few times, and the times were funny, awkward, and totally not something worth mentioning.

Van and I were a regular couple. Van spent the night at my house, or I spent the night at his, and we made love unlike the people we were at work. Sometimes it was in the dark, with me on my stomach and him lying on top of me, slowly moving himself inside of me. It was sensual, with whispering and quiet orgasms, and nothing like the circus–freak show of a shoot, where dudes and I fucked on our tippy toes and got leg cramps from the incessant pounding. Van and I went snowboarding together, and often we were unable to make it home without pulling over to the side of the road and taking each other in the back of his truck. When we went to hip-hop shows, he smiled because I knew every single word. It wasn't until I met his mom, and realized how important she was to him—and what a big deal it was that he'd introduced me to her—that I began to worry about exactly where the relationship was going.

I bought four tickets to the music festival Reggae on the River, which I hadn't been to since Marc and I broke up years before. This time I was going with Jacob and Kurt, two of my besties, who made me feel safe. The third ticket was supposed to be for Van, but his addition to the group made me totally uncomfortable. I talked it over with Camilla one drunken night at a diner.

"I mean, what?" I said. "It's just a concert, right? Are we gonna get married?"

"Probably not, I'd guess, from the way you're acting," said Camilla's makeup artist, Angel, whom I'd just met for the first time.

"So, then why am I freaking out?" I demanded.

I suddenly felt much drunker than I thought I'd been at the club we'd just left.

"Because you obviously have a problem with intimacy," Angel said, laughing.

"Shut up, Ang," Camilla said. "Don't tell her that now."

Camilla turned to me.

"How are you getting home, Penny?" she asked.

"I'm fuckin' covering one eye to compensate for that double-vision shit, and then I'm driving like a gangster!" I yelled, wobbling as I stood up.

"No, no, that really isn't a good plan," Angel said. "You should give me your keys."

"How about you gimme your number and I'll call you when I'm home safe?" I said. "You can make me pretty sometime?"

I had been looking for a makeup artist.

I bet I wouldn't look so drunk if I had a professional do my goddamn makeup tonight, I thought.

"She's not gonna listen to you, Angel," Camilla said. "Let her go before she really starts yelling. Penny, go home; we can talk in the morning when you remember."

"BAH!" I yelled in the otherwise quiet restaurant.

I stumbled stupidly out the door to my BMW.

The next morning, I was totally surprised to wake up in my own bed, which is never good. When I read through the previous night's texts, I had no memory of who this new Angel person was, so I called Camilla.

"What the fuck happened last night?" I asked. "My brain feels like ouchie and my car is in the driveway. How'd I get home?"

I lit a joint and lay down on my couch, fully prepared to remain stationary for the entire day.

"Yourself," Camilla said, sounding grumpy as always. "You were a hot mess, dude. You yelled at everyone, even Angel, when she tried to take your keys away. Lots of yelling, dude."

"I know, it's the volume control thing," I said. "I just lose it when I drink. Who is Angel?"

I was displeased that I'd driven myself home and couldn't remember doing so, but I forced the thought to the bottom of my worry list, like I was good at doing.

"Uh, one of my best friends, and now one of yours, too, probably," Camilla said. "She was really worried about your drunk ass driving home. I'm glad you made it. You don't remember anything?"

"Meh, I remember, um, driving there, and then the first, like, five drinks," I said. "After that, there's some fog."

"You invited me to Reggae on the River," she said. "Do you remember that?"

"No, but good," I said. "Do you wanna come? I don't think I wanna bring Van."

"You said that last night," she said. "You were freaking out over how serious the relationship is. I told you I can't go. You said you're taking my brother instead, that 'it's almost like taking me.' Then you got all pissed off when Angel suggested you have issues with intimacy."

Camilla laughed her grumpy laugh and I heard her puff on her smoke.

"Ha!" I burst out. "Intimacy issues? I have intimate relations every day! I may have been drunk, but I wasn't totally off."

"Whatever, dude," she said. "Anyway, my bro's down, if you're serious."

It was decided. I was taking her brother to a reggae festival in Northern California, instead of my boyfriend. Now all I had to do was tell my boyfriend.

A FEW DAYS before I was meant to drive to Northern Cali with the troop of boys I'd assembled for the reggae festival, I was sitting on Noah's bed at his big shoot house. I still hadn't told Van that he wasn't invited, and I didn't know how to approach the subject.

"Just tell him, PF," Noah said.

"Yeah, but then what?" I said. "Tell him I don't want to bring him to the show? I haven't talked to him in like a week."

Noah tsk-tsked, hopping off the bed to go look for his dog.

"I don't know," he said. "What would you say if I were him?"

"You're easy, though," I said. "I'd just say, 'You hate reggae and I don't want to introduce you to my friends.' You don't count."

Noah unleashed his laugh that I loved. Though I was grateful for our uncensored, unguarded honesty with each other, it sometimes hurt to acknowledge the truth, which was that he was not interested in me the same way I was interested in him.

"It's true," he said. "I don't like reggae and your friends are *scary*."

Noah often told me that my friends were scary because he had heard the war stories of the wild nights we had survived together in the name of fun—like the time I'd gotten arrested in a G-string and sparkly marijuana leaf pasties for drunk driving a Jet Ski with Kurt.

"They aren't any scarier than me," I said in all sincerity.

"Mmmm'kay, PF," Noah said.

I wished I could be as honest with Van as I could be with Noah.

Van had never implied that our relationship should be more than it was, and in actuality, he had put no pressure on me whatsoever. But I had convinced myself that we had to progress into something or fade into nothingness. So I pulled a Ted. I stopped answering Van's calls pre-Reggae. But I had changed since the days of my relationship with Ted. At one point during the weekend-long festival, my blood coursing with mushrooms and E, I had an epiphany about the situation.

This isn't the way to do it Penny, I thought. *Go home, tell him you need space, and be a fucking adult.*

When I got home, I drove to Van's house to inform him of my spatial needs. We sat on the modern couch in his brightly lit Porn Valley condo.

"Yeah, I kinda figured, when you took Camilla's little brother to Reggae," he said. "That fucking hurt, Jennie. I was really looking forward to spending time with you. Space is fine."

I held back the tears that seemed to crop up out of nowhere.

"Space is fine," he repeated.

And, just like that, we had space. I left wondering if I'd just made a mistake, or if *I* was the mistake. A year and a half later, I entered *Sex Rehab,* and I began addressing all of the mistakes I had made in every relationship I'd ever had, and what came next.

12

"EXTREME FEAR CAN NEITHER FIGHT NOR FLY."

—WILLIAM SHAKESPEARE, *THE RAPE OF LUCRECE*

My little brother, James, had started Marine Corps boot camp the same week I checked into *Sex Rehab,* both of us having decided to make drastic changes in our lives. After jumping through the required hoops, James was graduating boot camp four days before I finished filming *Sober House.* My entire family was gathering in San Diego to celebrate his achievement, and because I hadn't seen either of my parents in what felt like years, I was a bit nervous about the unpredictable nature of the get-together. Because of this, and the fact that I didn't want to take away from James's day, I refused to let any cameras follow me.

The last time I had seen my mom, we got shit-house drunk together. That was Christmas of the previous year. Our relationship had seemed to disintegrate as both of our drinking habits escalated. Since I'd gotten sober and begun working with Dr. Drew, he had generously offered to fly her out so we could do a therapy session together, but she refused.

"You want to blame all your problems on me, Jennifer," she said. "And I don't want to be on television looking like I do."

It broke my heart that she wouldn't participate, as I had no intentions of blaming my issues on her. I had only hoped that we would be able to sit in a session and learn how to communicate, so that I could perhaps separate my feelings from her own. Jill said that one of my biggest issues was that I didn't feel like I deserved to feel my own feelings, and so I took on my mother's instead. Perhaps it was because of this that I never told my mother how much it hurt me that she'd refused Dr. Drew's airplane ticket.

Dr. Drew also offered to fly my dad in for a therapy session, but because I literally couldn't remember the last time I'd seen my father on friendly terms, maybe five or six years earlier, I didn't wish to reunite with him on television. I had visions of the commercials they'd cut together to tease the episode: "Porn star and father reunite." It felt like some Oxygen channel made-for-TV melodrama, and even though I used that as my excuse, I'm sure that both Drew and Jill knew that, really, I was terrified of what my dad would say. It was one thing to start building a relationship by phone with my estranged father. It would be another thing altogether to see him face-to-face, to hug him, and to weep for the years we had lost because I had taken on my mom's anger and hatred toward him. I felt I had already cried enough on both of the television shows, and didn't want to share any more of my tears with the VH1 crowd.

When I arrived in San Diego, I quickly found my way to the bleachers filled with families of soon-to-be Marines, their smiling faces basking in the Southern California sunshine. The first person I saw was my sister, a skinny string bean of a twenty-one-year-old girl. We immediately snuck off to smoke.

"You seen him yet?" I asked, handing her one of my Parliaments.

"James? Or Dad?" she asked, taking the cigarette gratefully and chugging down her second or third Rockstar energy drink of the day.

"James. Dad, too, but James," I said. "How does he look?"

I puffed on the cigarette and tried to blow the smoke away from the child-oriented, family-friendly crowd gathering nearby.

"He looks like such a man!" she said. "Like, superman style. Not, like, S-on-the-chest super, but you know what I mean."

I started laughing, which made Lyss laugh too. We spoke in almost exactly the same way: our tone, our love of made-up words, our overuse of "super," "-ish," and any other means of expressing excitement.

"Yeah, dude, supermannish style and kinda anti-little-bro-ish," she continued. "Gimme another smoky treat."

I handed her a follow-up cigarette, which she lit with the butt of the first.

"Whatevs, he'll totally let me beat him up still," I said. "And Dad?"

I was curious, but also hopeful that whatever she said would cushion the upcoming reunion.

"Dude! He's *superexcited* to see you," she said. "Like, pumped. Oh, and the aunts and uncles are here too. Everyone. Oh, and Mom."

Lyss had an interesting relationship with our mom as well. As I had learned in therapy, since Lyss was the middle child growing up, she tried to mediate. When I left home, and she became the oldest child, she got a little footloose, and Mom put her in a rehab facility for overusing cold medicine. As a result, Lyss was very guarded about what she shared with Mom, and about her life with anyone, period.

"How's she looking?" I asked, knowing that it was easy to tell the current level of Mom's alcohol use by the puffiness of her skin.

"Eh, still drinking," she said. "Pretty red. Puff monster. Sadsville."

Lyss stubbed out her smoke and walked over to a clay trash can to dispose of her waste. When she came back over to me, I fluffed her hair and hugged her under my big-sister wing.

We walked back to the bleachers, watching the heat rise from the pavement as we crossed the parade grounds. The trumpets announcing the beginning of the ceremony cut through the crowd's noise. As we climbed the metal stands, I spotted Aunt

Suzie and then the rest of my family, with Mom and her husband, the same boss from the video my dad showed me all those years ago, side by side, smiling, and taking up the very last row. Everyone in the stands stood and faced the marching ground to honor the strong young men and women who had completed the long and arduous boot camp training. As I hugged Suzie and waved to Mom, I spotted Dad, wearing a black USMC DAD shirt. Though it had been years since we had seen each other, we immediately hugged. It almost felt as if the applause that surrounded us was in honor of that hug, which was enough to make me feel like I had a dad again. Unbelievably, the huge hurdle of reuniting with my father was less difficult to overcome than I had imagined.

Dad put his arm around me during the ceremony and I, a bit worried that Mom would be upset because I'd chosen to sit by him, waved to her. Her skin was as Sadsville, red, and puff monster–like Lyss had said. She waved back and quickly turned her head to the parade grounds to watch her son graduate, tears in her eyes. As the ceremony came to an end, the audience surged from their seats, and each group of family and friends sought out their new Marine. Seemingly out of nowhere, my brother, who now stood with perfect posture and had strong shoulders and a lean, cut Marine's body, came and wrapped his arms around Lyss, Dad, and me. Dad started to cry, overwhelmed by how great James looked and that, after fourteen years, he had all of his kids together in one place, as a family. Mom watched the reunion from five steps away. Then she stepped up and gave me a hug.

"You look good, Jen," she said. "I hope you're happy."

I didn't know exactly what she meant, because she didn't look like she hoped I was happy. She looked pissed and butt-hurt that the reunion didn't include her. But I tried not to feel like that was my fault.

SEX REHAB MADE it clear that there were lessons for me to learn, which would help me chart my progress away from porn:

> *Lesson Numero Uno:* Just because I made a decision at eighteen years old (the decision to be in the adult business, which led to the decision to be a porn star) did not mean I had to continue making the same decision for the rest of my life. I could change my mind at any time, and as many times as I wanted.

> *Lesson Numero Dos:* Just because someone might need to *ask* for help did not mean that that someone was weak. Sometimes, it takes more strength and courage to ask for help than to not ask.

On *Sober House,* there were two more lessons to be learned:

> *Lesson Numero Tres:* Boundaries are not simply physical barriers between one thing and another. There are emotional boundaries, mental boundaries, even spiritual boundaries, and all of these invisible protection devices can be used to keep me safe.

> *Lesson Numero Cuatro:* If I was not going to be a porn star, that meant I had to be something else—anything else. Implicit in this outwardly simple lesson was an inwardly complex realization. I didn't know what I wanted to be.

The biggest lesson that I needed to learn, which combined all of these seemingly rudimentary lessons, involved exploring the possibility of alternative occupations and learning to live within my means. I felt like I needed someone in my life who would teach me how to make money without doing porn, and how to save the few dollars that—with my clothes on—I might be lucky enough to earn, assuming some potential employer would be able to look past the video-streamed evidence of my earlier poor choices. I brought all of this up when I sat down with Dr. Drew in one of our final one-on-one sessions.

"I don't know what else to do," I said.

I looked at him from my uncomfortable chair in the double-wide therapy trailer.

"Well, Jennie, what are you *willing* to do?" Dr. Drew asked, pen in hand, head slightly cocked to the side.

"Anything," I said. "I don't care. That's the whole thing. I'll do anything in the world if it means I don't have to sell sex. I'll be an assistant, work at a bagel shop, coffee place, waitress, I don't care. Anything."

I held on to my tissue. Dr. Drew had the incredible power to make me cry with a single question.

"Well, have you thought about school?" he asked.

"I only have five more units until I have all of my general education stuff out of the way, then I'd be a junior," I said. "I'd love to go back to school. But for what? I have no clue. I feel like a fucking kid again, like I have these huge life decisions to make and no resources to make them."

I began folding my tissue into triangles.

"Well, hold on," he said. "You have some pretty serious resources here, Jennie. You have me, you have Jill, you have quite a bit to help you get on the right track. Now, if you're *really* willing to do *whatever* it takes to stay out of porn and get better, I think we can help set some things up for you. And if you're that close to being finished with your bachelor's, I think you should put some serious thought into going back. You're very bright. It's one of your biggest problems"—he looked at me and laughed—"because you've cleverly figured out how to exist in the world without emotions. But now that they are coming back, it's important we figure out how to use that brain for good."

Dr. Drew smiled at me, a smile that said: *We are done here.* It also said: *I am down to help you if you let me, and I believe you can change because I see you changing.* I smiled back at him, wanting to believe that he was right.

Three days before *Sober House* ended, Dr. Drew and a super-producer named Steve Longo set up an interview with the effervescent Lisa Gregorisch-Dempsey, a senior executive at *Extra* and the executive producer of all things awesome. I did a little research before going to the interview, just so I knew whom I'd be sitting down with, but no amount of research could have prepared me for this successful bombshell of a woman. Her clothes were kind of like the clothes I brought to porn sets when shooting an office scene, but they were nicer, and more expensive, and not the kind of apparel that would be carelessly thrown to the floor or used as kneepads or cum wipes. Her hair and makeup were perfect, and her smile lacked the smoker's crinkles I saw accumulating around my own. She was the epitome of business and class but swore like a sailor.

You, Lisa Gregorisch-Dempsey, are my hero.

With trepidation, I took my seat next to Dr. Drew, miles away from Lisa, across her huge, executive-producer-of-awesomeness desk. I hadn't been on a job interview where I remained clothed in eight years, except for the *Sex Rehab* interview, during which I would have gladly disrobed had they allowed it. I had no idea how to sell myself without the use of my tits or ass or pussy. Dr. Drew very delicately guided me through the fully clothed interview process, encouraging me to tell Lisa my story and divulge my struggles and the changes I'd committed to making. My heart raced as I told her the truth: that I'd been a camera whore for approximately eight years and was now done selling my body for money.

One of my biggest fears in leaving the adult business was explaining to potential employers where I'd been for the last eight years. But, with Dr. Drew's help, I maintained composure.

Lisa listened to my whole spiel before responding.

"So, what are you wanting to do, Jennie?" she asked.

"Anything," I said, holding on to her desk to stop my hands

from shaking. "I'll get you coffee. I'll sweep the floors. I don't care. I just need a job. Any job."

Lisa leaned back in her tall-backed chair and smiled at me.

"You know, most people come in here and want Mario Lopez's job," she said. "It's nice to hear you'll start from the bottom. I think you'll do fine."

Even if no actual job came from the interview, the experience had been invaluable. It gave me the confidence that if I could simply get in front of an employer, I could get a job.

The following day, my field producer, Louie, had set up an interview with Gary Miller, a music producer out in Malibu who had worked with artists including David Bowie and Kylie Minogue and was looking for a personal assistant. The knowledge that I'd be interviewing with a man, coupled with an image of what women generally wear in music videos, inspired me to dress a bit sexier than I had for my *Extra* interview. Dr. Drew was not there to get me in trouble for showing skin, so I threw on a pair of sexy low-rise jeans and a backless turquoise shirt. As far as I was concerned, this was a totally different opportunity to shine. Old habits . . .

Lisa might have hired me because of my story and desire to succeed, whereas a music producer will, foremost, require that his assistant be superhot, I thought.

As I prepared for the interview, I started to feel as if I might actually have a job waiting for me after *Sober House.*

Louie and I pulled into the long gravel driveway, which cut across an immense front lawn overlooking the ocean, and we parked next to the other production cars that had pre-arrived to film the "arrival shot." Cameramen were already stationed behind bushes and baby trees. Still in a fantasy world where everything would go my way and I'd have a job that would pay for my Benz, I clip-clopped in higher-than-high heels down the cement walkway to Gary's front door without noticing any of the production crew.

The front door opened into a big recording room with a grand piano, a keyboard, multiple microphones, a drum set—everything a musician could want in his or her living room. A private listening studio sat behind soundproof glass above the recording room. Gary's thick, heavy hands rested on a control panel with millions of buttons and switches.

"Welcome," he said, extending his hand to shake mine.

As I graciously thanked him for seeing me, I sat daintily on a bench across from him, crossing my legs at the ankles and placing my hands on my knees.

"So I'm looking for an assistant, I'm sure they've told you, and I'm wondering what it is that you'd like to do," he said, speaking as if he reading from a script.

I immediately suspected that this entire interview was a fake and that he didn't need an assistant at all. But I decided to play along. I quickly repeated the exact same thing I'd told Lisa. If this whole interview was simply for filming purposes, I didn't want to exert any more energy than was necessary.

"I'm down to sweep floors," I said. "I don't care. I just need a job."

He sat up and drummed his hands on his knees.

"Yes, you will have to sweep floors," he said. "But you don't sing by any chance, do you?"

His question hit me like a truck, not only because it was random and possibly impulsive, but also because I used to sing and I'd always loved it. I'd taken voice lessons throughout childhood and into my teen years, along with piano lessons, dance lessons, and any other kind of artistically inclined lessons my mother came across. One by one, I had quit them all. I quit singing after my high school choir teacher called me out on a bus filled with my choir and classmates.

"You would sing much better if you didn't smoke," he said.

Instead of quitting the cigarettes, I quit believing in my ability to sing. The only time I sang anymore was in the shower, and the only two songs I sang were Elton John's "Rocket Man" and

Little Willie John's "Fever." I was terrified of anyone hearing my scratchy, cigarette-damaged voice.

"I used to sing," I said. "I don't really anymore."

His response made me want to throw up in my mouth.

"Will you sing something for me?" he asked.

I looked at Louie, who sat off camera smiling from ear to ear. Beads of sweat gathered on my forehead and the small of my back. I figured there were two options:

Option Number One: Sing for the man. Possibly throw up. He likes the voice, not the throw-up.

Option Number Two: Sing for the man. Possibly throw up. He doesn't like the voice or the throw-up.

But the opportunity was too much to resist. So I sang:

"Never knew how much I love you / Never knew how much I care . . ."

I DIDN'T THROW up, but I couldn't tell if he liked my singing or not. He didn't react, except for a millimeter lift of his eyebrows. When I finished, he smiled.

"You know what's interesting, Jennifer?" he said. "It's interesting that you can indeed sing. But it's more interesting that the song you've chosen happens to be a song that I remixed a year or two ago. I set it aside to wait for the right person to sing it. Here you are. How would you like to come back and sing for me instead of sweeping my floors?"

I couldn't believe my ears. I was too shocked to do more than meekly agree.

"Yes, yes, of course I'd like to sing instead of sweep floors," I said.

I walked out of his home in more of a daze than I'd arrived. Suddenly, my keeping-the-Benz fantasy had been replaced with the fantasy of owning ten Mercedes, reenrolling in dance classes, and finding someone to watch Saucy and Kitty as I traveled the world on my first-ever pop-not-porn tour.

When I reached my car, I lit a cigarette as Louie bounced onto the soft leather seat beside me.

"Girl! Look at you!" he said. "You're gonna be a fucking star! And you better quit those. But give me one first."

The next day, after recording at the studio with Gary and feeling like the fucking star that Louie insisted I'd be, I sat in the double-wide therapy trailer across from Dr. Drew for our final one-on-one session.

"So tell me about the interview in Malibu," he said.

I was surprised that he hadn't already heard about my new-found stardom.

"It was amazing, Dr. Drew!" I said. "I went in to interview for an assistant's position, and he wants me to do a record. A whole record! He's already talking about a record deal!"

As I relayed this information, the color drained from Dr. Drew's face. He adjusted his glasses and recrossed his legs before he spoke.

"Now, that isn't exactly what we had in mind," he said. "See, what's important right now is to become right-sized. Which means your ego isn't bigger than it should be, and it isn't smaller than it should be. It means that you have an appropriate job, working among other right-sized people. Now, I imagine that a record deal sounds very seductive, but I don't know that it's best for your recovery. It kind of feels like an extension of Penny Flame."

Dr. Drew was totally on point, as usual. When the possibility of a record deal came into play, all of the things that he'd worked hard to help me desire, which supported the four lessons I'd learned in the rehab and sober-living process, all went flying out the recording studio's window. My right-size goals had included the desire to return to school, form healthy friendships, find a job appropriate for my qualifications (which were none, a fact that was definitely humbling to my oversize Penny Flame ego), and get rid of the super-unaffordable car. As part of my new fantasy, I also began thinking about the men who would love me once I'd gained worldwide vocal stardom. I had even found myself thinking about one of the really hot crew guys from the show—Christopher—and how I could maybe seduce him with my smoky, jazzy sounds.

Christopher and I had run into each other at a random Venice Beach house party on the Fourth of July and, in a 100 percent harmless moment, had exchanged phone numbers. At the time I hadn't been drinking, smoking weed, or sexing it up with any guys, so it just felt like it was a good thing that I was gaining the number of another person who knew that I was a changed woman. Once I'd decided to become a pop star, though, that number suddenly became a golden opportunity. I was already planning to text him: "We should kick it once I'm outta here."

Dr. Drew had silenced me with his assessment of my pop-star plan. Now he brought me out of my Christopher daydream and back into the reality of the therapy trailer.

"Jennifer? Is this something you're going to pursue?" he said. "I hope you still intend on returning to school."

"Oh, yeah, I'm still going to school," I said. "I signed up for the New York Film Academy. It starts in September. I'm not sure if I'm going to pursue the singing thing."

As I spoke, I tried to stay present and in the moment.

"Well, good on the Film Academy," he said.

Then he paused and looked up, making eye contact and smiling.

"I think you'd do well at a four-year institution though, as well," he continued. "So think about that some more. You now know you can do anything. I know you'll make some good choices."

The words "four-year institution" definitely brought me down to real life as they reminded me of how badly I had fucked off during my academic career at San Diego State University.

"Dr. Drew? Can I have your number so I can check in with you?" I said. "Also, you know, like, if I need a letter of recommendation?"

I tried to sound confident, even though I was unsure if I really had the balls to text him, or to ask him to write me a letter of recommendation, or even to apply to school.

"Of course, I'd love to hear how you are doing," he said. "I know you will do well."

His concluding statement did more than just inspire me. It made me feel that I *had to do well.* And not as a pop star. It reignited my desire to continue down the path that he, Jill, and I had created. I was struck by everything this man had done for me.

There is no way I can let him down: people don't get chances like this, I thought.

"Thank you, Dr. Drew, for this chance—for everything," I said.

The bright lights of *Sober House,* with its heightened reality of constant therapy and living my life on TV, came to an end, and it felt like I blinked and was back in my apartment in Hollywood. It was as if my month on *Sober House* had never happened. My return to normal life meant that I was hiking Runyon Canyon with E-Deez and avoiding Duncan, whose e-mail had damaged our friendship; that I was over at Noah's beautiful mansion, having *Whale Wars* and Ben & Jerry's sleepovers, cuddling Saucy and Nutmeg between us in his king-size bed. The transition was abrupt but remarkably easy. I found myself thinking about how much smoother the comedown was from the second show than from the first.

It was a good thing that I had let go of my pop-star fantasy. When I finally heard the finished "Fever" recording, I knew my choir teacher had been right. My voice was good, but not good enough to sell millions of albums, even if we could Auto-Tune the cigarettes out of it. Gary still talked about signing a contract for a full album, but in the same way that the bright lights of reality television had faded so fast, I knew it was all a fantastic pipe dream.

Reality was healthier for me, but it was still harsh. I gave myself some tough love:

I'm not going to be a star. I'll be lucky if I can be a normal girl with realistic dreams. My best chance is to stay sober and get as honest about myself as I can. 'Cuz that shit was a big, fat lie. And lies aren't part of my life anymore.

PURSUING SOBRIETY ENTAILED quite a bit of work. Sexual and emotional sobriety felt more challenging than substance sobriety, because substance sobriety only required that I not drink/use. Sexual and emotional sobriety required the circle plan, which meant attention to the smallest details of my behavior in everyday life:

Am I checking out someone's tits because I feel uncomfortable about not knowing anyone at this meeting?

Am I talking about sex because I don't feel I bring anything of value to the conversation?

Sexual and emotional sobriety required 100 percent attention to 100 percent of my actions. On top of that, Dr. Reef Karim, my unofficial advisor/mentor since the end of *Sex Rehab,* who specialized in addiction and other compulsive behaviors, advised me to keep a masturbation log.

"Just write down a few quick sentences about what your feelings are," he said. "Are you horny? Are you upset? Are you sad?"

"Really?" I asked. "Every time I think about masturbating I have to write it down?"

"As much as you can," he said. "It'll be interesting to see what motivates you. How are the meetings going?"

He seemed to have superpowers in his ability to call me on shit, which was unlike any other person I'd ever met. I was totally incapable of bullshitting him, which was great for my recovery but totally sucked as it was happening.

"They're going," I said. "I mean, I go. But I wish there were more women in the rooms."

"What about the Love Program?" he said. "There are plenty of women there."

"Yeah, but I can't relate to loving people so much that I'm borderline obsessed," I said. "I relate to running away from people. Opposite problem."

The Love Program—where people chased after the object of their affections, often to their own detriment—was indeed the polar opposite of the Sex Program, which was a program for men, and a few women, with feelings of shame and low self-worth who were terrified that if we were seen as we truly were, we would be denied love or affection, and who used sex as a means to dull these fears.

As I drove home from our meeting through Beverly Hills, I received yet another call from the IRS. They'd called a few times about some Penny Flame money that I owed them from 2006, but I had been ignoring their calls entirely. So I called another mentor from one of my substance programs.

"What the fuck do I do?" I asked. "They keep calling me!"

"Dude, everybody owes money to the IRS," she said. "It's their money. Stop thinking of it as yours. Stop complaining. You made some money from that show thingie, didn't you? So pay the man. Stop bein' a little bitch."

I had her on speaker phone, with my windows down. As she reprimanded me while I sat at a stoplight, I quickly rolled up my windows, fearing that the person next to me would hear the financial trouble I'd caused myself and judge me for driving this car they now knew I couldn't afford.

"But it's like five Gs!" I said. "Five Gs is a shit-ton of money right now!"

"Look," she said, "the IRS will only quit calling you if you *pay* them *their* money. So don't be the old you that runs away from everything, and that's afraid of everything. Be the *you* right now.

Today. Stop whining, go to the bank, pay the man, and stop living in fear."

My substance mentor was a genius, but each time I thanked her for the advice, her response was completely humble.

"It's only what *my* mentor told *me*," she said.

I wished to become more like her: to live with her humility and grace instead of my fear and shame.

BOTH MENTORS—DR. REEF and the substance program girl—had asked that I compose lists, which I have always loved doing anyway. Dr. Reef's masturbation list seemed like it'd be more fun, though, so I started that list first. The first entry into my masturbation log was:

> 7:03 a.m.—motivation: awake.
> 8:13 a.m.—motivation: coffee brewing and bored.
> 9:40 a.m.—motivation: frustrated that Hulu only keeps the five most recent episodes for viewing.
> 10:23 a.m.—motivation: anger, because I didn't have a television to take up my time.
> Noon—motivation: because I just hiked Runyon and there are super-good-looking people on that hike.

And so forth, and so on. By the end of the first day, I'd taken up an entire sheet of college-lined eight-by-ten paper, and I quickly saw the ridiculousness of the motivations behind my desire for self-pleasure. It was all over the place. Out of the nearly twenty different times that I'd wanted to masturbate during the day, only once was it because I was actually in the mood for sex. Realizing how superficial my other motives were made it impossible for me to follow through with getting off, and so I found myself writing in the log and going on to do something else instead.

Ultimately, when I brought my list back to Dr. Reef, I had to laugh at myself and my inability to deal with normal, everyday stillness, which was the quintessential problem for me.

"If I'm bored, I want to masturbate, if I'm happy, masturbate, sad, masturbate—it's all such silliness, I don't even want to do it anymore," I said.

He nodded and jotted things down while maintaining eye contact with me.

"Good, keep doing it."

I don't know if he realized how much the log had ruined my enjoyment of compulsive masturbation, because after ninety days sober from substances, and only having pleasured myself two or three times during those three months, the clearness with which I was now able to see my prior actions was actually a bit disturbing. But I continued to keep track, even though we didn't discuss it again.

Next up was the two-part list that my substance mentor had asked that I make, which I went through with her first. She had given me the assignment one day as we sat at her kitchen table, talking about life and the anger festering inside of me, and she told me to make a list of everything I resented.

When I began the list, I started broad and then worked my way into specifics. And when I revisited her kitchen table three weeks later, I had a ten-page taped-together list that resembled the lists of girls' jobs that Derek used to keep in his office.

"Wow, very thorough," she said.

I started reading.

"Men. All of them."

"Women. All of them as well."

"Hold on, kid," she said. "We have to talk about *why* before we move on."

She smiled and leaned back in her chair.

"Why do you resent every man in the world?" she asked.

"Because they are predictable," I said, stone-faced and positive about the absolute correctness of what I said. "They only want sex, and they use me."

"Really? Every man in this world only wants sex from you?" she asked. "No man has ever surprised you? They *all* use you?"

As she talked, she went to the cupboards for two glasses.

"Well, no, not all of them," I said. "But I think most of them."

"Have you met most of them?" she said, laughing as she dropped ice cubes into the glasses.

I looked at my list and realized it would be a long night.

"No, no, I haven't," I said. "But I feel like most of them have met me."

"Wow! So every man in the world knows who you are, little ego monster?" she asked. "And they all want to have sex with you and use you? Use you for what, may I ask? You can't even pay the IRS, so apparently they can't use you for money."

She filled the glasses with water and walked back to the table, an ear-to-ear grin on her face as she sat down.

"Okay, no, not every man knows who I am," I said, succumbing to the obvious logic of what she said. "And the IRS is further down the list, but we'll get to that. Fine, I see your point. But that doesn't stop me from feeling that they want to use me."

I traced a straight line in the moisture on my glass from the top to the bottom.

"So, whose fault is that?" she asked.

"What do you mean, 'whose fault'?" I asked, a little pissed that she'd question my feelings like that.

"I mean, why do you think that every man thinks of you as *sex*?" she asked. "Because that's what you're arguing, right? That they all want you for sex, and only sex, and that's why you are resentful of them all?"

She sipped from her glass and leaned forward, elbows on the table. I searched my mind for the answer, and because it didn't occur to me then that my dad had told me that's how life worked when I was all of twelve years old, the only thing I could think to say was more of a question than an answer.

"Men only want sex from me because I was a porn star?" I said.

"Who made that choice?" she said with a smile.

"Me," I said, looking at my hands.

I suddenly realized where this ten-page list pointed: right back to me.

"Did you give them any other thing to like about you?" she asked. "Besides being a sex object?"

"Fuck, you're telling me that every resentment on this list is because of something that *I* did?" I asked.

I wanted to crumple the list up in my hands, not because it was bullshit, but because she was right. It was ten pages of misdirected anger.

"So, what's the next right action?" she asked.

"Like, what can I do to not feel like they only want sex from me?" I asked. "I guess present them with a person who is not super-oversexualized. The action would be to present a woman who is respectable and not a mega-whore."

I drank from the glass after I said the word "whore," needing to wash it from my tongue, as it was part of a language I hadn't used since I quit porn.

"'Whore' is a pretty ugly way of thinking of yourself," she said. "Let's not do that anymore, okay?"

She smiled at me.

"Next?" she continued. "You had said women?"

"Yeah, because they aren't trustworthy," I said, also fairly positive the statement was a mere fact, even after the moment of self-discovery I'd just had.

"Do you trust me?" she asked. "Or Jill?"

"Yeah, but you don't count," I laughed.

"Why the fuck don't I count as a woman?" she laughed back at me.

I saw her point.

"Okay, fine, specific women can't be trusted," I said.

"Who, may I ask, should not be trusted?" she said, leaning in as if she already knew the answer.

"Me: I shouldn't be trusted because I'm a liar and thief and a whore," I said. "No. Ex-whore. No. Ex–porn star slash woman who sells sex for money. God, you're such a bitch. Next resentment."

I tried to move forward, but she frowned and stopped me.

"Really? You really think you're a liar, a thief, and an ex-prostitute?" she asked. "That's how you see yourself? We need to work on that."

"Whoa, I was never a *prostitute*," I said, suddenly proud of the distinction that I'd made between porn and prostitution.

"You said you sold sex for money, and that's prostitution, right?" she inquired gently, somehow knowing what a sensitive subject this would be.

"Yeah, but it's different," I said, gripping the cool glass. "I pay taxes."

"Obviously you don't pay taxes, or the IRS wouldn't be calling you!" she laughed.

Again her point was clear.

"Fine, I'll fucking pay the IRS the five thousand," I said. "Fuck!"

We continued through my ten pages, covering everything from San Diego State University, for being a party school and too scary to return to, all the way down to people who ride bicycles on the road like they are cars, because they are in my way when I'm driving my supersweet car.

All the list did was reveal how ego-driven my resentments were—how everything I hated about other people was really something I hated about myself.

It took us two hours before I came to the final resentment, which was the obvious conclusion of my list.

My biggest resentment was: me.

I resented myself for being afraid to love anyone; for being unable to say "I love you" in the mirror; for needing help; for squandering every dollar I made in porn. For abusing drugs; for being obsessed with perfection; for being a compulsive cheater/liar/masturbator; for making idiotic decisions while intoxicated. I resented myself for failing at college; for wasting eight years of precious life in a business I'd ultimately be discarded from like yesterday's headlines. Most of all, I resented myself for cutting my dad out of my life for twelve long years. I resented each misspent year that I couldn't get back. By the time I was finished reading her this list about how much I hated myself, I was sobbing uncontrollably, because all of it explained why I made so much effort to destroy everything around me that was good.

"We can do the fears list next week," she said, giving me a big hug.

She let me cry until my tears stopped. When I got home, remarkably, I didn't want to masturbate, or watch television, or do anything except sleep.

It was the best sleep I'd had in a very long time.

———

THE SECOND PART of the ten-page list was a list of fears, and after telling a few of my more entertaining anxieties to Dr. Reef and Jill—who both told me I joked about my fears in order to deflect away from their seriousness—I read them to my substance sponsor. She asked that I differentiate between the real and imagined.

"So, after you read this list, you have to agree to only be afraid of things that are happening at that precise moment," she said. "The real fears. Like, if you are in the process of drowning, you are allowed to fear drowning. Also, no fearing things that have already happened, because that's living in the past."

At first, I didn't quite understand the line she'd drawn in the sand.

"Deal, but most of my fears are real, and happening right now," I said. "So here goes."

I looked down at my long list and took a deep breath before beginning.

"I'm afraid of being a failure," I said. "Of never finding love, and drowning, and sometimes I'm afraid of heights. I'm afraid of being fat and out of shape, of Saucy or Kitty dying, and of being homeless, broke, and forgotten."

I lifted my eyes to hers, and she nodded her approval, so I continued.

"I'm afraid of being kidnapped and beaten," I said. "Of cancer, dark alleys, being raped again, and microwave ovens. I am afraid of being hurt, being stuck in the desert with no water, and of my brother dying in a war. I'm afraid of choking, small places, and being disliked. I'm terrified I'll end up back in porn, and that I don't have anything more valuable to offer than my vagina. I'm afraid of being laughed at, my family dying, of third-degree burns, of relapsing, and that my paintings all look like shit."

I stopped to take another breath, because I was getting down to the nitty-gritty.

"I'm afraid I'm not special," I said. "I'm afraid I'm mediocre, and that mediocrity is the best I can do."

Tears filled my eyes as I read the list to her, and I realized that not a single one of these fears was happening at this precise moment in time.

"Sounds like a lot of wasted energy," she said. "Imagine what you could accomplish if you stopped being afraid of all these imaginary things and started living?"

She was right. While there were some fears I felt unwilling to let go of, I knew it was time to stop being afraid of being human.

"Okay, next step is to go back home and make a list of people you've harmed," she said. "It's probably going to look like your resentment list. . . . Just so you know."

She patted me on the shoulder.

A fucking ten-page novella? Try a hundred-page novel, I thought.

Yet, I agreed to the task, because I'd told Dr. Drew, Jill, Dr.

Reef, my dad—everyone in my life—that I'd do anything to change everything. That also meant that I'd made the promise to myself as well. And I intended to keep it.

———

AT THE END of July, I received an e-mail from a professor at Harvard University interested in hiring me as a guest lecturer. He found me through my blog and said he'd previously interviewed Sasha Grey, another adult-film star, and was contemplating writing a paper about adult-film stars but wanted a more thoughtful and less numbed perspective than Sasha had provided. We sent letters back and forth and became friends over the course of a few weeks, so when I mentioned to him my desire for a New York adventure, he said he would make his way down from Boston and we could have lunch. I bought an airplane ticket to the Big Apple and headed in to see Dr. Reef and tell him the good news.

"I've been invited to speak at Harvard!" I said. "Sick, huh? He's still gotta set some things up, but it looks like an almost done deal."

As I talked, Dr. Reef scribbled so quickly on his papers that I could barely follow his hand moving.

"Harvard, huh?" he said. "So what's the plan?"

"Well, I'm gonna meet the professor in New York to talk about a paper he might write, and he's gonna try to line up the lecture for the spring," I said while searching for gum in my purse.

"New York? Isn't there a guy you like in New York?" he asked, remembering that I'd mentioned the crew guy Christopher in a previous session.

I had thought a little about Christopher, and the thoughts were well documented in my masturbation log, but rarely did I act upon *those* thoughts.

"Yeah, but it's not like we're gonna *do* anything!" I said.

Scribbles and eye contact.

"No? Okay good. Well, let's make a plan, then. I want you to write a behavioral contract covering your time there. You said this guy is cute? That sounds like you're planning on doing *something*."

Fuck, I thought.

"I don't wanna do *that,*" I said. "I mean the contract. I will, but I don't really want to."

"Why don't you want to?" he asked, smiling. "It's the same as your circle plan, just a redefined commitment."

"I said I'll do it," I said. "Fuck! All these lists and plans and contracts! Fine. I'll do it."

AFTER TWO WEEKS of avoiding it, and only a few hours before my last session with Dr. Reef pre–New York, my friend Angel called me to find out if I'd written my contract.

"You haven't done it, little Pie, and I know you haven't written it because you would have read it to me if you had," she said.

"Fine! Jesus! I'll write the goddamn contract!" I yelled into the phone.

Busting out my Parliaments, paper, and a pen, I got myself ready.

"We'll do it right now," I said. "Okay? Happy?"

"Read it out loud as you write, Pie," she said, laughing even more. "Then I'll believe you."

I read the contract out loud as I wrote, using my most serious voice:

"This contract applies to all men seen, and pertains to the sobriety that I, Jennifer Ketcham, wish to maintain. This contract is to confirm and establish a behavioral code to which I must adhere during the course of my New York visit."

"Such a little lawyer, Pie!" she said, causing us both to laugh.

"Hush," I said. "Okay, as it pertains to my sexual addiction, certain behaviors and actions will put me in a lesser position than my current. This contract is not a punishment, it is merely the code by which I wish to live, and by contracting myself, I am taking a step further in my sobriety."

This final bit hopefully provided the reminder I would need if I found myself in some sexy, hottish trouble.

"Pie, get to the point," Angel urged.

"The following behaviors/actions are in my inner circle and should be considered unhealthy for me and my recovery, and thus be considered a relapse: sex (including but not limited to oral), drugs, alcohol, kissing, making out, ass-smackery of any kind, and lip smoochies. The following behaviors are in my middle circle and should be considered slippery territory: kissing on the cheek, handholding, alone time, and excessive knee grazing. The following behaviors are totally acceptable: arm linking, flirting, hugging hello or good-bye, and occasional knee grazing."

"You better tell Christopher about this contract, Pie," Angel said.

I wanted to yell at her, but she had a point.

"Fine, I will inform my man companion of this contract, so he is aware of the commitment I've made to myself," I said. "I have 127 days sober, emotional and substance, and I'd like to come home with more."

My biggest qualm with informing Christopher about my contract wasn't that it revealed my sexual sobriety—he knew and had filmed that whole thing—it was that he didn't know how hot I thought he was. Reading this contract to him would be a total reveal of how high he scored on my hot-o-meter. The jig would most definitely be up.

"Sign it, Pie, sign and date it," Angel laughed.

I couldn't help but laugh with her.

"Who does this?" I said. "Who needs a behavioral contract to behave like a fuckin' lady?"

"You do," Angel said in her matter-of-fact way.

I knew, as was almost always the case, she was totally right.

13

"WHEN I EXAMINE MYSELF AND MY METHODS OF THOUGHT,
I COME TO THE CONCLUSION THAT THE GIFT OF FANTASY
HAS MEANT MORE TO ME THAN MY TALENT FOR ABSORBING
POSITIVE KNOWLEDGE."
—ALBERT EINSTEIN

New York in August feels like freshly fucked sheets, and I was excited to have an adventure in the hot city streets. Before I hopped on my plane to LaGuardia Airport, I had a short talk with Christopher, who had agreed to be my tour guide during my brief vacation.

"So Reef had me write this behavioral contract, like he's worried I'm gonna bang you," I said to him over the phone while sitting at Los Angeles International Airport.

Sexual innuendos had been designated as slippery territory on my behavioral contract, but direct, open statements had not, and so I'd decided to just go for it.

I read it to him quickly, rushing over the slippery stuff like flirting and knee grazing, hoping that he wouldn't hear what I was saying.

"This doc thinks I'm a bad man?" he said, his accent even

thicker than I remembered it. "Like I ain't gotta hawt? Like ima take youse out here, after all I's seen you do, and just do you like that? Naw. That ain't me."

"Yeah, I told him you were the respectable sort," I said. "But I think it's for me. Not you."

After I hung up my phone, glad that my conversation with Christopher was out of the way, I turned my focus to alcohol, and the fact that I wasn't allowed to drink any.

How the fuck do people fly without drinking?

Most every flight I'd taken as an adult had felt like time travel: I drank at the airport from which I was departing, and then woke up at a new airport. Magic.

The flight to New York City was going to be much longer sober.

ONCE I ARRIVED in New York, my worries shifted once again.

How do people explore a new city without drinking?

In Los Angeles, with its millions of familiar things to do that didn't require drinking—hiking, yoga, meetings—I barely ever thought about having a drink. In New York, it was all I thought about—until, that is, I saw Christopher in all his tall, skinny cuteness.

I'm either gonna need a nice cold beer or a good hard penis.

"Good flight?" he asked as we climbed into what I soon found out was his mom's Mercedes.

"Quick, what's on the agenda?" I asked.

Just like that, he whisked me away to the city, pointing out interesting buildings and bridges as we passed.

"Can we go to the Marcy Projects?" I asked.

"Why tha fuck ya wanna go there?" he laughed. "You fuckin' think you're fuckin' Jay-Z?"

"I'm not fuckin' anyone, son," I responded in my best gangsta

New York voice. "Just show me shit that is off the map. That's what I want."

He shook his head. "Yo, you crazy," he said. "I'll take ya there, yeah, but then we gonna go someplace nice. Go see some fuckin' art."

He said the word "art" like it had an *h* in it—"ahrt "—and I made fun of him throughout the rest of the day, from the projects to the Metropolitan Museum.

Humor will be the best way to secure this deal, I thought, still intent on fucking him, even though I knew it was against the rules of my contract.

But once we finished our tour of the city, he dropped me off at my hotel.

"I'll be back out here tahmarrah," he said, transferring my bags from his trunk to the bellhop. As I rode up in the elevator with the bellhop, I tried to make sense of what had just happened.

Man, this guy doesn't wanna fuck at all? Serious?

As soon as I got settled into my closet-size hotel room, I called my dad for a pep talk.

"I don't understand the vibe I get from him," I said, telling him about Christopher. "I always understand the vibe. I think I'm broken, Dad."

"You aren't broken, pumpkin," he said. "Maybe he saw you change and he actually respects you. Maybe he wants you to succeed."

"Yeah, but really?" I said. "I mean, really. How am I supposed to not flirt with him?"

It felt like a strange question to be asking my dad, but I didn't know who else to ask at that point.

"Well, what do you want to do out there?" he asked. "Why are you in New York?"

"I'm visiting the Harvard professor," I said. "We're having lunch. That's why."

This was part lie and part truth. I would be having lunch with the professor, but I couldn't deny a nagging feeling that the real reason I'd flown across the country was to try and seduce this dude.

"Focus on that, Jennifer," my dad said. "Guys will come and go. Besides, while he's not driving his mom's car, he's riding the bus! Just think of how sexy a bus rider is!"

Dad started busting up, well aware that I'd soon be a bus rider as well. I let him laugh, not mentioning my inability—after twenty-six years—to focus on anything other than the guy, or to imagine a world where sex wasn't the number one priority.

"Thanks, Dad," I said. "I'm getting off the phone now."

———

I WAS NERVOUS about my lunch with the Harvard professor. I hadn't met any strangers as Jennie. Meeting people as Penny had always felt safe, because there was a name and an attitude to hide behind. I covered my face with the same heavy foundation that I once wore as war paint for scenes, and dressed carefully. But beyond that, I had nothing except for my constant cigarette. And I wanted, badly, to convince this man that I was capable of a speaking gig at Harvard; it would be the first item on my first résumé outside of porn and I hoped it would lead to inspirational speaking gigs at colleges across the country.

Somehow I managed to get through it, even when I'd discovered that the upscale outdoor café where we were meeting was both anti-smoking and anti-cheap; even after I admitted that my only teaching experience was dick-sucking classes at the bondage/discipline/sadism/masochism convention, Dark Odyssey, in D.C.; and even after I was forced out of my Los Angeles recovery cocoon for the first time when he drank two beers over lunch. At least when it came time to discussing porn, I found that I felt at ease talking about this stuff with him.

"So the paper I wrote, on Sasha, it was good but I didn't feel like she was really . . . honest?" he said, referring to his earlier interview with porn star Sasha Grey. "It felt like she was holding back. As if there was something to the story that I wasn't getting."

"She's young," I said. "It took me a long time to realize that I'd turned off emotionally. And even then, I'm sure if I'd kept having sex and not taken the rehab break, I'd still be numb. I have no doubt that if you tried to interview me when I was her age, I would have presented the same emotionally void girl that she does. . . . But I would have been more fun."

"What happens?" he asked. "Inside? That makes it viable? Is it abuse? I keep trying to imagine a singular reason, and I know there isn't, but could there be some underlying common denominator?"

"I don't know," I said. "I never thought I'd sell sex. But you put one foot in the pool, even a toe, next thing you're fucking swimming."

It was apparent from his expression that this wasn't the kind of conversation he'd had with Sasha.

"There's constant attention and validation," I continued. "And you surround yourself with people that are doing the exact same thing. It makes it easy to turn off any inner monologue wishing for more from life. Easier, anyway. I don't know that I can pinpoint one precise thing, though, like the emotional off switch. My mom certainly wishes I could. She's fairly convinced all my mistakes are her fault, no matter how many times I say they're not."

I realized that I wasn't nervous anymore, and it almost felt like a given when, during a post-lunch walk in Central Park, he made up his mind about the speaking gig.

"I'd really love for you to come to Harvard to speak," he said. "I think it would be incredibly interesting for the students. I'll see what I can line up once I get home."

When I heard this, I felt like hugging him. But I knew that would be totally inappropriate, because we'd just met a few hours earlier, and I assumed that Harvard professors are pretty good about maintaining personal boundaries.

"That would be so awesome," I said. "I'm down."

I tried to act cool, as if I were invited to speak at Harvard every weekend.

"Besides, it'd be sweet to teach with my clothes on," I continued. "Not that I'd be teaching. Just speaking."

As I corrected myself, I felt silly for presuming that I had anything to teach anyone. He smiled kindly and patted me on the shoulder.

"You'll do fine," he said.

We shook hands and parted ways. On the way back to my hotel, amped up at the thought of maybe having just lined up the first real thing I could put down on my professional résumé, I called Christopher and we confirmed our plans to hit a baseball game the next day.

When I returned to my hotel, I decided to spend the evening working on the list of people I'd hurt, the second part of the two-part list that my substance mentor had asked me to write. I plopped down on the hotel bed with a pen and paper, ready for some truth, not realizing until I wrote it that it was going to be the longest list of all.

THE METS GAME the following day was awesome. Still in try-to-seduce-Christopher mode, I wore a black backless top and low-slung jeans topped with my A's hat, which Christopher promptly replaced with a Mets hat the second he saw me. Somewhere around the bottom of the third inning, as we were walking from our seats to the smoking section, someone in the stands yelled out: "Penny Flame!"

Christopher threw his arm around my shoulders and led me away before I had time to process how it felt to be recognized as a person I no longer wished to be.

After the game, we headed back to Brooklyn, where Christopher's best friend, Vinnie, lived.

This is the kind of neighborhood I could rock, I thought. *Vinnie is cute too.*

We fixed ourselves up, I threw on some Saturday-night-special-sexy-attire that I had hiding in my bag, and decided to hit the town, first to a bar where Christopher had the homie hookup, and then to see my friend DJ Odi, who was spinning in the warehouse district somewhere out in Brooklyn.

By the time we got over to Odi's club, Christopher was obliterated. He'd been drinking steadily since the game, after starting with beer and moving on to the hard stuff. I stood at the bar with Vinnie, looking super-fly in a little red dress, when Christopher did an awkward little stumble walk over to me.

"You think Odi can get some yay?" Christopher asked me.

Vinnie, real quick, tried to shut him down.

"Man, naw, not tonight, not cool," Vinnie said.

I agreed but felt the need to please after the fun day Christopher had shown me.

"I can ask him," I said.

"Naw, he doesn't need it," Vinnie said, shaking his head. "Don't get him anything you don't want to get him."

It hadn't occurred to me that I had a choice about whether or not to find him drugs. I felt like the unspoken deal we'd made, with the awesome game and the first club he'd taken me to, meant that I should do something to help him out in exchange.

"I'll just ask," I told Vinnie and Christopher.

I walked over to Odi.

"Can you get any blow?" I said into Odi's ear. "He's fuckin' waste-o."

He looked at me closely.

"Aren't you sober?" he asked.

"Yeah, but I'm not getting any for me," I said. "For him."

As I nodded my head in Christopher's direction, Odi stepped up close to me and put his hands on my shoulders.

"No, Jen," he said. "And he shouldn't have asked you."

"He's fuckin' blasted, O," I said. "He doesn't know. I said I'd ask. I asked, and no is a totally acceptable answer."

I kissed Odi on the cheek, thankful that he had the courage to say that Christopher's request wasn't okay, even when I did not. I wasn't upset with Christopher. I figured it was just a result of how drunk he was. As we left the club and crossed the deserted, warehouse-lined street, it occurred to me, however, that his drunkenness might be just what I needed to seduce him. After we all climbed into Vinnie's car, I sent Christopher, who was sitting in the backseat, a text: "You can spend the night at my hotel. I will behave."

When I glanced back to where he was sitting, he shook his head no and looked away.

How much of a jerk do I have to be to turn a drunk guy off? I thought.

"Vinnie, you don't have to drive me," I said. "I can sleep on your couch. I don't want you to have to go out of your way so late at night."

It might have seemed like a morally upright offer on my part, but really, I was still thinking about the possibility of seducing drunk-ass Christopher.

"No, you can have the bed," Vinnie said. "Me and him will sleep on the pullout couch."

Fuck, fuck, fuck, I thought.

"Thanks, Vinnie," I said.

We drove back to his house in quasi-silence.

Once we got home and decided that I would indeed be taking the bed, I threw on a pair of Vinnie's sweatpants and climbed in. I lay there for twenty minutes, my body stretched out in a way that I knew it looked best, on my side, legs split ever so gently, covers barely covering me, mind racing, hoping that Christopher—or Vinnie—would get the urge to snuggle.

Is he coming in here? I thought. *How much longer am I going to stay awake, hoping he comes in?*

I'd left the door ajar, and suddenly the floor in the hallway creaked, letting me know that someone was walking around out there. I waited eagerly, wondering which guy it would be and what would happen when he came in. Then Vinnie walked to the bedroom door, turned off the hallway light, shut the door, and returned to the couch.

As I accepted the fact that I would remain alone that night and surrendered to sleep, I was unsure of whether I was more frustrated that I'd failed in the art of seduction, or that I'd chosen such respectable, pro-female men friends to hang out with.

What the fuck is wrong with me? I thought. *Why am I intentionally trying to fuck this up? Why am I so desperate for someone to be with me? Why can't I just be alone? Why can't I stand myself?*

The next morning, after I had returned to the safety of my hotel room, I tried to rinse off the shame of being an idiot in a strange town, but feelings don't simply wash down the drain.

Fool, I thought. *You fucking fool. Almost fucked up all you worked for. Time to get serious and stop looking for loopholes like knee grazing and snuggling. Time to stop sabotaging yourself and using sexiness and flirty time to distract you from the course.*

When I got out of the shower, I retrieved the half-finished list of people I had hurt and decided to finish it, then and there, while I still had the motivation and drive to take the task seriously.

Time to do whatever it takes to be someone else, I thought. *Time to be the new Jennie.*

THE LIST OF people I'd hurt was proving to be a chance to take an in-depth look at the behavior that had gotten me in trouble in the first place. It clearly displayed how arrogant my ideas about life were, how I constantly wished to control people, places, and things, and how I used the subtle tactics of manipulation and sexuality to do so. It all began with my family, and then, from there, I worked my way through each of my girlfriends, my boyfriends, my semi-boyfriends, and then on to broader relationships, like acquaintances and institutions. The list ended with me and with the damage that I had done to myself on a daily basis, from the way that I thought, to the way that I acted. Out of all of them, this was the most difficult entry to write. All together, the list was over ten pages, and once I had finished writing it, I realized that I had a ton of apologies to deliver and, even when I did, not a lot of hope of being forgiven. Even more than that, I had to change how I lived now in some pretty fundamental ways.

In order to right my selfish behavior toward my father, I committed to living differently, to asking for help only if I really needed it, and to making a major effort to nurture our young and budding relationship. I knew I couldn't make up for the time we had lost, and so the new memories had to be extra special. They had to be real.

To repair the unrealistic expectations I had had of my mother and my siblings, and the unfair resentment this had caused me to have toward them, I committed to accepting and loving them for who they were and allowing them to know and love me as I really was.

To fix my damaged relationships with my girlfriends, I had to acknowledge where I'd failed by lying, choosing men and cock over them, and refusing to share my real feelings, even when they were open and honest with me. And I had to become a good friend, listen attentively, and risk being vulnerable.

I owed each of the men I had ever dated an apology, making amends face-to-face if they'd allow it. But the thought of seeing some of them made me sick to my stomach. I could deal with the hatred that I imagined each of them felt toward me—in my mind. But the thought of actually having to face it directly, sitting across a table from them, looking into their eyes, made me feel like I'd crumble beneath the weight of my mistakes and the guilt I now felt about the insensitive ways in which I had left all of them. Seeing them would make the hurt I'd caused them real. It seemed impossible to deal with all of this, but I knew that it could be a good thing too.

Maybe, if I do this, I can understand why I should never do it again, I thought.

Finally, after working through my tear-splashed laundry list of mistakes and fuckups, I came to the biggest fuckup of all.

In what ways have I caused myself pain? I asked. *And how can I make it right again?*

I wept as I wrote, wetness leaving my eyes and blurring the words I scribbled on the page:

> *I forbid myself normal, human feelings. I forbid myself to be imperfect—perfectly imperfect, as Jill says—and I hated everything I did that wasn't breathtaking. I sold my body for money, my emotions for a Mercedes and a three-bedroom house I didn't even own. I refused to imagine a life in which I was valued for my thoughts and opinions instead of tits and vagina. I lived in fear of everything that could go wrong, and couldn't see how many things often go right. I didn't think I deserved to be happy. I was ashamed that I could experience jealousy and envy, angry that I felt love, that I could fall in love and not allow myself to be loved in return. I didn't think I deserved to be loved because I didn't think I was lovable. I've caused myself pain by choosing a profession in which there is no room for spiritual growth, no space for artistic expression, no positive outcome for years of devotion. I've pigeonholed myself into being a sex worker. I've become a woman whose only way of relating to others is by virtue of her sexuality. I hurt myself by believing that I am a one-dimensional fictional character by agreeing with my fans who believe porn stars are always and only horny, that sex is the one thing that constitutes who I am and who I can be.*

I read and reread the words I had never let myself think before. And then I tried to figure out how to make amends to myself.

How do I make it right? How do I begin loving myself? How do I become convinced that I am worth more than a thousand dollars a day—that I am, in fact, priceless? How do I undo the years of trauma I've caused myself, trauma I didn't even realize I was causing until I stopped?

I looked over at my face in my bathroom mirror.

"You've already started, Jennie," I whispered. "Jill says 'Acknowledgment is the first step.' Then comes the change."

I splashed cold water on my face, as if it would clean away all of the self-hatred I'd just outlined. I was amazed at how easily the ways in which I'd caused damage came spewing forth, and how difficult it seemed to change myself or my life.

I stared at the droplets of clean water, still present on my freckled cheeks.

It's progress, I thought. *There was a time when you couldn't admit to hurting at all. Admitting that you've hurt yourself is a good step for today. Just worry about today.*

I grabbed a washcloth, pressed the soft towel to my face, and then folded it gently and left it on the sink. I decided to pack my belongings for the trip home. Making my list had brought up so many painful memories and thoughts, but I was more focused than I'd felt in a long time. I knew exactly what I had to do to move forward. I had to face the past.

A MONTH AFTER my trip to seduce Christopher, Dan, a good friend who was one of the organizers of the EXXXOTICA Expo in New Jersey, called to ask if I wished to make one last appearance that year. The girls generally enjoy the EXXXOTICA Expo—a spin-off of the Adult Video News Expo—more than AVN because at AVN they can only make money signing autographs, but in New Jersey they can also sell DVDs, which brings in additional money. Some of the girls—at both shows—also choose to make additional money on the side, and not by selling DVDs, either. At the Jersey show, if a girl is staying at a small hotel in New Jersey, it's safe to assume that she is only selling DVDs and eight-by-ten photographs. If a girl is staying in New York, though, there is a good chance that she is on the island to hook, and that her appearance at the Jersey expo is merely to produce the illusion that she's in town to sign autographs for her fans.

Many of the girls in porn sideline as hookers—"escorts who do privates," in the lexicon of the San Fernando Valley—and it always made me laugh to watch girls show up to the expo superlate, excusing their tardiness by saying the taxi driver got lost. Of course, everyone in the biz knew that a private from the previous night had run long and she had overslept. At $1,000 an hour, many girls brought in crazy money from privates that "ran late." I had always thought it beneficial to stay up on who was hooking and who was not, as such extracurricular activity added additional sexual partners to the girls' tests that would not be accounted for through AIM. But during this, my final year at the expo, hookers and johns were irrelevant to me.

The only thought on my mind was the plastic tubs in my closet that were filled with stripper heels and plastic skirts, and the hundreds of DVDs that had once sat in the dirt of the Malibu hills waiting to be burned for the entertainment of reality TV viewers. At the time of the bonfire, I had calmed down enough to throw a few of the more worthless things into the flames so that Production would get their special "cathartic" TV moment. And now I wanted nothing more than to sell the rest and be rid of them forever. But I also knew to be cautious. I made sure I could bring Angel as my sober companion before I agreed to attend.

Then I began to plan for what would be the final showing of Penny Flame. I pulled out the tubs of porn stuff I'd hidden in the closet after the Malibu hills breakdown. As I sorted through the first fully stuffed tub, I called Angel to discuss our upcoming trip.

"I got Dan to buy you a ticket," I said.

"To Hookerfest?" she said, laughing. "Sounds fun! I've had, like, four other girls ask me if I'll be there. They want me to come to the City to do their face before they do privates. Silly hookers."

I smiled, sitting down on the hardwood floor in my living room and lighting a cigarette. The DVDs were covered in Penny Flame's face and body, which I no longer thought of as my own and found hard to look at. As I began to delve into the clothing tub, filled with feather boas and various feature dancing outfits, the scent of strip clubs that had been trapped in the cheap fabric came wafting forth. The smell was intoxicating, as pungent as the memories they stirred.

Packing the suitcase quickly morphed into what felt like funeral preparations for Penny Flame. Every single piece of physical evidence I had that proved my involvement in pornography, strip clubs, and the seedy underworld of sex had been locked away in those tubs. And as long as they had sat in my closet, I didn't ever really have to look at what I'd done for those eight years. But when I brought everything out into the living room, where I surveyed at least one hundred DVDs, thousands of eight-by-ten slicks, dildos, vibrators, skimpy clothes, and wigs, I remembered why I'd felt it necessary to hide all of this away and try to avoid what I still felt like all of this proved about me.

I ran upstairs and knocked on Deezy's door, a pack of cigarettes in one hand. After taking one look at me, he knew something was wrong and went to his freezer for the ice cream. Then he brought an empty ashtray to the couch for me and sat down.

"You okay, buddy?" he asked.

"No, no, I don't think I am," I said, smoking my third Parliament in a row. "I was down there trying to pack for Jersey and I started to break down."

No matter how hard I tried, it seemed I couldn't stop crying.

"Once I sell off this merchandise, there will be nothing in my home physically connecting me to that alter ego," I said. "Once the closet is empty, the only thought that will remain of a woman it took eight years to perfect will be in my head. Destroying my entire career only took six months, and selling all my stuff will only earn me a few thousand dollars."

"That's good, isn't it?" he asked.

"Yeah, but I can't get over the idea of selling off my entire career."

The cigarettes continued to smoke themselves as I wept, unable to be anything but openly wounded at this point.

"Your feelings are totally valid," Deez offered. "This is a tough process. You have to go easy on yourself. Penny protected you for a long time, and it's understandable that you'd be sad to see her go. But now Jennie is taking care of things."

His words touched me so deeply that I had to leave and be by myself for a while. Although I appreciated his empathy, I couldn't stand to think that what he'd said was actually true. I still wasn't sure that I could take care of myself.

I went back to my apartment to finish packing. And then I was ready for what would be Penny Flame's last dance.

OUTSIDE NEWARK LIBERTY International Airport, our friend Camilla swooped us up curbside, and as the three of us girls drove down the coast to her beach house, a few blocks from the Jersey Shore, we ate pizza that she'd brought for us and talked about the convention ahead.

"You sure you're okay with all this, Penny?" Camilla said. "Fuck. I mean Jennie. Sorry."

I couldn't fault her for her flub, because even though we'd been friends for four years, we rarely called each other by our real names. I smiled and meant it, feeling cleansed from my waterworks display in Deezy's apartment the night before.

"Yeah, I'm good," I said.

The next morning, Camilla and I painted on our porn star

masks. We used Make Up For Ever foundation to create a flawless porcelain finish; high- and low-lighted our cheekbones; accentuated our eyes with M-A-C eyeliner and sultry fake eyelashes that we stuck to our lids with clear, strong glue; and brushed our lips with rose-colored lip gloss. Then, we threw our heavy bags, filled with DVDs, eight-by-tens, and other schwag, onto our backs to lug out to Camilla's dude's giant truck.

As we drove north to Edison, where the convention was being held, Camilla made a confession.

"You're so lucky, Jennie," she said.

I laughed.

"Why?" I asked.

"You got the rehab show and everything," she said. "If you didn't, you woulda been stuck forever, just like the rest of us. It sucks, dude. I'm so fucking sick of it."

She looked at her nails and then lit a cigarette as we raced along the Jersey Turnpike.

"Camilla, you can quit whenever you want," I said.

"Yeah, right," she grumbled. "Just quit paying all the bills and say fuck it to Camilla Bangs Entertainment. I put everything into it, dude. I don't have shit."

I knew exactly how she felt: the frustration of looking back over years of selling your pussy and having nothing to show for it except for the gonorrhea and chlamydia that returned every five months, and the chance to maybe keep selling your pussy for a few more years, as long as there was still a demand for it.

"You don't have anything socked away?" Angel asked, leaning into the front seat and smoothing the extensions in Camilla's hair.

"No, dude," Camilla said. "I told you. It all goes into the company. And what doesn't goes into bills. I gotta go fucking hook in the City to make ends meet, and I can barely afford the hotel room."

I thought of Camilla sitting alone in a hotel room in New York City, impatiently waiting for the arrival of strangers who would pay her to fuck them. . . . It broke my heart.

"I know it's scary, C, but you can quit," I said. "You can go out and get some lame job, just a little McJob that gives you money to eat, move back in with your parents, and say fuck all of this. You don't have to keep going so hard. You don't have to spend as much money as you do. We aren't as tight as we thought, you know? We really aren't the ballers we pretended to be. And that's okay."

I reached over the seat and put my hands on her shoulders.

"Yeah, nobody is ballin' anymore," Camilla said, looking at me in the rearview mirror. "I had to lower my rate to five hundred an hour. I'm thinking about doing three. It's bad out there right now."

"Duh, hookers are like the first thing to go when the economy is bad," I said. "Hookers and haircuts."

I was so nervous, I felt like barfing as we pulled into the convention center, unloaded the bags, and made our way onto the show floor. I was terrified that if I went through with this funeral for Penny Flame, I would be totally cut off, not only from my fans, but also from my friends in the business. Even though I had quit, I wasn't quite prepared to say good-bye to the entire industry face-to-face. I assumed that my retirement was a big deal only for me, and I didn't like how easily I assumed that fans and friends alike could say good-bye to me and simply move on.

And so when I got to my booth and both fans and porn girls started coming over to say good-bye, I was more than touched. I was a total tear factory on the verge of a meltdown.

"I'm getting a little choked up looking at all your DVDs," one of my fans said as he stood at my booth.

The table had been set up with a spread of my movies and pictures covering the very beginning of my career to the very end. Even though only half of the things I'd brought to New Jersey were displayed on the table, I was amazed at how much crap I'd purchased over the years.

"I'm going to miss you," he said, grabbing my hand.

This guy, like many other porn fans, made an effort to travel the country to meet and support his favorite girls. I'd seen him in Vegas year after year, and in New Jersey and Miami too.

"You are very brave for putting yourself out there," he said. "I don't want to say the other name, so I'm not going to say any name. But you are very brave."

Instantly, I knew he'd read my blog and that the truth was out. He knew my real name. He knew that Penny Flame had died and that this was essentially her funeral. I fought back the tears that threatened the glue on my fake eyelashes.

"Thank you," I finally managed to say. "For the support."

I walked around the table and hugged him. He appeared to be holding back tears as well. I realized that he and a bunch of my fans had really watched me grow up and had supported me in their own way. I suddenly felt bad that I had never even asked them their names. Being in—and getting out of—porn was a lot more complicated than I'd ever thought it would be when I first posed naked for a paycheck.

That night, when I got back to Camilla's house, I decided to leave my remaining bag of schwag in her dude's truck so I wouldn't have to haul it back downstairs the next morning. I also didn't want to think about what was left in that bag. I had come to New Jersey wanting to sell off everything. After a full day of hawking DVDs, I had made less than $500 and I still had the majority of my movies. I didn't want to bring any of that shit home to Los Angeles. I didn't want it to even exist after Jersey. The schwag bag had morphed into a body bag containing the remains of the old me, and I was so tired of carrying her around and mourning her.

Fuck it. Fuck it all, I thought.

This evening was more solemn than the previous night had been. I think Camilla and I were exhausted, and Angel could see the struggle that we both were experiencing, me as I tried to say good-bye, and Camilla as she dealt with the fact that she had no obvious escape plan. I curled up on the couch with a vat of frozen yogurt and fell asleep before the tasty treat had melted.

The next morning, after waking up to the sound of Camilla and her man fighting, I showered, applied my porn mask, and wandered downstairs to the patio for a morning smoke. As I sat outside alone, trying to pretend they weren't screaming at each other inside, Angel crept out and took the chair next to me.

"Car got stolen last night," she said, super-nonchalant, like it wasn't a big deal that a giant diesel truck had vanished.

Her words caught me so off guard that I spilled coffee all down the black shirt I'd chosen as the appropriate funeral attire for my last day as Penny Flame.

"What?" I said. "My shit was in there!"

"Yeah, well, it's probably somewhere on Canal Street now, Pie." Angel laughed.

She walked inside to grab a towel for my coffee-soaked shirt.

"They've been screaming at each other all morning, like either of them can fix it," Angel said. "Idiots."

"Oh my God," I said. "My stuff is gone. It's gone! What am I gonna sell now?"

I jumped to my feet and grabbed her by the shoulders.

"It's gone!" I continued, getting excited now. "I only need to sell the other half and then she's gone! It's all gone!"—clever realization.

"Pie, you might not wanna act so happy when Camilla comes out here," she said. "She's kinda pissed. You know. 'Cuz the car was stolen."

Immediately, my joy over not having to stay at the show any longer than necessary was dampened by the bigger issue of the loss of the truck. When Camilla walked out onto the patio a few minutes later, Angel quit laughing and lit a smoke and I dropped my happy face and went into serious mode.

"Dude, there are three options with this stolen-car thing," Camilla said. "Oh, and sorry, Jennie, your stuff was in there."

I shook my head.

"No way, lady, huge favor," I said. "Probably the only good thing about the car being stolen."

"Good," she said, quickly returning to her detective mission. "So it's either really stolen by, like, a car thief, or . . . a fan followed us home and stole it like a psycho . . . or . . . or it was his ex-wife."

I nodded, not sure what to say, since all of these possibilities sounded bad to me.

"We can take a cab there today, so don't worry," Camilla reassured me.

She might have thought that I was really set on going to the show, but the truth was that I didn't care anymore. I didn't want another day full of on-the-verge-of-tears conversations with my fans, or encounters with random porn girls whom I had to give an explanation to about why I didn't have a drink in my hand or a blunt in my purse.

"Whatever happens, I'm not worried," I said. "I'm selling off all my shit today. And then it's bye-bye PF forevs." I had one bag left of the two that I had brought to Jersey, and never in my life had I thought I'd feel blessed by being robbed.

"Lucky," Camilla said.

THE CAB RIDE was easy, and the morning passed even more quickly than I'd hoped it would. It seemed like every time I turned around, there was someone from my life—now my past—in porn.

I ran into Audrey Bitoni, a mega-dream-girl escort, who hugged me warmly.

"Ohhh, I'm sad you're going!" she exclaimed.

I saw Sasha Grey, who raised a suspicious eyebrow at me, as if she wondered what angle I was working, but she made no mention of my decision to end my career.

I saw little Lexi Belle, one of the sweetest, most innocent porn girls I'd ever met. She wrapped her thin arms around me and whispered into my hair.

"My Penny," she said. "I loved you most."

The morning was filled with good-byes of all kinds: quick good-byes, sad good-byes, inauthentic and dispassionate good-byes, and heartfelt and loving farewells.

As I hugged most of the girls, I made the same promise, even though I didn't know whether or not it was a promise I could keep.

"I'll see you again one day," I said again and again.

When time began to run down, and the crowds became more and more sparse, Angel stepped up to my table and started shouting at the top of her lungs.

"Penny Flame must go!" she yelled. "Last time ever! Get your Penny Flame stuff!"

Taking her lead, I began screaming as well.

"I'm never coming back here, or to any convention, so buy this shit now!" I shouted. "Half price! It's all gotta go!"

Soon my stack of sixty DVDs turned into forty, and then thirty, and then twenty-five. When we hit twenty, Angel began walking out onto the show floor and grabbing people by the hand.

"It's free!" she said, leading them back to my table. "You want it!"

"Free! Free! Free!" I yelled, waving eight-by-tens and movies at anybody who would look.

The girls signing autographs at the table next to me shot me furious glares, because they were still trying to sell videos. I didn't care. As they could tell, I was straight fucking over it.

The last twenty movies went quickly. Once they were gone, Angel looked at me and smiled.

"There," she said. "Now she's gone. What should we do tomorrow, Pie?"

Originally, I had intended to spend three days signing at the show, but now, with no more schwag, there was no more reason to stay.

"Try to take over the City, my love!" I yelled.

I threw my arms around her and buried my head in her shoulder.

"Thank you," I whispered. "I couldn't have done this without you."

"Shut the fuck up," Angel laughed. "Don't make me cry at Hookerfest."

By quarter past ten that night, my hands were empty and my heart was light. The funeral was officially over. The body bag had been emptied. My career had been sold off. I'd made less than a thousand dollars. But I was free.

Angel and I spent the next day in Manhattan, and suddenly, everything seemed possible. It felt as if selling the rest of the memories that had been hidden in my closet had been the most important, final step in letting go of my old life and identity. After everything I'd been through, I was done with Penny at last.

It was after two in the morning when we arrived back at Camilla's house. I could think of nothing but sleep. I had just lived my first day totally Penny-free, and I was exhausted from all of the emotional upheaval.

We slept long into the morning. After I'd showered and packed, I dragged my now very small bag down the stairs and walked into the kitchen where Camilla sat.

"Your stuff is back," she said.

"What do you mean, my stuff is back?" I asked.

"His psycho ex took the car," Camilla said. "She dropped your stuff off last night. Aren't you excited?"

I couldn't tell if she was serious or not. I was the furthest thing from excited that I could be; I was pissed.

"I don't want this shit anymore," I said.

I looked down at the bag filled with images of my body, furious that the items zipped safely inside weren't floating around Canal Street, on sale for a crazy bargain.

"Well, it's not going away," Camilla said as she walked outside to smoke. "Guess you gotta deal with it, huh?"

Guess I gotta deal with it, I thought, *because there is no way I can throw this stuff away.* Instead, I called a cab to take me to the airport.

It was time to go home.

A WEEK AFTER I returned home from New Jersey, VH1 started airing *Sex Rehab with Dr. Drew*. The first night it was on, I padded up to Deezy's apartment so that I wouldn't be alone for the premiere episode. As I sat and watched the girl on the screen—dressed in black spandex, tits hanging out everywhere, all about flirtation, flirtation, flirtation—I didn't recognize her as myself. It was hard to see the fakeness that seemed to ooze from every pore, and below that, the sadness that revealed itself in her eyes, and the hopelessness that resonated in every one of her words. I couldn't believe that I had changed so much in so little time. The old me looked like a very sad girl.

"Thank you for watching this with me, Deez," I said when it was over, as I gathered up the plate of cookies that I'd brought up for our viewing pleasure.

"Next week, buddy?" he asked.

"Maybe we could kill some aliens instead," I said.

Something about watching myself had always made me uncomfortable, whether it was watching my porn videos before or watching the show now. I didn't like the girl I saw on any of those screens, because I didn't know that girl.

I returned to my quiet apartment and sat smoking cigarettes in my kitchen, which I'd transformed into an art studio. My phone rang.

I could just ignore that. Ignore everything, I thought.

The sadness of seeing the person I'd become at the end of my porn career was reverberating through every cell in my body, but remembering what I'd learned from Jill; Dr. Reef, my substance mentor; and everyone who had been helping me along the way, I forced myself not to isolate. I picked up the phone, even though it was the opposite of what I wanted to do. It was my dad.

"Hi," I said, not knowing whether he'd seen the show or not.

"Well, Jen, I just finished watching the first episode," he said, his voice sounding soft, a million miles away. "Did you see it too?"

"Yeah, I saw it," I said, still unsure about how I felt about seeing it. "You know, Duncan said I should write a book about my story."

By changing the subject, I hoped to put some space between the first episode and my feelings about it.

"Well, I think that would be really great, Jennifer," my dad said. "I think that this show was the best thing that could have happened to you, and that you are very brave for doing it. I think the book would be a nice follow-up."

It sounded like he was crying, very quietly, perhaps trying to hide his emotions from me.

"You really think it was okay?" I said, pinching back my own tears. "I hate seeing myself like that, Dad."

I wished that I'd stayed at Deezy's place a little bit longer, so I wouldn't be alone with this conversation and my feelings right now.

"Seeing you at James's graduation, talking to you all the time like we do, knowing what you are doing to get better . . . that girl on TV isn't you anymore," Dad said. "The girl on the show is what you can become if you are careless. But it isn't who you are today."

He was clearly crying now. I hadn't heard my dad cry since he and my mom divorced nearly ten years before.

"But if I write a book," I said, weeping as well now, "and that book is a follow-up, I don't know that I can be as brave. I don't know that I want to tell everything, to share everything. I don't know if I can. And what if it involves you?"

"You are going to help people with your honesty," he said, "on the show, and in your life. Just keep being the woman you are today, and you will help millions."

"But what about you?" I asked.

"Write whatever you need to write about," he said. "They are your memories. I'm only a part of them. I love you, kiddo."

"I love you too," I said.

After we said good-bye and hung up, I turned off my phone. I sat in my kitchen, staring at the last painting I'd been working on, a black-and-white image of hands growing out of a clenched fist, holding a paintbrush dripping with blood. It was one of my first paintings that I had ever thought was any good.

Maybe I can be more, I thought.

The following morning, I went to my computer and logged on to Facebook. I began to search for every man I'd ever hurt, fully prepared to honestly look at the mistakes I'd made and try to repair the pain I'd caused. I figured I'd go in order, but since Marc didn't exist on the Internet, I decided to start in college, with Jeff. I had seen him once since the end of our relationship, but because that reunion had been fully saturated with massive amounts of marijuana, I wanted to see him again in order to really have a clean start. I wrote to him and asked if we could meet up. When he agreed, I started planning my apology, never imagining that he'd be where he was, or that he'd receive me as he did.

14

"HIS HEART WAS AS GREAT AS THE WORLD, BUT THERE WAS NO
ROOM IN IT TO HOLD THE MEMORY OF A WRONG."
—RALPH WALDO EMERSON

My ex-boyfriend Jeff was still living in San Diego, but he'd given up dope and become an art dealer. He was doing well, working at a small showroom and living about fifteen minutes east of town in a pimped-out condo he'd bought with money he'd saved. I'd always wanted to buy a property of some sort, but I didn't have the determination he did. And so I was doubly impressed with his success.

The afternoon I drove from Los Angeles to make amends to Jeff, I was a ball of jumbled nerves, uncertain of how he'd respond, especially given his many successes. Jill and I had discussed the various ways in which the conversation might go, and she had told me that I would have to accept whatever he said to me. As she had reminded me, I couldn't be concerned with what he thought of me because it was none of my business, as they often said in recovery. The truth, though, was that I was very concerned with what he thought of me, because after years of being apart from him, I still thought of him often and wondered if he ever thought of me. I still wanted him to be in love with me, as I wanted all of the men I'd loved to still love me, because I wanted so desperately to feel loved. The only difference was that now I was no longer willing to do whatever it took to ensure that these men loved me.

———

THE GALLERY WAS in a wealthy neighborhood north of downtown. It was familiar to me because a young, wealthy company owner I had once fucked lived there, and I knew it was filled with men and women exactly like him. These are people who go to yoga in the middle of the day, five days a week; people between the ages of twenty-five and fifty who drive Porsches, Aston Martins, and Ferraris, and don't mind paying $5 for a tomato at Whole Foods or Bristol Farms. It's an area where a starter home runs a cool million but doesn't have an ocean view. When I used to drive through there in my E350, high on herb and sex appeal, I felt like I belonged, like it could one day be my home as well. Now that the weed had worn off, and I had shelved my sexuality in order to develop genuine self-esteem, I saw what a phony I'd been, driving a car I couldn't afford and thinking that smoking weed made me cool. This was for millionaires and billionaires, and I wasn't even a thousandaire; I was more like a couple hundredaire.

Jeff's gallery was no more than a two-minute walk from the beach. As I walked into the display space, where Jeff had discovered that his true talent was slinging modern art to customers who pulled up in $100,000 vehicles, I realized once again how out of place I was. When Jeff came around the corner and smiled at me, I stood quietly in front of a vibrant photograph, breathing in the reds and greens of the image and waiting patiently for him to say something first.

"I knew you'd like this one," he said.

As he looked at me, his smile grew wider. It was the same smile I recognized from my late teens, a smirky grin capped by twinkly eyes, which were a teensy bit hazy from a long day on his feet.

"It's sick," I told him, grinning back foolishly. "But you know how I feel about trees."

"Yeah, I know," he said. "There's another one. It's always made me think of you."

He nodded his head toward the rear of the studio and led me to a private screening room that was normally reserved for serious buyers. He shut the door and sat down on a couch. I hesitated before sitting, waiting for the reassurance of an invitation to join him there. When he put his hand on the soft leather sofa, I delicately lowered my body next to his. Our outer thighs were mere inches from touching. He smelled the same as he had when we were younger, but cleaner, and now he smelled like a man.

"Look," he said.

As he clicked buttons on a small remote control, the lights in the room dimmed and the space on the wall in front of us lit up. A picture of my favorite architectural structure in the world, the Golden Gate Bridge, appeared and began to glow with cars' headlights as the ocean below it reflected the light. It was San Francisco at dawn, lit up from the east, and slowly coming to life. In the dark, I touched his knee, feeling awe for the picture and thinking back to our trip to the city together.

"It's perfect," I said.

"I always think of you when I see it," he said. "And now here you are."

When he smiled, he kept his lips together. These were lips I knew so well, having kissed them a thousand times. I had forgotten them over the years, but I could easily remember them now that I was only a foot away.

"So what's up?" he said. "Everything okay?"

His words reminded me of my reason for the visit, and thoughts of his lips fell from my mind.

"What is the original photo printed on?" I said. "I'd love to use it for my work."

I stood and approached the picture. He laughed quietly, know-

ing well how I dealt with discomfort by taking up a new subject.
Even though I'd changed so much over the recent months, and had
tried so hard to be a new, healthy, and different woman, some of
my old habits had yet to shift at all. These little things that were
perhaps unchangeable were many of the same little things he had
once confessed to loving most about me.

"Let me clock out and we can go get some coffee," he said.

While I waited patiently in the private room, I thought back to
the time we'd spent together in San Francisco and found myself
wishing we were back there now. But I knew that was impossible.
I shook off the feeling. I had an amends to make.

We walked across the street to Starbucks and then, with vanilla
lattes in hand, shuffled down across the grass to the sand and sat
overlooking a jogging path that bordered the Pacific. Sitting in the
fading sunlight, with my left leg gently pressed to his right, we
smoked cigarettes and exhaled with the crash of the waves. I knew
I had to say something, but I didn't know how to begin. Finally, I
worked up my nerve.

"You deserved better than me," I said.

I leaned forward to set my coffee on the ground. Then I rested
my elbows on my knees and put my head down, letting my hair
fall around my face. I began counting my heartbeats, consciously
slowed my breathing, and urged myself to move forward.

Be the woman you wish to become, I thought.

"I was so selfish," I said. "You deserved a woman who could be
with you fully. You didn't deserve to be the other man. It was selfish of me to ask that of you."

I fought back tears and looked into his eyes, which continued
to smile at me.

"You're trippin'," he said. "You know I didn't mind. I knew your
deal with Marc. I didn't give a fuck. I got you all the time anyway."

I felt the excitement of being near him again, the lightness in
my heart, and remembered why I had been with him. I had been
so convinced he would be pissed that I hadn't planned what to say

if he had forgiven me and moved on. The blood rushed to my face. I laughed.

"Fucker, I'm trying to make amends," I said. "Can you just be a *little* upset with me?"

"Remember when you said to me that we were like a lightning storm?" he asked.

He stubbed out his cigarette, threw both of our butts away in the trash can next to him, and then lit two more and handed me one as soon as he sat down next to me. It was as if nothing and everything had changed.

"They always end in thunder," he said.

I did remember telling him that. Years after we broke up, we had run into each other at a random porn convention, where he was selling time-shares, even though it had absolutely nothing to do with porn. We had sat in the parking garage after the show was over and smoked a bowl in my car while discussing the explosive fight with which our relationship had ended.

"I remember," I said. "But that doesn't mean you deserved the kind of storm I brought. You gave me butterflies, and I didn't know how to deal with them, so I exploded them in the sky. You still do. Give me butterflies. But I'm not going to explode them."

He put his arm around me and squeezed.

"It's fine," he said.

He took his arm back and leaned forward, elbows to knees, like I was.

I couldn't believe how well this conversation was going. It suddenly hit me that, when I had left him, it wasn't at a bad place in our relationship where leaving would have been logical. Instead, I had left when the relationship had become serious, after he had tried to be there for me following the deaths of my friends. Then it hit me that I'd done the same thing in all of my relationships: when things were going well, I'd sabotaged them and run. And because I was a supreme failure at communication, most men never knew what was coming and never understood why it had happened.

"Yeah, it ended kind of abruptly," I said. "I was never good at talking, you know?"

"I know," he said and nodded. "Like in San Francisco, when Marc called and said Arianna died, and you just hung up the phone and didn't cry or anything. I didn't know what to do. You wouldn't talk to me about it. You started taking cough medicine, and drinking booze like a fool, and refusing to sleep in your bed. I didn't know how to help you."

I could remember back to those days in my life, but not the feelings themselves, because I'd refused to ever experience them.

"That was brutal," I said. "I didn't think you knew it was Marc on the phone. Not that it matters now, but I should have told you."

Jeff put his hand to my knee.

"I always knew when you were on the phone with him," he said. "Your whole body changed. But that's fine too. It's the past."

"You know, I've had at least two friends a year die since then?" I said. "So shitty. I think that was the time it started to go wrong. With Arianna, and the drugs, and booze, and everything."

I could see him nodding in my peripheral vision, stubbing out his smoke and leaning over to the trash can. He held his hand out to me, palm open, so he could throw my smoke away too. I hadn't noticed that it'd gone out.

"I know," he said. "You wouldn't let me close after that. I still loved you, though. I didn't start hating you until I found out you went to Vegas with Ted for your birthday. I was so pissed when I heard you guys fucked. I was so fucking pissed."

I couldn't remember the Vegas trip, because, while there, I'd made friends with a coke-dealing limo driver named Cedric and then proceeded to drink thousands of dollars in alcohol and snort thousands of dollars in cocaine. I had but two memories from that trip. The first: losing Ted in a casino after a round of birthday shots to celebrate my twenty-one years on the planet. The second: finding Ted as he stumbled wildly from a bathroom in an entirely different casino, his shirt covered in blood. Actually, that wasn't the first time I'd had sex with Ted, but it was apparently the first time Jeff had heard about it.

"I shouldn't have fucked your friends," I said. "It was wrong. And by 'wrong,' I mean fucking horrible. I would totally understand if you hate me."

I wished I still smoked weed, so I could take a big hit and stop the self-loathing that was creeping up the back of my spine.

"I don't hate you anymore, Jennie," he said. "I did for a long time, but not anymore. Especially not now. I'm just glad you're okay."

Jeff wrapped both of his arms around me, and we sat in front of the western sea, taking in the vast blueness before us, breathing in and out as one, as if I hadn't done all of the horrible things I'd done. The dam broke, and tears began to fall from my eyes.

"Remember when we used to sit at Rock Spot?" he asked.

The memory was so clear that I could still feel the spray of the ocean as we had sat for at least an hour a day on the sandstone rock formation that jutted out over Sunset Cliffs, smoking weed, sometimes talking, more often than not, completely silent. It was definitely *our* spot.

"I think that's where I fell in love with you," he continued.

Jeff kissed my hair. We sat awhile longer, watching the joggers, the ocean, finally cleansed of all the atrocities I'd committed. It was a magnificent day to be forgiven.

———

THOUGH ANGEL AND I had been friends for nearly four years, I had never once taken notice of her birthday. There were other things I felt necessary to make right, apart from being a superbad friend, but as most of my blunders revolved around my ineptitude when it came to friendship, I decided to start there. I hopped online and bought us a weeklong cruise to Mexico. It was actually relatively cheap, considering the destination, but priceless when I saw the look on her face.

We were scheduled to leave from San Diego in early October, but in the second week in September I received a call from the super-awesome VH1 publicist Scott who told me that Oprah Winfrey wanted to interview me the first week of October. I called Angel.

"Oprah wants me to do one of her shows," I said, chain-smoking as usual.

"Wait," Angel said. "*Oprah* Oprah? Like, 'This is my couch, everyone gets a car and a washing machine' Oprah?"

I laughed.

"Yeah, totally the same Oprah," I said. "But it's the week we are scheduled to cruise. I'll turn it down if you want."

"Pie, shut the fuck up," she said. "Seriously? Shut the fuck up. Turn down Oprah—who do you think you are now? Nobody turns down Oprah."

As Angel so gracefully and generously agreed to change our plans in the face of this once-in-a-lifetime offer, Duncan, whom I'd only recently been in touch with again, phoned me on the other line.

"Dude, Duncan is calling me. Hold on one sec," I said.

"You're talking to *him* again?" she said.

I lit another cigarette, fully prepared for the quickest explanation ever.

"Yeah, we are talking again," I said. "But it's, like, from a distance, you know? I think I just relied on him too much, too quick because of that rehab romance shit. I think maybe if we can build our friendship slow, instead of the hyper-quick way that we became besties, that'll be healthier."

Both Jill and Dr. Reef had said that healthy relationships were built in 10 percent increments. First, trust the person only if they do something trustworthy. Then give them 10 percent of your trust. Then another 10. Then, if you are let down because they prove to be someone other than the person you thought they were, it won't hurt as much as trusting someone 100 percent right away. I had given Duncan 100 percent of my trust from the moment I met him, simply because we were experiencing the same things at the same time, and because we both ran from people we cared about when things became too intimate. Then, when he pushed me away after the death of the Big Dog, I felt betrayed, like what I can only assume every guy I've ever run from has felt. It sucked balls. So now I was rebuilding our friendship, but with boundaries.

I clicked over to Duncan.

"Did you hear they are doing show publicity on *Oprah*?" Duncan asked.

I felt like lying, but I didn't.

"Yeah, I heard," I said, "I just got off the phone with Scott at VH1. I'm gonna interview with O's people tomorrow."

"'O'?" he said. "Is that what you call her? I want to go on 'O' as well."

Given how he had reacted when I got on *Sober House* and he didn't, I was immediately worried about how all of this would pan out.

"Well, nothing is for sure for anyone," I said. "I doubt they'll even have us. It's kind of, you know, a taboo thing to do on daytime television."

I got off the phone with Duncan as quickly as I could and called Angel back.

"Fuck, dude," I said. "This could be bad."

"Maybe time to think about moving, Pie?" Angel said.

THE NEXT DAY, after the interview with Oprah's people, Scott began to plan the details of my trip to Chicago. Unfortunately, my excitement about going on one of the most famous talk shows in the world was tainted by my fear of Duncan's reaction, and my sadness over the soon-to-be-canceled ladies' getaway to Mexico. I had intended upon making my real amends to Angel somewhere out to sea, in open water, where the ocean was deep and the horizon long. I tried calling Royal Caribbean to ask if I could switch the dates. When they refused, I called Scott to tell him I was considering ditching out on Oprah and her super-comfy couch. Scott called Oprah's producers, who called Royal Caribbean. Suddenly, the power of the 'O' changed the cruise company's mind, and I was left with one singular worry: Would Duncan Roy be accompanying me on the show?

A week and a half later, when I was on my way to Chicago with Amber and Phil from *Sex Rehab,* it was clear that Duncan would not be joining us. I'm not sure who made the decision to exclude him or why, but after he posted a blog post entitled, "Fuck You Oprah," the Harpo producers were probably relieved he wouldn't be appearing on the show.

The next morning at the Harpo Productions studios passed like a windstorm. One moment we were in the dressing room, eating delicious, fresh pastries. The next we were being escorted to Oprah's couch. Suddenly I found myself sitting next to the lady herself.

"Have you ever been in love?" Oprah asked me.

I thought of all the men I'd been with, how I'd treated Jeff, Marc, and Ted—especially Marc and Ted—and of the amends I had yet to make.

"No, I don't think so, because I certainly haven't treated them as if I loved them," I said.

Oprah applauded our courage for talking about these difficult things on the show and congratulated me on my months of sobriety. Before I knew it, the taping was over. After a brief hug from Miss Winfrey, we were ushered offstage.

Once we returned to the dressing room, we were given goodie bags. Mine contained a crazy soft blanket, a candle, and a journal. I held the journal in my hand.

So this is it, I thought. *This is what you get for being healthy, for starting over, for taking a chance on a new way of life. Recognition from Oprah, and a journal. You did good, Jennie.*

As I fingered through the gold-trimmed pages of the red, Japanese-looking journal, I decided to begin my memoir on its pages.

Once I've finished, I thought, *I will send her this notebook with a thank-you letter that says, "You, Miss Winfrey, are super-awesome. Thank you for helping me start my book."*

As quickly as we had lifted off for Chicago and raced through the filming of a monumental show—or at least monumental for me—we were headed back to Los Angeles. From there I rushed to San Diego to hop on my cruise to Mexico with Angel. It was all go, go, go, and as a result of the constant motion, I had very little time to think about what I'd say to Angel once we were on board. Perhaps it was better that way.

THE CLOUDLESS SKY over San Diego on the day of our departure was an excellent reminder of why I so loved that sandy city. We took funny pictures of ourselves wearing giant hats as we boarded the boat, and we stood at the bow of the ship like Jack and Rose in the movie *Titanic*. As the boat crept slowly out of the bay and into my beloved Pacific Ocean, we headed to our small interior room. That first night we entered the dining hall and found our assigned tables, immediately checking out our table companions. We would be eating dinner with the same couples for the remainder of the week.

"I say 'cunt' a bunch," I whispered to Angel. "Do you think that is going to be a problem at this table?"

We surveyed the guests: one devoted Christian couple, complete with matching Christ-oriented jewelry; one super-quiet and nervous couple; one couple from Texas that included a woman with hair that was teased mad close to heaven. As they say in Texas: "The higher the hair, the closer to God."

"No, I don't think 'cunt' should be a problem, as long as you don't say it multiple times in a row," Angel whispered back. "No 'cunt, cunt, cunt, cunt.' Just one or two 'cunt's.'"

I giggled. Throughout dinner, we both said swearwords under our breath, and the devout couple looked at me nervously each time I swatted Angel's leg under the table.

OUR CRUISE TOOK us from San Diego to Rosarito Beach, Ensenada, and finally, to Cabo San Lucas. Because Angel and I were having so much fun, I gave very little thought to the amends I knew I'd soon be making. I'd been to Rosarito Beach and Ensenada before, during drunken college trips. Aaron Carpello and I had traveled to Cabo San Lucas the year before I entered rehab, and I had fallen in love with the infinite amount of alcohol and ceviche, fish being something I had learned to like after a few margaritas. The fact that I wasn't drinking now created a deep sense of worry within me as we continued to float south. The closer we came to Cabo, the more I could taste the tequila, and the more I thought: *Perhaps one small drink won't hurt.*

The morning we dropped anchor, I was up at seven, drinking coffee like water and chain-smoking cigarettes on the upper deck. We took a small taxi-ferryboat thingie into town. As we got closer, I pointed out the ME by Meliá hotel, with Nikki Beach and my favorite pool bar. We walked through the town for less than five minutes before making friends with one of the many guys that drive the small, dangerous-looking glass-bottom boats around Bahia de Cabo San Lucas. As we boarded his treacherous ship, our water taxi guy greeted us with a big goofy grin and two six packs of Tecate sitting patiently in a cooler.

We started out to the last fingertip-shaped beach on the stretch of land separated from mainland Mexico by the Gulf of California. Called Land's End, it has this amazing arch formed out of the rocks, through which one can watch the sun dip below the horizon. This arch has been re-created on every piece of Cabo touristy crap, from ashtrays to coffee mugs—both of which I'd bought on my previous trip with Aaron.

That night, back at the ship after having managed to resist the Tecates, Angel and I went to our shared couples table dinner. I let a few extra "cunt's" slip, a little louder than the previous nights. I couldn't help it. I was so excited about the new escape plan I had formulated earlier that day, in which Angel and I would run away to Mexico and run a pink charter boat for tourists.

I hadn't thought about sex in months, because it was something I no longer did. I'd masturbated a couple of times, but it had felt contrived after Dr. Reef insisted I keep a log. And now all of my previous impulsivity—the desire to escape reality via orgasm that had once ruled my life—was being funneled into my new Land's End pink boat escape plan. It was much easier for me not to think about sex when I was planning an escape route, making a list, doing something that was completely opposite from sex.

But then, in the middle of a bite of a very mediocre free-range chicken, it hit me: the truth of what was happening on this boat, every single night.

"Angel pie, is everyone on this boat having sex tonight?" I said. "I mean, everyone except us?"

Angel nearly choked on her equally mediocre bite.

"Um, really?" she said. "You're really asking me this at dinner?"

I shot a glance at the Christian couple next to us, who both looked like total virgins, complete with halos.

"Dude, do you want me to ask them?" I said. "I will."

Angel started to giggle and shoved salad into her mouth, as if to stop herself from getting further into the conversation. I looked to the couple, with their crosses around their necks, their empty wineglasses, and their napkins folded politely by their plates until the next portion of the meal arrived.

"Seriously, though, I'd prefer you answer me," I said. "They aren't even drinking! Are they fucking? Is this boat filled with fuckers?"

Angel swallowed her salad.

"Pie," she said, "most of these people came on this boat with someone they love. They are all vacationing, so, yeah, they are having sex. Don't look so horrified. Just because you stopped having sex doesn't mean the whole world stopped having sex."

I tried to wipe the look of horror from my face, but I felt betrayed.

"Everyone, though?" I whimpered. "Even the Christians?"

I looked to the virgins at the table.

"Pie, you're using your judgmental eyes," Angel said. "Stop judging them. All people have sex, even the Christians. And you will, too, again—not today, or tomorrow, but someday. You're going to fall in love and have sex, and it'll be wonderful and awesome, and you'll laugh about the day you freaked out at the strange couples table over a boatload of people having sex."

Angel folded her napkin in her lap, looked at me, and then placed it on her plate. "Let's go before you freak out again," she said.

THAT NIGHT, I sat in the ship's cigar room, smoking and writing in my Oprah journal. I hadn't thought about having sex in so long, I hadn't considered that, one day, I would again be sexually active, or that it would be with someone whom I thought was very special. Finally, Angel came into the room to fetch me.

"No more, Hemingway," she said. "Come dance."

We went up to the top floor of the boat and hit the teen disco, tossing our shoes to the side of the dance floor. Long after soreness crept into our dancing legs, we crawled into our beds where they rocked in the motion-filled darkness.

Now is the time, Jennie, I thought. *We go back to real life tomorrow. The time is now.*

"I know I haven't been the best Pie to you, Pie," I began, speaking quietly to Angel, who knew about the amends that I had to make.

"I know, Pie, it's okay," she said.

I was thankful for the darkness, because of all the amends that I knew I needed to make, this was one of the hardest, because she was one of the people I loved most.

"No, it's not okay," I said. "I'm not gonna be a bad Pie anymore. Or a bad friend. I love you very much, and I will show up for you from now on. I'm sorry I didn't."

I heard her roll over in her bed and laugh as she threw a balled-up washcloth at me though the blackness.

"Oh, hush, Pie," she said. "I know you will. You already have been a good Pie. Ever since you left rehab. I'm so glad you went. I missed my friend."

We were quiet then, floating in the darkness of the earth, not in Mexico or America, but in a space that was entirely foreign. And in that foreign space, with wet eyes and pillow, in complete darkness, awaiting the day that was to come, I was so grateful to finally feel like all had been forgiven, at least by Angel.

INSPIRED BY MY successful amends with both Jeff and Angel, I decided on a whim to send a Facebook message to Ted. I hadn't seen him since he screamed at me through my door that he'd been accepted to film school, and I had refused to let him in or look him in the eye. It was a short message: "Hey . . . I was wondering if I could see you sometime. I know we didn't end well, and I understand if you don't ever want to see me again, but if you have any time you can spare, I'd love to sit with you, if just for a moment. Hope you are well."

After a week, when I had almost forgotten that I'd written to him, he finally replied: "Hey . . . talk about something random to wake up to, I would like to see you, when were you thinking? My number is the same . . . if u want give me a ring or write back and we can figure it out . . . hope things are going well . . ."

Things had been going well. So well, in fact, that I'd been high on how good life could be.

After reading my blog, a literary agent had reached out and offered me representation. As a result, a producer had reached out and offered me a genuine and sincere platonic friendship, as well as potential business deals. He mentioned that he was interested in optioning my story once it had been published and that he'd like me to write the screenplay. We often met for lunch or dinner, and he became a mentor, solidifying something that my friendship with Deezy had first introduced: what it meant to have a man as a friend. I was being invited to appear on talk shows like *The Tyra Banks Show* and *The View* to discuss the changes I'd made in my life. And my blog was featured on Carson Daly's show. With each passing blog post, I was becoming increasingly confident in my writing. And I was starting to believe that I might really have a future outside of pornography. I didn't, however, see how Ted could respond in such a positive manner—or how he could respond at all—given the state in which I'd left him.

When I saw Ted's reply, instead of feeling happy, I felt sick to my stomach. It didn't make sense to me that this man could still find compassion and empathy in his heart for me after everything I had done to him. So I put Saucy on her leash and took us on a walk through the dark streets of the Hollywood Hills, plotting our conversation as we went.

As I worked out my amends in my mind, I prepped myself for his hatred—welcomed it, even, because it would explain my own self-loathing. It would legitimize every bad feeling I'd turned inward, forming the foundation for every night I'd drunk myself into oblivion, justifying the pounds and pounds of weed I'd needed to numb myself.

When there were no more hills to be walked, and both of my legs and all four of Saucy's were too tired to continue, we made our way home and to bed. I prayed that evening, not to God, but to the universe, looking out my window to the moon above, trying to discern the faintest of stars in the haze of the city sky.

"Please, give me the strength to make this right," I said. "Give me the courage to look him in the eyes."

In the morning, I walked to my favorite Hollywood coffee shop at Cahuenga and Franklin Avenue, bought a latte, and sat outside to chain-smoke until Ted arrived. I didn't eat breakfast, afraid I'd throw up from nerves, and my stomach growled with each new Parliament I lit.

In a moment of magnificent strength, I typed a text to him that read: "I'm out front." And then, in a moment of incredible weakness, I began to think that part of what I deserved included him standing me up.

If I press SEND, then he will definitely know he has the option of standing me up, that I've made good on my word and really want to see him, and he can now treat me as I deserve to be treated.

Finally, I pressed SEND and sealed my fate. But when Ted finally came around the corner and I stood, flicking my cigarette into the filthy city gutter, I forgot what fate I'd been so afraid to seal. When I saw his eyes, his fluffy hair, his tired smile, I knew he was the same man, but better. We looked each other over, and I felt a pull into his body. I wanted so desperately to hug him, but I worried that I would wake up from this dream if I wrapped my arms around his neck. I didn't know how one should proceed when seeing someone she loved, someone who had literally saved her life, after years of hating herself for things that she had done to him that could never be undone. So I hugged him. I laced my arms around his strong body and I breathed in his laundry detergent, his soap. His smell made me feel as if we'd just been together yesterday. I was so afraid to let him go—that if I did, he would vanish or, worse, that he wouldn't be hugging me in return. But his arms were wrapped firmly around me.

"Thank you for coming," I whispered between shallow breaths, trying to keep it together long enough to make it right.

We sat across from one another on a giant wood table outside the coffee shop. I held on to his hands, drinking in the courage to start the conversation.

"I didn't think you would respond," I said. "I figured you hated me."

"I did. Hate you. Not for long, though."

He dipped his chin down, his gaze on our hands, mine clutching his, and his soft hair fell across his forehead.

"Why did you get in touch with me?" he asked.

Just like that, the doors between us had been opened.

"I just . . . I needed to . . . ," I said.

I could barely breathe; my throat was closing down with each word. I wished that he, like Angel, could read my mind.

"I saw some of the show," he said quietly, squeezing my hands in return.

"I was wrong," I spewed forth. "Everything I did to you was wrong. I was a liar, a thief, a cheat, so arrogant and selfish, Ted."

The sleeves of his knit sweater grazed his knuckles. He had hands that were perfectly shaped and had touched every part of me.

"I think about you all the time, about all the wrong I did you," I continued. "I need you to know that, through this whole recovery thing, you were the person I worried most about seeing, because you have the most reason to hate me. To hate every part of me. I was abusive to you, and you saved my life. I disappeared on you, and I should have thanked you, taken care of you. You were an angel."

I wept openly, hoping that he could understand my breathy apology, that my words were coherent between the sobs.

"I know I can't undo it, but if there is anything you need from me, anything that will make any of it better, please say so and I will do it," I said.

None of the words that spilled from my lips were words I'd practiced on my walk or with Jill. And my tears felt infinite. Ted brought his hands to my face and dried my eyes with his fingers, tracing the outline of my cheeks down to my chin. Our eyes met and his face broke my heart into a million pieces. He sat back and took a deep breath, running his hands and fingers through his own hair, which I'd run my soiled fingers through so many times before.

"Why?" he asked, his voice almost inaudible.

It was a question I'd asked myself for years. The answer wasn't satisfying. It didn't even make sense. But I knew that I had to try to explain myself to him.

"You were so good," I said. "I couldn't stand that someone so good would love *me*."

As the words continued to spill from my mouth, he sat motionless and absorbed what I told him.

"I never wanted to hurt you," I said. "I just . . . we . . . you were so close. I couldn't look you in the eye. So I ran."

We sat outside that coffee shop for a long time and continued to hold hands. I continued to cry. And he continued to brush my tears away, just as he had years before. We even laughed. I touched his face, not fully comprehending until that moment how deep my love for him had been and how much I'd denied myself those feelings. When we used to sleep in his bed, with him as the big spoon behind me, I would look down at his hands where they wrapped around my body. They were so strong and clean and covered with the memories of my body, which felt so weak and dirty.

Across the wood table from him, still staring at his hands, I felt as if I knew every part of him. I knew his hands and his face by heart. I remembered the way his fluffy hair fell across his eyes; the sad smile he offered up when things weren't going his way; the way he leaned back to laugh. I knew this man, and even though so much time had passed, every feeling I had once had for him remained inside of me because of the way I'd left so suddenly, without any kind of closure. We were unfinished, and because of this, it still felt like it had the first time I ever touched him.

I could fall in love with you all over again, I thought.

Ted walked me home from the coffee shop. I showed him my walls, covered in my artwork. I introduced him to Saucy, and he said hello to Kitty. I walked him out to the street, and when it was time to say good-bye, I threw my arms around his neck again, burying my face in his shoulder, pressing my entire body into his. He pushed his face to my ear, his lips grazing my skin.

"I went through waves of hating you," he whispered. "Then the hate would leave and I'd feel empty. I forgave you a long time ago. Maybe you should start trying to forgive yourself."

As we hugged and I thanked him, I breathed him in, repeating his impossible suggestion in my head and wondering where he had learned such grace.

15

"I BELIEVE A LEAF OF GRASS IS NO LESS THAN THE JOURNEY-
WORK OF THE STARS."

—WALT WHITMAN, *LEAVES OF GRASS*

Ever since I'd met Noah in 2005, we had sleepovers at his house. When I got out of rehab, he knew I wasn't having sex with anyone, including him, and he was fine with that setup, because he was having sex with other women. It wasn't until one afternoon in late October, during a session with Jill, that I began to think these sleepovers might be a problem.

"So we need to talk about how you're going to start dating again," she said.

"I think I need to stop having sleepovers with Noah," I said.

She sat back in her oversize armchair, looking a bit shocked that I'd segued from the topic of dating into use of the word "sleepover."

"Okay, not where I was leading," she said, "but we can talk about that. I didn't realize you were still having sleepovers with Noah."

"They aren't, like, sexy-time sleepovers," I said. "But I spend the night at his house, like, two nights a week."

Not only did I feel like I needed to talk about my relationship with Noah, but I was also trying to wiggle my way out of the more general dating conversation. The notion of dating, and especially having sex with someone, still frightened me. It had ever since Angel told me that I'd sleep with someone someday. Her attempt at reassurance struck me more like impending doom than logic and reason.

Jill brought me back to our session.

"Why do you think you need to stop the sleepovers?" she asked.

"I was talking to my dad, and he asked how the relationship with Noah was going. It got me to thinking . . . it's kind of not going. It's, like, a non-relationship. I don't know, if I go on a date with someone, then I'll have to say, 'Oh, I have cuddle sleepovers with this dude, Noah, but don't worry, we don't bang, we're just in a non-relationship.' And that's just not a conversation I'd like to have."

Jill nodded her super-accepting-of-everything-I-said nod, and I shrugged my shoulders to dismiss the idea of confessing harmless sleepovers to an imaginary man on a date that I couldn't imagine going on.

"I don't even know how to date," I said. "But that doesn't seem like a good opener."

"Well, let's talk about dating, then," she said. "You don't know how to date?"

Jill raised her eyebrows a fraction of an inch as she waited for my response.

"I've never been on a date," I confessed.

I felt ridiculous to admit this out loud after so many years of interactions with men. I had always liked to act like I was so well equipped when it came to guys, like I knew what they'd want, how they'd want it, and when they'd want it. But it was becoming clear that the only thing I knew about guys was how to fuck them. And, of course, how to fuck them over. Dating, on the other hand, was a total mystery.

"I usually fuck a guy before we go anywhere, so that whole 'dating' thing just doesn't make sense by then," I said. "Dating is what you do to get in someone's *pantalones,* right?"

Jill took a deep breath. Though we'd been meeting once a week for nearly eight months, she could still sometimes be brought up short by my ability to rationalize anything.

"No, dating is what you do to see if you want to spend time with someone," she said. "Being intimate with them is what you do once you've decided they are the only person you want to spend time with. And it's a show of love and an act of devotion. It's very special. It's not just to get in someone's *'pantalones.'*"

I relaxed back into the couch. I didn't want to hear any of that "act of devotion" shit, so I changed the subject again. She was well aware of how I used this trick when a conversation topic made me uncomfortable, but she allowed me to use it as I felt necessary.

"Noah and I never had sex like that," I said. "It was awkward. Never, like, 'Oh, I love you so much,' even though I do totally love him. I think that's because he's not a get-married, have-kids type of guy. He's the forever-bachelor type. He can't even have a girl-friend, because he's worried about people in porn gossiping about him."

Jill tilted her head, and her eyes revealed a hint of a smile.

"So you see yourself as the one-day-marrying type of girl, then?"

My throat did that closing-down thing that it does when I start to cry.

"I don't know about all that, but . . ."

The thought of loving someone forever made me sad, and the thought of someone loving me forever seemed impossible.

". . . but maybe a boyfriend or something?" I continued. "You know, like, a real one. Not that the others weren't real, but I wasn't very good to them. It doesn't feel like they were real relationships because I lied so much."

My throat kept sticking. I unfolded my legs from the Indian-style sitting position I'd taken and reached for a tissue.

"Well, that's why we need to start talking about dating," Jill said. "You're probably going to have to go on a bunch of dates before you meet a guy who you really want to be with."

I dabbed at my tears and folded the tissue into triangles, grateful that she'd changed the subject from eternal love to first dates.

"I don't want to date multiple guys at once, though," I said. "That feels like cheating. It feels like old behavior."

"It's not going to be old behavior, because you won't be committed to any one of them in particular," she said. "And when you decide who you want to be with, he will be the only one you see. We don't have to worry about that, though. We still have some time before your one-year anniversary."

I had been sober and porn-free for eight months, and I wasn't allowed to start dating until I reached the one-year mark. Emotional sobriety seemed like a more important goal for me than substance sobriety, and it was much harder than being sober. But staying clean from drugs and alcohol had certainly helped me to reconnect with the emotions I needed to process in order to heal. I intended to continue not using drugs or alcohol for at least as long as I'd committed to being single. Plus, I'd discovered that I could actually live on a super-minimal budget when I wasn't spending a hundred fifty bucks a day on booze and pot. You learn something new every day.

"Do you feel like sleepovers with Noah are old behavior?" she asked.

Fuck, back to this, I thought.

"Yes, and no," I replied, fidgeting and bringing my knees back up by my chest. "My dad gave me this car analogy, about test-driving cars and renting them and leasing them, and how I don't have to buy every car or thank the salesman who let me drive it. And I got a little lost in the analogy, but I guess it's kind of like what you were saying about dating multiple guys at once."

I put my triangle of tissue on my knee and looked at Jill from over my folded arms.

"I guess I always knew Noah was a lease," I continued. "He's like a lease and a rental. I lease him for the month, but I only get to rent him on certain nights, because other girls also have him on lease-rental agreements, and they get him the other nights. It's like I'm on a Monday- and a Thursday-night agreement."

As soon as I expressed this feeling out loud, I felt like a huge piece of used shit.

"So you don't mind putting your head down somewhere, knowing that pillow was slept on the night before—and will be slept on the night after—by different girls?" Jill said. "How many girls do you think he sleeps with?"

"I don't know," I answered. "He could have three other girls in a weekly rotation, with a night off for himself, or he could have ten who each get one day."

"How would that make you feel if he had ten different girls in that bed?" she asked gently.

Before that moment I'd seen it in a different light, which I tried to describe to her now.

"It used to make me feel special, like I was special enough to get two days a week," I said. "But it doesn't anymore, which kinda sucks."

Actually, it sucked a whole lot that the things that used to make me feel special no longer did. Sometimes, when I was alone, I worried that nobody would ever make me feel special again.

"I don't think it sucks that you don't feel special to be the number one of potentially ten girls," Jill said.

Jill had once told me to hug Saucy and tell her everything would be okay at the times when I felt sure that it wouldn't. I wished that Saucy was there for some hugging now.

"I want to be special," I said. "I want to be special to one person. I want one person to be special to me."

For once, I managed to get the words out without crying or folding my tissue triangle.

"I bet your dad thinks you're special," Jill said.

Then tears welled up in my eyes.

"I hope so," I said.

I made a silent vow to speak with Noah.

Two days later, I went to Noah's for our regular Thursday-night yogurt-DVR sleepover. After we finished watching *Rock of Love with Bret Michaels,* I tossed my empty frozen yogurt container in the trash bin and started to put my things together to leave. Noah was sitting shirtless on his California king-size bed, finishing off the remainder of his fro-yo.

"You goin' home, babe?" he asked.

"Yeah," I replied, and left it at that.

I didn't want to say out loud that I wouldn't be spending the night anymore. I had been hoping, since my conversation with Jill, that we could fade quietly into the non-sleepover, non-relationship friend zone, rather than having an actual conversation where I stated needs and he responded however he responded. But, in the moment, something came over me.

Fuck it.

"I don't think it's a good idea if we have sleepovers anymore," I confessed, my voice high and squeaky, like a helium balloon letting out its air superfast and without any control. "I don't think it's healthy for either of us. At least, I know it isn't for me."

He laughed. It was probably caused more by discomfort than because of any desire to be mean, but it definitely sounded snarky to me.

"Why, babe?" he asked. "Are you falling in love with me?"

I should have told him the truth as he sat there, scraping his near-empty frozen yogurt carton, smiling, and waiting for one of my clever, smart-ass responses.

I should have told him that I'd loved him from the first day I met him, that I should have said "I love you" a long time ago, and that everything I did, including accepting our non-relationship as sufficient, was because I loved him. That there was a time when we were perfect for one another because we both only wanted superficial things from each other, like nice vacations and chitchat about workouts. That he was the one reason I never felt alone in the industry, because I knew that I could call him anytime, and as long as my words didn't involve serious emotions, I could tell him anything that was on my mind and it wouldn't change the way he thought of me. I should have told him a million things, like how I was beginning to understand that true love occupied an authentic space we never could; it had to do with a level of honest intimacy we couldn't reach.

"No, I'm not falling in love with you," I said. "I'm just afraid I won't be able to fall in love with anybody else."

I walked over to the bed and kissed his forehead, his perfectly moisturized skin melting into my lips as I put my hand to his strong chest and held back feelings I should have felt years ago, if I hadn't been suppressing them the whole time. I scratched Nutmeg on the head and whispered in her big dog ears: "Your mama loves you so much."

Then I left that big, beautiful home overlooking Porn Valley.

Once I was in my car, I broke down in tears because I knew that everything had really changed. There would be no more vacations to San Diego, no more *Whale Wars,* no more fro-yo, and that hurt. Quitting all the other destructive things in my life felt easy compared to quitting my emotionally inept relationship with Noah. He had been the crutch that made everything else possible. He made me feel safe. He made me feel like I still had value, even though I wasn't a porn star anymore. Intellectually, I knew this was silly, but I couldn't help feeling that his approval after I quit performing implied that I also had the approval of the entire industry. Once I cut him from my life, I felt like my final connection to Penny Flame would die.

I saw Noah just once more, and like the sex we occasionally had, it was awkward. It turned out that, once our sleepover, non-relationship relationship ended, so did our connection. This hurt, but a lot less than I had feared it would. I think I had already let go of Noah when I left his house that night. As scared as I was that I might never find another man who made me feel as safe as he once had, I knew that I couldn't hide out in the past anymore.

IT WAS OBVIOUS to me why my relationships with Carpello and Noah were over. The real sting came from the disintegration of what I had thought were more stable relationships. One of the hardest to face was the end of my friendship with Jacob. I visited Jacob in San Diego a few times after I got sober, but it was tough, because he took smoke breaks during our time together. When he locked himself away in his bedroom to smoke pot, he left me sitting on his couch alone. When he returned, reeking of that musty, stanky herbal odor, it never felt entirely comfortable.

I wish I could spend more time with you when you aren't high, I thought. *That way, we could see if we even like each other without weed.*

I quit visiting him, and he didn't fight for our friendship. I think he saw how much I was changing and knew we no longer fit, even though I'm sure he didn't think of it in quite those terms.

My relationship with Duncan had morphed over the course of nine months as well, undergoing such an accelerated rate of change that it was sometimes almost painful. We continued to talk after I was booked for *Oprah,* but I was cautious about what I said to him. I feared my words would be used against me. I didn't feel like I could trust him as I once did, and so I hesitated to share my dreams with him, even as these dreams were slowly coming true. But, overall, my new, cautious relationship with Duncan was fine. As Dr. Reef said, "People grow at different rates." And I loved spending time with Duncan when he was happy. The only problem was that his happiness was delicate, like a flower that could be stomped on at any moment.

One evening, when Duncan was feeling particularly happy, he

accompanied Deezy and me to a party that Deezy had been invited to. Thankfully, Deezy seemed to grow right alongside me, and our friendship continued to provide the safety we both sought. He was in recovery as well, and we had taught each other what it means to have friends of the opposite sex whom you don't have sex with. The dictionary might define this as platonic, but both Deezy and I thought of it as super-awesome and new.

The party was at a ballet studio and consisted of lovely gay boys and lady dancers who moved to music in ways I could not; they would bust out an arabesque or the Michael Jackson kick-ball-change-grab-crotch maneuver. So, instead of pretending I could dance, I hung around the IBC root beer. Deez and I had strategically planned our beverages for the evening, bringing root beer that so closely resembled actual beer, it would be impossible to tell the difference without a taste. I thought having a bottle to clutch would make me more comfortable at a party where I didn't know anyone except Deez and Duncan. Even so, the birthday girl's friends all seemed to be unbearably attractive. I watched Duncan move about the party from young man to young man. In lieu of going on my own flirt-astic studio adventure, I stepped outside into the cool Santa Monica air to smoke a few cigarettes with Deez.

"How long you wanna stay here?" I asked, knowing how much he hated parties, socializing, and anything outside of his warm, safe home.

"I'm ready to go whenever, but you know that already," he said. "I hate people."

Deez's personality was much like a stand-up comedian's: self-deprecating and sardonic, yet incredibly bright and occasionally hopeful.

"You don't hate all people," I said. "You just hate being in large groups of them."

"No, I'm pretty sure I hate them," he said. "Even when they are alone. Or with me."

I laughed.

"Okay, so we'll stay another thirty minutes?" I said. "That way, we will do the do, like we said we'd do, and then home again and Halo. I'm feeling murderous."

I lit another cigarette and happily thought of the video games that sat waiting for us at home. Deez still lived one floor above me, and we had nightly root-beer-and-chain-smoking sessions with the occasional addition of ice cream, cookies, or brownies. I had experienced a major crescendo in my sweet tooth when I stopped drinking. But while I might have gained a few pounds on the old hips as a result, I never woke up in a stranger's bed after eating too much chocolate.

"I'm fine with that," Deez said as he took a long, hard drag on his cigarette.

A red Ford Ranger pulled into the parking lot as I lit another cigarette—my cigs always seemed to burn faster than Deez's—and I flicked my recently finished butt toward a row of cars before realizing a party guest was walking toward us from the Ranger. He was wearing a straw fedora on his short curly hair and he had a super-friendly smile, which I thought he was directing at me. As he came closer, though, I realized that Deez was the actual recipient of the smile. When Deez recognized him, they both laughed and thrust out their hands.

"Garrett! My man!" Deez exclaimed. "How ya been?"

Garrett had a little gap in his teeth, like I did, and he was supercute.

"Not too bad, just dishin' out birthday wishes," he said. "What about you, man?"

As the men carried on the man talk, I surveyed Garrett from hat to heels. Nearly six feet of man. Kind face. Warm energy. And muscular thighs like I'd never seen before, even at a party where I was surrounded by ballet dancers; his thighs were the size of my waist.

I immediately checked myself from wondering what would make a man's thighs so strong.

Do not sexualize Deezy's friend, Jennie, I thought. *Stop looking at those delicious thighs.*

"Garrett, this is Jennie," Deez said.

I was startled out of my thoughts.

"Oh. Um. Hey," I said, feeling like that same old third grader getting ready to kick the boy she likes in the shins.

"Hey," Garrett said to me.

"You just get here?" he said to Deez.

"Naw," Deez replied. "Thinking about leaving soon, but we'll go in with you. I'm going to get wild on another root beer."

I realized with dismay that my superpower flirting and guy-getting skills had vanished. All that was left was a shy, nervous girl in pink spandex pants and a pink knit beanie.

Goddamn you, Dr. Drew, I thought. *How am I ever going to hit on this cutie when I can't even say hi like a normal person? I'm a fucking mega-goon!*

Garrett led our three-person parade into the party. I punched Deez in the arm.

"Why didn't you tell me you have a supercute friend that wears supercute hats?" I whispered. "You're so selfish!"

Deez laughed and rubbed his arm, even though there was no way my little punch had hurt him.

"Actually, Garrett is totally the kind of guy I would hook you up with," he said. "I didn't introduce you to him before now because I knew you had that one-year goal, and you and Jill were doing that dating plan thingie. But this is kind of perfect."

I hung back one more second, grabbing Deez by the shirt and watching as Garrett opened the dance studio's front door.

"Perfect schmerfect," I said. "His thighs are like Superman's thighs. Did you see those things?"

"No, I did not check out another man's thighs, if that is what you're asking," Deez said. "But why don't you get to know him and see if you like his personality too?"

Deez smiled, and I gave a little huff.

"Thanks, Jill," I said to Deez sarcastically.

I hurried through the door that Garrett had been holding awkwardly for us as we stood in the parking lot whispering to one another.

"They got a cake in this place?" Garrett asked.

If this guy loves cake, we are going to get along fine, I thought.

I looked into his eyes, which I hadn't realized were baby-boy blue until we were in the well-lit dance studio, and felt like butter sitting out in the sun.

"I, um, think she's waiting to bring it out," I said. "She knows I'll eat it all and then leave."

Moron, just be quiet and look pretty.

He grabbed a bite-size block of cheddar cheese and tossed it in his mouth.

"Ah, I only go to parties for cake," he said. "She's a nice girl and all, and I'm glad we're friends, but mostly I'm here for the cake."

I was so grateful that he hadn't said, "Wow, fat kid," or given me some cheap, half-assed laugh that I found the courage to continue the conversation instead of running to hide behind Deez.

"So you don't know anyone here, either?" I asked. "I mean, besides the birthday girl?"

I swayed back and forth from my heels to my toes, trying to flirt, but not so obviously that it looked farcical, and not really understanding what obvious flirting looked or felt like anyhow. Jill and I hadn't talked about how to flirt appropriately. And my old patterns had required that I have sex before flirting, to see if the flirting was actually worth the effort.

"Naw," he replied. "I was a little worried I'd be here talking to the wall."

I thought I detected some flirting on his end too. I laughed, only the laugh sounded way louder than it should have. Deez raised his eyebrows as if to say, *Holy fuck, you meet a cute guy and totally lose your cool,* and excused himself to find the birthday girl.

I knew what Deez was doing, leaving us there to dance the

flirtango. I had never experienced the delicate digging that is a first encounter, but it felt like Garrett was working up the courage to ask for my phone number, and I was working up the courage to say, "Let's hang out." That's when Duncan flitted over like a hummingbird and injected himself into our conversation.

"Hello," he said, crossing his arms.

Garrett politely introduced himself and they shook hands. Duncan looked at me as I smiled at Garrett sheepishly, then he looked back to Garrett.

"And what exactly do you do?" Duncan said.

"I'm a runner for a production company right now," Garrett said. "I moved here from Chicago a year ago. Wow. It goes fast, huh? A year? Anyway, yeah, that's what I do. It's okay, the job, and there's room to grow, which is nice."

"Do you know who you are speaking with here?" Duncan said, nodding his head toward me.

Instantly, I wished I could crawl under the easy-fold table covered in cheese cubes.

Please go away, Duncan, I thought. *Please, please, please go.*

"I was sure her name was Jennie," Garrett laughed, "but now I'm a little bit worried."

"This is one of the biggest porn stars in the world," Duncan said. "Did you know that?"

I knew he meant his comment to be silly and fun, but it felt mean and hurtful, especially because I wasn't one of the biggest porn stars in the world. Not anymore.

Duncan turned to me and placed his hands on my shoulders.

"You shouldn't bother with assistants," he said. "They will always be assistants."

Then he fluttered off to another group of attractive young men while I attempted to stutter out some sort of cohesive explanation.

"I, um. No. Well, he's, I mean, I was. But I'm, um. I'm sorry."

I didn't know what exactly I was apologizing for, or if Garrett could sense the tsunami of tears that was building up behind my eyeballs, but it was a huge relief when he put both of his hands on my shoulders and smiled.

"It's okay," he said. "I grew up with two gay brothers, so I can take the abuse."

"But about what he said?" I asked.

While I was grateful that he'd shut down the assistant comment, I was still concerned that my past had been revealed so bluntly.

"I was a porn star," I said. "For a long time, but I'm doing something different. Like, super-different. And . . ."

I was about to reach my breaking point. I felt I couldn't recover from my previous life. Even though I was trying so hard to leave that life behind, it still followed me everywhere. I couldn't sell the proof in Jersey. I couldn't clean up the memories in therapy. I couldn't forget any of it in reality. It had just become glaringly clear that no matter who I hung out with, what kind of friendships I forged, or what kind of progress I made, at some point my pornographic past would resurface. Even if I moved on, the world might not.

"I'm sorry," I said again, hanging my head.

I was totally defeated and already planning to walk home so I didn't have to ride with Duncan.

There goes any chance of seeing this guy again, I thought.

"Seriously?" Garrett said. "It's not a big deal. Everyone has some sort of past, and that guy's is obviously making him unhappy. It's good you're doing something super-different."

Still holding his hands on my shoulders, he gave me a little shake.

"Really, it's fine," he said.

The birthday girl brought out the cake, and Garrett dropped his hands from my shoulders. I wished that we could go back to just before Duncan came over and ruined the moment, when he was getting ready to ask for my number. I wished I still had the courage to say, "Let's hang out." But the only thing I could muster made me feel like a mega-nerd.

"Do you Twitter?" I asked.

Maybe Twitter can help me do some damage control, because he will see my Tweets and think about me, and it will put this whole mess into a new, not-messy context, I thought.

I still had no idea who this totally incapable little girl was who had taken my awesome skills at hitting on guys and squashed them into oblivion.

Garrett laughed, a nice, sincere laugh.

"Yeah, do you want to cyberstalk me?" he asked.

I dug my toe into the floor and looked down, feeling more vulnerable than I ever did when I was naked and sucking dick in front of a camera.

"Yeah, but not like scary stalk," I said. "Just nice cyberstalk."

The conversation continued in this fashion for another twenty heartbreakingly painful minutes, with him laughing sweetly at my kindergarten attempts to flirt, and me hating myself for my complete and utter lack of interpersonal skills.

Where the fuck did my confidence go? I kept thinking. *Does it only exist in six-inch stilettos? Is it at home hidden in the tubs of leftover porn from Jersey? If I can't get this guy's number, how will I ever be ready for a date? What the fuck does a date even look like?*

IT WASN'T UNTIL two weeks later—two weeks of innocent flirtations that unfolded in the standard Twitter format, 140 characters at a time—that Garrett finally gave me his number before I could even work up the nerve to ask for it. All I had done was send him a direct message on Twitter about how much the Cleveland Browns sucked and how my Oakland Raiders would be the team to watch, even though I knew the statement was only half-true.

In return, he sent me his number with a short message: "In case you ever want to watch some football."

When I opened it and saw that he was still interested in hanging out with me, my heart skipped three beats. From there, he eventually asked me to dinner and a hockey game. I accepted his invitation superexcitedly. When I arrived at dinner, wearing a sideways Oakland A's hat and pink leg warmers over black spandex, I was brought up short by his dress pants, collared button-up shirt, and tie.

Oh, fuck! This is what a date looks like! I thought.

A date looked like a chair being pulled out for me, and his sweater over my shoulders when I got chilly at the ice rink. It looked like an introduction to his best friend from childhood, who was also at the game, and a kiss on the cheek at the end of the night, with a request to repeat the evening again sometime soon. It looked sweet and innocent, and nothing like Penny Flame. Because Penny Flame was a girl I used to play in porn movies, not a girl I had to be in real life.

EACH MONTH, MERCEDES-BENZ sent me a bill for one thousand one hundred and forty-something dollars, and each month I begrudgingly sent them a cashier's check. In addition, I also paid a car insurance bill, which ran two hundred and thirty-something dollars. These figures were a stark reminder of that which I could no longer afford. Dad knew all of this, because I was forced to ask him to help me cover my rent that November. We often discussed my financial future, or lack thereof.

We talked about it again one sunny winter afternoon as I stood in my kitchen painting a picture of the Golden Gate Bridge that had been commissioned by one of my blog fans.

"How long are you going to keep holding on to the Benz, Jen?" he asked.

"I don't know what to do with it, Dad!" I said. "Can you really just give a car back because you can't afford it anymore?"

"Well, you can't squeeze lemonade from rocks, pumpkin," he said.

I tapped ash from the end of my cigarette and stood back to look at my work.

"So I just walk in and give it back?" I asked. "Like, 'Here are the keys'?"

"Have they left you with any other option, Jennifer?" he asked.

Each time Dad said my name, I smiled. He said it a bunch, like he was trying to make up for all the years he couldn't say it.

"No," I said. "The lady said I can't lower the payments. They wouldn't let me trade it in for one I can afford. December's payment is the month they said I could tack onto the end of my lease agreement, so it's kind of my get-outta-jail-free card. Come January, I'm fucked."

"I think you know what to do, Jennifer," my dad said. "Think of it like paying off a college education. Now you know better than to sign a five-year lease if you don't know where you'll be in five years. Consider that your twenty-thousand-dollar lesson."

I put down my cigarette and went to the freezer for a spoonful of my favorite comfort food.

"I know," I said. "It's just a shitty lesson."

I wished that I'd invested my money in Ben & Jerry's Half Baked low-fat fro-yo as I took a bite, instead of the car I knew I'd eventually have to return.

"So you're going to do it, then?" he said. "You know, Lyss and Jim are both coming up for Christmas. It would be very special if you were here too."

I tried not to think about the last Christmas we had spent together. It had been nearly twelve years ago, when he had showed me a video of my mom cheating on him. I hadn't really enjoyed Christmas since then, perhaps because my young life had steadily fallen apart, perhaps because something really big had been missing from it.

Maybe he's what was missing, I thought.

"I'd love to, Dad, but I don't have the money to buy a ticket."

"Jennifer, I can help you," he said.

I wanted to cry as he offered his help, because a big part of me knew that he was the missing piece of the holiday puzzle: the smell of his coffee in the morning, the way he sat next to the Christmas tree while we opened presents, laughing and putting sticky bows on our heads.

"I'll make it happen," he said softly.

I held back my tears.

"Thanks, Dad, for everything," I said.

THREE WEEKS LATER, and following a few more dates with Garrett, I was heading to Portland, Oregon, to spend time with my family for the holidays. Before and after each date with Garrett, I called my dad for a pep talk.

"Don't be afraid to let him pick up the tab, Jen," he said.

Or: "A guy should open the door for you."

When I told him how the dates went, he was optimistic but cautious.

"He sounds like a nice guy, but you don't have to rush into anything yet, kiddo," he said.

I knew he was right, but I was excited to be dating one guy, and to have that one guy be Garrett. He and I clicked so well and laughed over the same silly things. As I became less and less obsessed with my own nervousness, I began to notice how nervous he was, and that made me feel better about the whole situation. When I told Jill about Garrett, she seemed pleased with the rate at which the relationship was developing, and she was especially pleased that I had my dad as a go-to for fatherly advice.

WHEN I SAW Dad at the airport, he had tears in his eyes. As he hugged all three of his kids at once in a big, giant bear hug, he wept openly.

"This will be my first family Christmas since your mother," he said. "Twelve years."

I couldn't help but think of all the years I'd sent back his presents, the disappointment he must have felt as he opened the returned packages and found his gifts completely untouched and unappreciated.

"Thanks for bringing us all here, Dad," I said as we left the airport to head to his house.

The front door of Dad's home opened onto a hallway covered in graduation pictures. My throat began to swell shut as I looked over the pictures covering his walls and then explored the home from Lyss's bedroom upstairs, which was filled with our little-kid drawings, all the way to the kitchen, where our small clay handprints sat near the sink and our macaroni paintings were still taped to the fridge. The living room contained two man chairs—recliners—and two end tables. The kitchen table was devoted to a computer and papers. Except for the evidence of his kids around the house, my dad's place was the home of a bachelor. As I looked through the pictures of my brother and sister, I couldn't help but be devastated by my absence in them after the age of thirteen. There was no evidence of my existence in my dad's life after my parents' divorce, but I knew it was not from his lack of trying.

My dad and my brother moved a couch that was rarely used into the living room so Lyss and I had someplace to sit. As I sat down, I began to worry about the amends I had to make to my dad. All of the other amends had gone unbelievably well. I kept waiting for someone to be upset with me, to shake me and say:

"Why were you such a piece of shit? Why did you do that to me? How could you cut me off from your life? I can't forgive you for hurting me!"

But none of the people I'd made amends to had said anything even the least bit hurtful. I was grateful for how gracious they had all been, but I also wondered if their grace made the process even more difficult for me. I had always felt that as long as at least one person was still mad at me, then it wouldn't be as hard to make amends to Dad, which I feared the most because I knew he was the man I'd really screwed over.

Even though Jill, Dr. Reef, and Dr. Drew talked to me about how my dad's overdose when I was nine had driven a wedge into our relationship and created an unsafe environment for me as a kid, I knew that I was still accountable for refusing to be his daughter for half my life. I was painfully aware that he still had to wake up every single day knowing that the first person he created was waking up somewhere in the world hating him for things he couldn't control.

I had hated him because he had overdosed, and I didn't feel safe, and then, when I started to trust him again, he was too honest about what was actually going on in our family. I had hated him because my mom left. I had hated him because he had revealed the truth of her indiscretions. I had hated him because I hurt, and I didn't know who else to hate—or blame—for my pain.

Sitting in my dad's living room and looking at the wall—which was empty of memories from more than a decade of my life—while mentally preparing to make amends, I knew exactly who I could hate now. I saw her every time I looked in the mirror. But I was trying not to do so.

ONE AFTERNOON A few days into my visit, I found myself alone with my dad. My sister was outside smoking, and my brother was at the gym. I sat and silently worked up my courage.

If I just say what I have to say, I will finally know how upset he still is with me, I thought.

I grabbed a chair and sat next to him at the computer where he was surfing the Web.

"I'm sorry I didn't call you Dad," I said.

"You call me all the time, kiddo!" he said, not taking his eyes from the computer.

"No, I mean I'm sorry that for half my life I called you 'Gene' and not 'Dad,'" I said. "It was hurtful. I'm sorry for returning all your presents. And for cutting you off from my life. I wish so much that I hadn't been such an awful bitch."

"I'm sorry, too, Jen," my dad said. "We missed out on some really good years. We have a lot of making up to do now."

Tears were streaming down my face, and my open floodgate of a confession continued, long streams of words strung loosely together with no beginning and no clear end.

"I was so selfish," I cried. "I didn't think the choices I made would hurt you, but I look back now and I see how much they hurt me, and I know they had to hurt you too. I'm so sorry. I'm sorry I hurt you and that I was selfish and cruel, and I want to make it better. I want to fix it."

I was having a hard time breathing, and I couldn't see through the giant tears that filled my eyes.

"But I can't," I continued. "I can't make any of it better, and I hate myself for it every day, and I'm just so sorry."

He took hold of my shoulders and brought me close for a big Dad hug.

"We start now, Jennifer, we start fixing it now," he said. "We keep building the relationship like we've been doing and we just keep moving forward. We keep talking and being in each other's lives. And even though we can't get those years back, we can make new ones. We can make new memories. I always knew you would come back into my life. I just didn't know when. I'm so thankful it's now."

Then we sat in his kitchen and cried. We cried for the moments we could never share, the good days and the bad days we hadn't had together. We cried for the people we were twelve years before. We sat in that kitchen for two hours and let every single tear fall that needed to fall. Mine dried up long after his did, but he hugged

me until I was done weeping. Until, for the briefest moment, all
the regret and pain had drained from my heart. I had missed having a dad, but I didn't have to miss it anymore.

———

I CHOSE JANUARY 2, 2010, as the day on which I would return
the Benz.

Garrett and I had officially started dating, exclusively, after five
real dates, a bunch of phone conversations, and a kiss on the mouth
when the clock struck midnight on New Year's Eve. Even though
I had been single for only nine of the twelve months I originally
intended, I felt like that was okay because our relationship had
progressed in what Jill called "a healthy, natural way." Because of
this, I didn't want to deny myself the chance to be with a special
man. I really knew I had met someone worth keeping when Garrett said, "If you ever want me to go to Jill with you, you know, to
talk about stuff, I will."

Still, even though I was calling Garrett my boyfriend and
he was calling me his girlfriend, I was too ashamed of my failed
car-leasing situation to ask him to pick me up at the dealership. I
called Deez, and he agreed to come get me fifteen minutes after I
dropped off my car.

The morning of the second, I put on a proper pair of pants and
a button-up blouse and drove down to the Beverly Hills Mercedes-
Benz dealership.

*If I'm going to put my tail between my legs and give this car back,
I'm going to do it at the ritziest dealership possible,* I thought. *I know
Beverly Hills will give me the ultimate piece of humble pie.*

I expected the men on the receiving end of the car to scoff at
me for being such a colossal failure. I could hear them laughing at
me as I drove down Santa Monica Boulevard. I heard snickering
as I parked in the front of the dealership. I detected whispers as
I walked in the front door. As I approached a polite-looking car

salesman, I could have sworn someone said, "She even *looks* like a failure."

"Can I help you, miss?" the man asked.

As he smiled at me, all the whispers, snickers, guffawing, and running commentary fell silent in my head. The showroom was absolutely still.

"Yeah, I, um, I need to give this back," I said, holding out my hand. "I can't afford it anymore. The financial people said to give it back. So here. I'm done. I can't do it."

I turned my palm over to reveal the two keys I'd been clutching so desperately while holding in tears. He continued to smile, completely unfazed by my failure.

"You know, in Vegas last year, there was a three-mile-long line of people voluntarily surrendering their vehicles on the first and second day of January," he said. "The economy is shit."

He nodded as he took the keys from me and then stepped forward, a bit closer to me than a salesman normally would. He was so close that he could reach out and put his hand on my shoulder, which is precisely what he did—not in a sleazy way, but almost like a dad.

"This year will be better, kid, don't worry about it," he said.

I stared at him, waiting for the joke, until I heard an awkward forced laugh ring out in the otherwise still showroom. It took a few seconds for me to recognize the laugh as my own, and then it took me what seemed like years to stop laughing. I thought about everything that had happened over the past year, and before that, over the past twenty-six years and ten months of my life.

"Yeah, this year is already better," I said.

I left the dealership and went outside to meet Deez, who sat waiting patiently for me in his Honda Accord.

"Ready, buddy?" he asked.

We had a date with some video game aliens, a hot dog, and maybe some Ben & Jerry's.

The real work was far from over, but with the car gone, I felt a sense of surrender that far exceeded any high I'd had before. The paranoia that had consumed my brain walking into the dealership was replaced by a calm serenity as I left. Neither the car nor the porn made me who I am. And even though the state of "I am" is constantly changing and evolving, I *am* more confident in what I can be, and less afraid of what I've been. I am.

ACKNOWLEDGMENTS

WHILE IT IS entirely possible to film a lame-ass and borderline-skeezy porn flick with only two people, it is nearly impossible to create a readable book, especially a memoir such as this, without the help of a medium-to-large-sized village. I have so many people to acknowledge and thank, I'm positive I will leave someone out, and must apologize ahead of time in case I do. So, here goes: I'm sorry if I fail miserably and forget to thank you. You know who you are and, hopefully, how grateful I am for you.

That being said, I'd like to start this by thanking those who have devoted precious time to helping me through this recovery process and into this new, "healthy life thing." Dr. Drew, seriously, I am so grateful to have participated in *Sex Rehab*, and I will go to any length to pay forward the blessings bestowed upon me there. The therapy I received in treatment opened a door to such an incredible new life—words pale in comparison to the gratitude my heart holds for you. To Dr. Drew's wife and family, I am forever grateful for the precious hours with him that you've been generous enough to donate to me and all of those in recovery.

Jill Vermeire and Dr. Reef, I am thankful to the both of you, for similar but super-mega different reasons: Jill, you are the woman to whom I look in times of need. I trust your sage advice, and your compassion and empathy have inspired me to care for myself on a level I didn't believe possible. I would never be able to look myself in the mirror today and say, "I love you," were it not for you loving me first. And I don't mean that in an unhealthy way—which is neat, because you taught me the difference.

Dr. Reef, your mentorship has proved so powerful that I am already pursuing goals I never dreamt were obtainable. Thank you for teaching me the importance of boundaries, even seemingly meaningless ones like, the whole calling a doctor a "Doctor" thing. And thank you for helping me to realize that I am totally capable of making my dreams happen if I am willing to put in time and energy.

Jill Stern, a mentor, friend, and an incredible writer. You are, perhaps, the single biggest reason why this book is currently in existence. Without you, there would be no agent, no publisher, no belief that I could actually do it. Just a little blog on the internet called Becoming Jennie and big words inside a short girl. Thank you for helping me to find the right people and helping the right people to find me. There will never be a day that I am not grateful for what you've done for me.

Dad, thank you for every day that you were willing to rebuild a relationship with me. It wasn't until I allowed myself to be loved by you that I realized you could teach me how to be loved by others. Thank you for not fucking off when I told you to fuck off. Thank you for being my dad. I love you.

Mama and Papa, thank you both for understanding that there had to be some changes in my life, and in all of our lives, and for having the courage to make those changes with me. I am so proud to call you both my parents, and so blessed to be able to love you and be loved by you both.

The rest of the family, thank you for welcoming me back into the Ketcham crew, for understanding that sometimes we take a funny path to get to a normal place, and for loving me like you did when we were young. Lyss and James, I love you both so much and am proud to be your big sister. I only hope that I'm being the big sister, now, that you both deserve.

Friends: to those I Houdini-ed, those I ran away from, those I lied to, took advantage of, or abused in any sort of way, I am sorry.

From the bottom of my heart, I am sorry. It was wrong of me to treat any of you in the selfish ways I know I have, and you deserved better than I could give at the time.

To the people in the adult industry, I am sorry to have disappeared from your lives as I did. I wish that circumstances were different, and that we could all be together again. In a healthy, not-selling-ourselves-for-money kind of way. Never feel like you are stuck, or forever doomed to sell your body. You are and deserve more. Don't fear your life changing for the better, and never forget that sweet, innocent child deep inside of you.

To the men I've dated, especially Marc, I am sorry for all that I put you through. I was selfish, self-seeking, arrogant, and cruel. You never deserved to be treated the way I treated you. I hope that wherever you are, you are with someone who can love you like I should have.

To Mr. Man, who had to deal with me and love me through this whole process. Garrett, my dearest, I can only hope that this is but the first chapter of many in our life together. I love you and thank you for supporting me through this process.

To everyone in the book writing biz, from my first agent, Eve, to my first publisher lady, Kara, to the women who were here for nearly the entire thing. Terra, my agent, I am so happy that we met, so blessed to be under your wing, and so thankful for the hard work you put into pimpin' out these pages. Jen, my lady publisher, you are an awesome make-it-happen-captain, hooking me up with the perfect editor, Patrick, who was super inspirational to work with. Patrick, thank you for treating these delicate pages, and this delicate heart, so gently, for being the creative, chapter-re-arranger that you are, for spending countless hours making this book the thing it is. To the copy editor, who had to deal with my made up words and typos, sorry—it will (hopefully!) happen again—and the lawyer that is keeping us all from getting sued, I owe you a hug.

To Jeb Brody, thank you for being such a great friend and mentor. I was so afraid that I would forever be seen as a sexual, and

otherwise worthless, object. Thank you for gently reminding me
that not everybody wants to fuck me and not everybody wants fuck
from me. You are a good man and a wonderful dad. All your ladies
are very lucky to have you, and I am blessed to call you my friend.

A special thanks to E-Deez and Angel, who have both been
there from the very beginning of this journey, albeit slightly different journeys: Thank you, Deez, for the countless hours of alien-
killing madness, for the wonderful chain-smoking and crying
sessions (that'd be me doing the crying), and for being my rock
in recovery. There were so many times I thought, "Fuck all of
this"—having you by my side, struggling along with me, was tre-
mendously inspirational. You are a big part of why I felt capable of
moving forward. Thank you for sharing your life and your story
with me.

Angel, thank you for always being the best friend a person
could ask for. Thank you for being so selfless, even when I was a
bad, bad, selfish Pie. Thank you for being brutally honest, especially when I didn't want to hear it. Thank you for supporting me
through our friendship, and for allowing me, now, to be the friend
to you that you deserve.

The very last, and biggest, thanks goes to my Sherpa, editor, and
friend, Sarah Tomlinson. Without you, Sarah, this book would be
such stinky doo-doo, it probably would have been laughed out of
the Gallery offices. You inspired me to keep chugging along when
I thought my little engine simply could not. You sat silently and
patiently at the other end of our internet/text/phone conversation,
and when I needed you, you were always there. You said "write
more" when I thought "meh," and when I figured everyone knew
what some silly porn lingo meant, you always brought me back
into reality, where thankfully, people don't speak the Porn Valley lexicon. Thank you for being my teacher, my superior book-
mountain-guide-goddess, and for helping me to believe in the
impossible. Thank you for helping me to write this book.